The
Romantic Age in Prose

An Anthology

edited by

Alan W. Bellringer
and C.B. Jones

THE ROMANTIC AGE IN PROSE

NEW SERIES • VOLUME XXIX

COSTERUS

AMSTERDAM 1980

THE ROMANTIC AGE IN PROSE

An Anthology

edited by Alan W. Bellringer
and C.B. Jones

Department of English
University College of North Wales,
Bangor

Y λ0 2

Rodopi

AMSTERDAM 1980

CONTENTS

INTRODUCTION

In this anthology we present the reader with a selection of texts of English discursive prose of the period from the late 1780's to the early 1830's, the Romantic age. We present what we consider to be important texts bearing on key issues. Only Coleridge stands out as a major prose-writer in this period, and in the section devoted to him we have brought together examples of his early, middle and late work. The extracts from the works of the other authors represented in this anthology are grouped in sections around three themes which most occupied writers' minds during the Romantic period, Freedom, Imagination and Reform. Though several of the passages chosen are comparatively short and others considerably cut, we have, we believe, nowhere sacrificed continuity of argument or coherence of debate to mere variety. We have, however, confined this selection to the prose of ideas, omitting, for reasons of space, more 'literary' types of prose, in the forms of dialogue, character-sketch, autobiography, reverie, travel-description and comic anecdote. Our main purpose is to provide a wide representation of the literature of thought of the period.

The historical background to English Romanticism is, of course, no less than the three revolutions which shook the world of the ancient regime in the 1780's. The attainment of independence by the American Colonies in 1783 was the first of these. Though America's revolution had been successfully attained with the assistance of Great Britain's European rivals, it did in effect mark a significant shift of power away from Europe. The defiance of centrist aristocratic authority by middle-class intellectual and mercantile interests, supported by small landed proprietors, in a remote region of vast and unexplored economic potential, encouraged those forces in Europe which were willing to challenge despotism and re-shape the state on optimistic, rationalist models without the hierarchical dominance of the nobility and the church. The French Revolution, when it came, developed rapidly beyond the controlled constitutionalism of its predecessor and produced a nationalist populism which was at once vindictive and aggressive. Paradoxically, one of its main targets was the cosmopolitan aristocratic culture whose style and language were French. International respect for French sophistication in the arts was under-mined. In Britain the Napoleonic War brought overt hostility to things French. The main alternative cultural influence was German. In Germany the tradition of Lutheran pietism had combined with a disciplined educational movement to provide the basis of a distinctive and experimental culture. Taught by Herder, Goethe praised the Gothic architecture of Cologne Cathedral as Germany's national style, and in the 1770's the Storm and Stress writers had re-awakened interest in Shakespeare, in feudal heroism, in the primitive imagination, in idyllic nature and in the expression of wild feelings of rebellion, protest, restlessness, tragic love and youthful melancholy. The increasing emphasis on individual intuition, which is the principle feature of these German writers, received powerful stimulus from Britain, where the cults of the sentimental and the Gothic and the search for the origin of the Sublime in art and landscape had exposed gaps in neo-classical sensibility. In turn, German melodramas became the rage in Britain. By the beginning of the nineteenth century it was possible to chart a redirection of the European literary consciousness from the old Rome/Paris axis outwards, to the Teutonic forests to the east and to the Celtic and savage lands to the west, a centrifugal tendency of extraordinary novelty and force. The highest values of the new writers were openness and freedom, but they were also ready to explore the dark areas of insanity and guilt.

In Britain the 1780's also saw a development which accelerated the most important change of all to an irreversible momentum. This development was only the application of the rotary steam engine to the loom, yet this proved to be the central link in a series of technological innovations which suddenly freed the factories of the early Industrial Revolution from river-power and enabled the existing large towns to become manufacturing centres with unrivalled economic advantages. The subsequent mushrooming of Britain's cities over the next decades established the main conditions of modern society before they were properly understood. The demand for industrial labour stimulated a growth in population which was already under way owing to improvements in transport, numerous inventor's patents were taken out, output increased, wage-levels altered beyond expectations, and successful industrialists exerted a new type of influence, challenging the power of the landowners and the financiers. A new seriousness enters English prose around this time, hesitantly at first, since it is the product of uncertainties and conflicts. For the Industrial Revolution realigned men's moral thinking as well as their political loyalties. The pace of change was so rapid and the movement of population so bewildering that philosophers' trust in a natural moral order which converted private profits into public good was shaken. Commerce, generally regarded hitherto as a balanced exchange of goods, providentially convenient in a geographically various world, was now seen as a source of social injustices and evils. Even private property, long declared the guarantor of stability and of limited political rights, could come under attack as a scandalous sign of unfair ingenuity and conspiracy. Rural depopulation led to a literature of indignant contrasts and nostalgia. Conservatives and radicals alike disliked developments so out of proportion to expectations of a controllable tomorrow. Humanitarian concern, however, still largely took its bearings from traditional religious sanctions. Social insights came fitfully as the implications of the machine age were very gradually grasped. There was no sudden dawning of a new consciousness of economic reality. In the nature of the case, though the pull towards an ultimate reorientation of literature in line with social problems was irresistible, the most dramatic initial impact upon writers at the end of the eighteenth century came not from the Industrial, but from the French, Revolution.

It is true that the French Revolution has been viewed by many historians as the product of underlying economic and political forces, but its contemporary witnesses saw it primarily as the work of ideas and responded to it with the spontaneity of personal involvement. The revolution became the focus for many varieties of aspiration and its progress provoked a deep re-examination of personal and political ideals. Its early stages were celebrated as a blissful dawn by Wordsworth and Coleridge, when every new book dealing with the principles of liberty raised hopes of millennial proportions. As the 'revolutionary decade' came to an end, however, the radicals had largely recanted any revolutionary intentions. Shaken by the aggressive policies of France, intimidated by a campaign of repression which included a network of spies and *agents provocateurs*, and themselves fearing a dangerous outburst of popular disaffection in Britain, the English Jacobins could be pronounced dead as a political force by Godwin in 1801. Wordsworth, Southey and Coleridge were attacked as turncoats, but they reacted honestly to the quick turns of events and tried, in their political writings, to face contemporary pressures without totally relinquishing the progressive hopes of the age. Later disillusionment prompted such gloomy retrospects as that of Shelley; 'Methinks those who now live have survived an age of despair'. Hazlitt, who considered the 1790's his formative period, commented;

> The French Revolution was the only match that ever took place between philosophy and experience; and waking from the trance of theory to the sense of reality we hear the words "truth", "reason", "virtue", "liberty", with the same indifference or contempt that the cynic who has married a jilt or a termagant, listens to the rhapsodies of lovers.

The tendency to view the crisis of the 1790's in terms of the conflict of principles both in society and in man himself developed during the Romantic period.

The Fall of the Bastille was greeted in Britain with almost unanimous cordiality. France, so long an example of the horrors of despotism and supersitition, was casting off her chains, and many observers anticipated her attaining the same degree of liberty as that enjoyed in Britain. The Revolution seemed to Wordsworth 'nothing out of Nature's certain course', and came as a natural successor to American independence. Paine, Price and Godwin all tell the same tale of the development and diffusion of ideas of liberty from the time of the Commonwealth and the 1688 settlement. Yet the school of 'natural rights' which had developed especially in America went far beyond the compromises of the British Constitution, and Burke, who had supported the Americans on constitutional grounds, was one of the first to recognize the dangers of this new manifestation of radical ideas. Many radicals such as Major Cartwright sought to justify their claims by an appeal to ancient British customs before the imposition of the 'Norman yoke', but the principal danger came from those who ignored the authority of precedent and demanded freedom and equality on the basis of the Protestant right of private conscience and judgment or on the more metaphysical grounds of 'natural' equality. A Dissenting background was common to many of the leading radicals of the day. Paine was brought up as a Quaker, Godwin as a Sandemanian, a creed also shared by the proto-communist Thomas Spence. Priestley and Price were prominent members of the Dissenting fraternity. Most of them placed natural religion above revelation and many had close links with scientific thought. They were influenced by the works of the French enlightenment, especially those of Helvetius, who had asserted the original equality of man which is only disturbed by environmental forces; and in the Dissenting Academies the study of French materialists such as d'Holbach led a few like Godwin and Hazlitt into atheism.

Burke saw the threat which this combination of ideas posed to the traditional framework of British society, and responded even more to the spectacle of French popular tumult, as subversive ideas ceased to be the property of an intellectual elite and in England were disseminated through societies of artisans and appeared in novels and plays. The *Reflections* can be faulted as a perversion of the principles of the 1688 settlement and of the historical events in France, but its central importance lies in its reinterpretation of the idea of tradition and in its interpretation of the historic crisis facing Britain. Burke's defence of traditional ties does not depend upon ideas of rational order or harmony, nor primarily upon order as a bulwark agains latent chaos. Burke gives a positive value to tradition by basing it upon feelings, which are built up through life by associations of place and person. 'We begin our public affections in our families', he states, and goes on to construct a model of the state cemented by familial bonds of loyalty, obligation and heredity. Overshadowed and supported by this matured, age-old framework, the individual is denied the capacity to originate plans of conduct or of society by his own unaided reason. Burke values experience above speculation, and the test of time and of wide acceptance above individual conviction. Burke's choice of ground was deliberate and well-judged. Against the imposing edifice of his system, Paine might point out errors of historical fact, and pour scorn on individual passages, and Mackintosh might employ his keen lawyer's wit to reduce to absurdity Burke's appeal to precedent, but Burke's main positions were as much beyond logical refutation as they were above rational proof. Paine had developed during the American War a style of popular journalism which responded to issues of the moment with colloquial urgency, ignoring the niceties of political disquisition and using the metaphors of the stable and the highway to describe the manoeuvres of the Parties. He appealed to scriptural authority with the bold directness of a Dissenter and approached the mysteries of government with a similar lack of reverence. His 'common sense' approach reduced national finance to a mathematical simplicity comprehensible to the ordinary man, backed by intoxicating hopes of tangible social benefits. Paine led the paper armies of vindication and set the informal tone for writers whose strong feelings hurried them into print. Mary Wollstonecraft passed quickly from the rights of men to those of women, and her work shows a vehemence of personal feeling at the expense of both propriety and organisation. Her radical technique of comparing women with other oppressed or excluded groups sometimes gets out of hand, especially when she compares women to soldiers or to the aristocracy, but her lasting relevance lies in her attacks on ingrained social attitudes as well as on particular financial, educational and career disabilities. She raises perennial problems in feminist thought, such as the difficulty of re-conciling a mother's care of her children with the conduct of a career. Both Mary Wollstonecraft and William Godwin attacked the social shibboleths of reputation and honour, sexual and aristocratic, and both looked for an extension of the liberty of the individual and a more genuine freedom, equality and openness in personal behaviour. Godwin's demand for 'perfect sincerity' was as much a plea for a lifting of social barriers to unforced intercourse as it was a method for the ascertaining of truth. It was a mark of the informal mood of the 1790's so nostalgically recorded by Hazlitt and evidenced in styles of behaviour and dress. Godwin recognised the threat to progressive ideas posed by Burke's monolithic traditionalism, and set himself the task of erecting a similarly imposing radical philosophical monument couched in the old-fashioned form of the two-volume treatise. In fact, his thorough-going treatment of ideas and their logical conclusions produced some sensational spec-ulations which amply justified Burke's epigram that a strict logician is a

licenced visionary. Nevertheless some of Godwin's audacious speculations as to the status of marriage and the possibilites of technological
and medical advancement have proved more prophetic than his contemporaries might have dreamed. Inspired by the French Revolution to
envisage a simpler form of society, he took libertarian ideas to an
anarchistic extreme, while his sense of natural human sympathy, nourished by the eighteenth-century school of Shaftesbury and Hutcheson,
and a peculiarly exclusive and intellectual brand of dissent, imposed a
strict criterion of social responsibility. Man is released from political
coercion only to be bound by the inflexibly demanding rule of justice, the
obligation to contribute to the highest welfare of society, and to follow a
rigorous intellectual discipline to make this contribution effective and
free from the perversions of traditional emotional prejudices. His hopes
for the gradual 'perfectibility' of man rest squarely on the faculty of
reason, although he recognised the force of Burke's idea that men are
emotionally as well as intellectually formed by and attached to the
existing framework of 'things as they are'. In his novels, Godwin presents
sombre portraits of men corrupted by environmental pressures; but his
philosophy maintains that reason can look beyond the limits of the
actual, and recall the corrupt man or alienated criminal to the ideals of a
common humanity. His literary technique is deficient in imaginative
appeal but perhaps his main weapon is his clarity of logical definition.
His definition of a political party as a confederation to give dis-
proportionate weight to the opinions of those so associated is capable of
giving pause to many 'democratic' party-men, even before he goes on to
the other disadvantages of such conglomerates.

Godwin's ideas greatly influenced the early Romantic poets. The plan
of Coleridge and Southey to found an egalitarian Pantisocratic community in America was based on his theories. Coleridge projected a book
on Pantisocracy which would contain 'the best of Godwin'. Godwin was
also at one time a light in darkness to Wordsworth. Wordsworth, after a
first-hand experience of revolutionary France which left him with a
lasting impression of the power of a popular movement — 'my hope was
in the people' — quickly became disillusioned with the rise of Napoleon.
'A Pope/Is summon'd in to crown an Emperor', was his sardonic
comment. Wordsworth turned to Godwin for a political optimism which
drew its hopes from ideals of the mind, independent of actual events.
However, Wordsworth, ever seeking the palpable connection with the
'world which is the world/Of all of us', felt a sense of dissociation as he
was forced to consider man as he might be, rather than man as he was.
The restless critical analysis of traditional values seemed even to dis-
sociate him from nature and his own past. Eventually he worked out a
new, poetic faith which linked him with the here and now, a faith founded

on the emotional and moral worth of the social traditions of his boyhood Cumberland and Westmorland. While Godwin placed his chief hope in an elevated and purified version of aristocratic virtues such as knowledge, cultivation and rational benevolence, Wordsworth placed his in people of little learning and restricted opportunities, but possessing great knowledge of the human heart and of nature, and speaking an unsophisticated language which he praised as both poetic and philosophical. In a later political work Wordsworth praised the revolt of the Iberian peoples against Napoleon because their movement was 'social' in character and not motivated by rational objects.

In the radicalism of their youth, which both were later sedulous to conceal, Coleridge and Southey gave lectures in Bristol. Coleridge was forced, according to his own account, to publish his first moral and political lecture because of accusations of treason; it was later revised and published as *Conciones ad Populum*. Coleridge's strategy was largely to emphasise the points on which he differed from other radicals as he developed his own more radical ideas, expressed in religious terms. He seems to have held with Godwin that the political rights, forms and privileges for which other radicals campaigned were not as important as the abolition of property (or 'aspheterism' as he called it in his Pantisocratic days). 'It is a mockery of our fellow creatures' wrongs to call them equal in rights when, by the bitter compulsion of their wants we make them inferior to us in all that can soften the heart or dignify the understanding'. Thelwall, the noted radical orator, visited Coleridge in 1797, and his comments testify to Colderidge's extreme position on property, for the violent nature of which he reproached the poet. Even as late as 1799 we find Coleridge urging Southey to write a history of the levelling principle. In his published writings Coleridge showed a more cautious attitude, defining a Jacobin as one who believed in natural rights — on which grounds he could technically disavow Jacobinism — and stating that government 'must be founded on property for the present race of men'.

Both Coleridge and Southey made much of their difference from extreme radical rationalism. Coleridge felt that 'the intensity of private attachments encourages, not prevents, universal benevolence'; he moved towards a paternalistic attitude and towards management of the people, an idea he found in religious organisations such as the Methodists and Evangelicals, who would go personally among the poor, teaching them their duties that they might be rendered 'susceptible of their rights'. In Coleridge's late publication on *Church and State* these earlier ideas are developed into a scheme which embraces all aspects of moral and political life. His feeling that property should not be owned absolutely by individuals survives in his idea that all ownership of property is granted by the State on condition of certain duties. This concept of stewardship is implicit in his new name for private property, 'propriety'. The other category of property is the 'nationalty' which supports the National Church, an organisation dedicated to moral, social and religious ideals. Religion, education and medicine are the particular fields of activity of the 'clerisy', but its overall function is to preserve and foster the moral and religious ideals of humanity against the threat posed by rationalistic materialism. It ensures that the ends served by the instrumental sciences are human ends. In the practical administration of the State Coleridge planned a system of government which balanced the forces of permanence — the landed interest — and the forces of progress — trading, manufacturing and professional interests. Although the functions of the National Church are theoretically distinct from the political organisation, there is a certain overlap when Coleridge asserts that the Church should teach the basic principle of political life — obedience to the laws, or 'civility' — and should make the people aware of their duties, lessons which seem to inhibit dissent. The book was very influential among those who wished the Church to play a larger part in unifying society in the pursuit of moral and humanitarian goals. However, the 'ideal' method which Coleridge employed is equivocal. Things remain much the same for practical purposes; it is the way in which they are regarded which changes. Coleridge insists that the ideal 'National Church' differs greatly from the actual Church of England (itself a literal 'Godsend') in its enormously expanded influence, and this gave real inspiration to the Broad Church movement. But his views of constitutional arrangements implies little practical change.

Another centre of intense original intellectual activity was creative art. The aesthetic ideas of the British Romantics are of a very mixed complexion. Lacking the sense of unity that many of the continental movements possessed, they present an odd variety of ideas. The central document of British romanticism is Coleridge's *Biographia Literaria*. Emerging from his long working relationship with Wordsworth, it found receptive readers among the younger poets. Yet in the *Biographia* Coleridge conducts an extended argument against Wordsworth's Preface to *Lyrical Ballads* and is heavily indebted to German sources. Keats, in his definition of 'negative capability', objects to Coleridge's excessive attachment to theoretic consistency; Shelley with his typical synthesising method, assimilates Coleridge's ideas into his own conception of art as visionary inspiration, itself indebted to neo-Platonic sources. Byron rejected the ideas of Wordsworth and Coleridge, preferring to look back to eighteenth-century ideas of poetry, yet his grand gestures and the extravagant emotions of his poetry became for many the keynote of 'the romantic'.

The problem facing Wordsworth and many of the British Romantics was how to convey deep feeling without overbalancing into sentimentality. The approach which many followed was to stress the reality of their subjects and the specific, well-proportioned emotion of their reaction. This justification is not dependent on conventional situations with their over-ready emotional *clichés*, but is carried by the material itself and its comparability with situations in real life. The reader is almost forced to compare his own reaction to analogous situations in real life with the insights of the artist. Wordsworth, with a profound wish to ameliorate public taste and attitudes but wishing also to utilise habitual or traditional feelings, had to awaken a new appreciation of common reality — one might almost say forge a new image of reality. The Lake District life which he praised as an existence in which 'the essential passions of the heart find a better soil in which they can attain their maturity', was in fact a very selective image of everyday reality. Nevertheless the passions which Wordsworth elevates into principles convincingly correspond to basic human instincts such as familial love and independence; and the poetry, as well as the Preface, lays emphasis on the reality of character and setting, often to the extent of being authenticated by documentary proof or personal record. In fact so great is Wordsworth's stress on reality that he viewed the poet as 'mechanical' or servile, and the poet's power as small beside the power of actual suffering; and his poetic theory tends to ignore techniques of selection and presentation in favour of an appeal to experience. He wanted to recall poetry to the discipline of empirical reality. But the later additions to the Preface include the paean to poetry as the rock of defence of human nature and suggest that the poet is a man gifted beyond the ordinary, a man able to see and interpret the spirit of Nature working through all things, a claim expressed with a Romantic eloquence which looks forward to Shelley's rhapsody.

Coleridge criticised Wordsworth's theory rather than his practice. The Preface to *Lyrical Ballads* seems to advocate copying rather than imitating, whereas Wordsworth's poetry had impressed him by 'the fine balance of truth in observing with the imaginative faculty in modifying the objects observed'. For Coleridge a poem is a structure ordered by the originating impulse, less a description of outward things than a system of symbols representing inner experience. The poet cannot merely copy the observed language and behaviour of others but must rely on his own educated and intuitive choice of images and diction to correspond to the exact nuance of emotion. The discipline of observed reality is replaced by fidelity to inner experience which organically shapes the poem, its diction, rhythm and rhyme all working together to reinforce the progression and climaxes of a representation of emotional or spiritual experience. Coleridge's stress on the inward experience which a poem embodies — 'meditation' rather than 'observation' — is consistent with his philosophical views on the inner origin of all spiritual and moral values which are evident to the Coleridgean faculty of Reason. From the subordinacy of the material realism of sense comes the importance of the Imagination, which 'dissolves, diffuses, dissipates, in order to re-create'. In his second *Lay Sermon* Coleridge defined the Imagination as 'that reconciling and mediatory power, which, incorporating the reason in images of the sense, and organising (as it were) the flux of the senses by the permanent and self-circling energies of the reason, gives birth to a system of symbols, harmonious in themselves, and consubstantial with the truths of which they are conductors'. The function of the symbol, mediating between the individual and the general, sense and spirit, is integral to Coleridge's idea of poetry, but the emphasis on reconciliation is perhaps an indication of his particular interest; the analysis of emotions and states of being that are complex and often paradoxical, for which normal language and conceptions are inadequate.

Hazlitt attended Coleridge's lectures on Shakespeare, and Keats attended one of Hazlitt's. Keats, to whom Shakespeare's works were an education in themselves, develops the idea of the versatility of the artist's temperament in his letters, where he doubts whether the poet has a personality. The artist's relish in the intense dramatic representation of human passions can conflict with the demands of a stable moral character. The artist delights as much in the creation of an Iago as a Desdemona, an Iachimo as an Imogen; this suggestion adumbrates a moral irresponsibility that points forward to the Aesthetic movement. Hazlitt too adopts the Coleridgean criterion of dramatic impersonality; imagination is consequently denied by Hazlitt to Wordsworth, whose subjects are seen as mere vehicles for the artist's self-projection. Even in Keats, his own protegé, he finds a deficiency in 'action, character and...imagination' and a want of 'masculine energy of style'. It is strange to find Hazlitt, the immoral turbulent Romantic, criticising the Romantic poets for exactly the same deficiencies of weight of subject and dependence on 'expression' as Arnold some thirty years later.

Coleridge's account of the Imagination also influenced Shelley, though the effects were such as to demonstrate the difficulties of Coleridge's own formulations. For Coleridge the poet's secondary imagination is similar in kind to the primary imagination, which is a universal possession, a faculty by which everyone creates his own world, which is yet the world of all of us. The secondary imagination, though creative, fashions its worlds in a strict conformity with the ideals which order the communal reality. Yet however hard Coleridge tries to reconcile the insights of the artist with the everyday world, the figure of the poet in his work suggests the exceptional visionary, the vates with glittering eye and floating hair inspired by supernatural forces. In Shelley's 'Defence of Poetry' the poet is no longer seen as Wordsworth's common man, who, 'singing a song in which all human beings join with him, rejoices in the presence of truth as our visible friend and hourly companion'. Shelley's poet, struggling to eternise the transient visitations of supernatural power, is a nightingale who is little acknowledged by men entranced by the melody. The intensity both of the poetic inspiration and of the response to poetry is such as to escape rational consciousness; it is 'a going out of our own nature, and an identification of ourselves with the beautiful which exists in thought, action and person, not our own'. The idea of poetry as a record of moments of high intensity received eloquent expression in Shelley's rhapsody with its images of hot coals, electrical discharges, Promethean fire and lifted veils, while his emphasis on the momentary nature of inspiration licensed the fragment as a poetic 'form' and added to the conviction with which Poe was later able to assert that a long poem was 'simply a flat contradiction in terms'.

The inspiration for social reform at this period was not confined to artists. Among those who made the greatest practical impact in this field were adherents of a new form of puritanism, often legalistic in its approach. The moral earnestness of the Evangelicals was not a new thing in English life, but it did become organised into an influential campaign in the 1780's, and won converts among the most powerful establishment circles. Fashionable pulpits thundered threats of hell-fire, and the discrepancy between standards of behaviour and the practical implications of Christian doctrine seemed more obvious. The Evangelicals' writings were addressed to the responsible classes and inculcated the virtue of respectability. Their education of the poor was concerned to foster docility and appreciation rather than criticism and imagination. This conservatism is not, however, exclusive of energetic denunciation of human shortcomings, idleness and vanities, and it can produce an enthusiastic vision of an enlightened discipline in society.

The Evangelical temper was at first inimical to radical political reform. A more potent intellectual influence in this respect was the peculiar form of moral and democratic rationalism associated with the Scottish tradition. The combination of the elective, debating form of church government, and the tolerant 'new light' ethic of the moral sense, had given Presbyterianism a human face in the eighteenth century. The Scottish Universities proved more hospitable to adventurous enquiry in economics and jurisprudence than the English. Edinburgh was by 1800 a leading European educational and cultural centre, attracting young Englishmen denied the opportunity of the Grand Tour by the wars with France. The younger generation of Scottish intellectuals, Mackintosh, Jeffrey, Brougham and Lockhart, engaged in debating societies. The majority wrote in favour of progressive social principles. Their habits of intensive academic study and legalistic exactitude added weight to the case for reform which was being argued more idealistically in England. When James Mill, a rationalist advocate of educational and political solutions to the problems of the age, joined forces with Bentham, the utilitarian tradition lost for ever its dimension of hedonistic latitudinarianism, and allied itself to high seriousness and detailed proposals for the rationalisation of the bureaucracy, the colonies, the schools, the magistracy. Despite the material benefits which these measures brought, and the undoubted humanitarianism of their proposers, they were widely attacked for their concentration on materialistic benefits and their acceptance of 'natural laws' which set strict limits to benevolence. Rationalism, which to Godwin and many of the early radicals had seemed consonant with the greatest human improvement, became viewed as a cold sacrifice of human values to material advantage and administrative expediency. The defence of the imagination in Shelley's 'Defence of Poetry' was a counter-blast to the predominant spirit of government and an affirmation that true reform lay in a study of man's instinctual, emotional and moral nature. Shelley's ideas maintain a commitment to progress, and indeed to revolution. In Brougham, on the other hand, the radical cause found a skilful orator who applied the techniques of legal action, petitioning, pamphleteering and organising movements to secular ends. Brougham gained an influence in the Educational Institution set up by Joseph Lancaster, who invented the economical monitor-system of teaching. It became the British and Foreign Schools Society, with the aims of furthering secular, factual education and basic skills. The concept of Useful Knowledge embraced the sciences and practical arts, history and biography, and resulted in a widespread improvement in the abilities and confidence of the leaders of the working class.

The Owenite experiment in social and educational reform was at once more ambitious and concentrated than the Working Men's associations. Supported by Bentham and prominent Quakers, Owen reorganised his workers' lives on a strictly authoritarian and paternalistic basis with a strong though disguised bias towards secularism. Owen was himself a man of limited reading but wide experience in trade and manufacturing. In his writings he exhorts and demands without the embellishment of learned allusions, but with a fervid literalness suggestive of a revivalist preacher. Owen's hectoring repetitiveness, however, indicates his impatience with both the method of individual salvation and of Parliamentary Reform. He wanted his socialist organisations administered by strong governing bodies, and when he assumed the leadership of various labour organisations he was continually attacked for his autocratic methods. Hazlitt called him a man of one idea, that the individual's character is formed by his environment, and in his model village he set out to provide an environment that would produce happy, moral and productive workers. Above all ruled the principle of kindness: 'a firm, well-directed, persevering kindness'. Owen's fame in his later years rested on his projects for co-operative villages. He had originally prepared plans to organise the unemployed into independent productive units based on industry and agriculture, ruled by committees of elders. His ideas inspired many experimental communities, in Britain and America, some of which Owen himself helped to establish, and he persisted in grandiose schemes of national labour organisation, underestimating the resistance of entrenched economic interests, and of his own comrades, to the reasonableness of his measures.

Cobbett's reaction to the post-war economic crisis was visceral rather than analytic. When he rode by a fertile estate and learned that the owner was Ricardo he set his spurs to his horse and decamped with speed. Cobbett upheld the traditional values of an independent yeomanry. He championed the small independent farmers and lamented their decline as they were compelled or indoctrinated to support the accumulated wealth represented by the large estates and owners of the public funds. Cobbett attacked the palpable target, the economists or Scotch 'feelosophers', and those who were buying up the old estates, the 'tax eaters' and 'jobbers' who were capitalising on the new financial system, and the 'accursed hill' of Old Sarum which represented the corruption of political life. In Cobbett the gift for publicity went with a pugnacious, if erratic, political commitment. Every instance of oppression that met his eye on his travels gave rise to a 'rustic harangue' or article in his *Political Register*, tracing its cause back to enclosure, the grasping large landowners, the Poor Laws or the 'paper-money system'. The sight of the unemployed making roads while crops deteriorated in the fields especially roused his ire, and he cursed and avoided the turnpikes and canals, the improved communications which he saw draining the life-blood of the countryside to swell the 'wen'. Cobbett looked back to a childhood spent in 'merrie England', and often upheld nostalgically the old plain and substantial way of life when the rights of labourers were respected and a common sense of interdependence sustained social and economic relationships. He frequently returned to the example of the medieval monastery as the image of a beneficent social institution, a working community, settled and focal, and found it preferable to the insecurity, competitiveness and rapid urbanisation of the early industrial age.

Cobbett's anti-Protestant attitude contributed towards the increasingly medieval sensibility of nineteenth-century intellectuals of all viewpoints, for instance Scott and Carlyle, as well as Disraeli. Even Coleridge, whose style of thought and writing contrasted so sharply with Cobbett's, praised him as a great educator with a mastery of the popular style, who had become 'the rhinoceros of politics, with a horn of brute strength on a nose of scorn and hate', but who had also 'given publicity to weighty truths'. In many respects a reactionary, Cobbett also looks forward to the next age; he was not only a member of the Reformed Parliament, but a studious cultivator of his own personal image, with an individual, though not learned, style.

Cobbett's paradoxical combination of devotion to the pre-industrial past and commitment to political and economic reform gives his prose a representative significance which no doubt is too great for the actual quality of his writing to bear. Nevertheless his work contributes to what is an impressive array of the discursive prose of the Romantic age. The cultural shift which occurred in the later eighteenth century and early nineteenth century is, as has been indicated, of startling breadth and variety, affecting all subjects of enquiry, all fashions and all the fine arts. Prose is not only one of the arts so affected, but also, because of its amorphous nature, it uniquely reflects the details of the shift. Burke's *Reflections*, consciously cast in the mould of ancient wisdom admonishing upstart novelty, appeal rhetorically to the emotions, yet his style was soon outmoded. The characteristic form of Romantic prose is the narrative essay, individual, revealing, and capable of brilliant bursts of argument and spells of scenic clarity. Not all the best prose of the Romantic age is, of course, romantic. Yet even the most rigorous opponents of originality, idealism and intuitionism formulate their objections in a prose which seems sharpened in definition by the very energy of its adversaries. Certainly, compared with the ratiocinative prose of the Augustan age, the argumentative writing of the early nineteenth century utilitarians and economists is markedly austere, pointed and assertive. The prose of the whole epoch is characterised by swift transitions and densely concentrated climaxes, such as Coleridge's celebrated two paragraphs on Imagination and Fancy. Wordsworth's Preface has some spectacular short passages, and when he argues there that there is no essential difference between the language of poetry and the language of prose when prose is well written, his point cannot only be taken as the downgrading of poetic technique: the argument works just as well the other way, to a higher evaluation of literary prose. Indeed, for different reasons, both Wordsworth and Coleridge direct our attention to the creative achievement of prose-writers. Coleridge believed that the 'writings of Plato, and Bishop Taylor, and the *Theoria Sacra* of Burnet, furnish undeniable proof that poetry of the highest kind may exist without metre, and even without the contradistinguishing object of a poem'. It is not, however, such older eloquence or sustained elaboration of imagery that one seeks in Romantic prose. Shorter energetic flights are more typical, surprising turns, graphic sketches; they represent a loosening of the constraints exerted by Augustan principles of decorum and balance. It is true that Johnson's Latinate and symmetrical style was still widely regarded as a model in the early nineteenth century, but Coleridge attacked Johnson's antitheses as almost always verbal only, and Hazlitt criticised Johnson's mechanical rise and fall, his long words and his artificiality. De Quincey, too, objected to his triads. In 1832 Carlyle described Johnson's writings as laborious and obsolete, and by 1835 he could discern 'the whole structure of our Johnsonian English breaking up from its foundations'.

The change deserves to be regarded positively. Factors which contributed to it include the increasing suspicion of authority and desire to by-pass aristocratic patronage. Certainly many of the prose-writers of the Romantic age learned their style in a more open forum than the journals and letters in which an earlier generation had begun to practise prose. The development of journalism is particularly significant; the extension of political comment into full-scale articles on topics like the slave-trade, the colonies, the war, and penal and electoral reform can be observed in process during the period from 1790 to 1830. The journalistic essay had to be colourful and pressing, as well as topical; many of the writers of this period earned money by writing such pieces. Later the quarterly reviews were able to pay better rates and offer generous space; in their pages the writer had the advantage of anonymity and independence from booksellers. The breadth of the audience's interests fostered versatility in the reviewers, as well as an assumption of authority, the confidence to beat out an idea over several sentences and a weakness for familiar quotations and dismissive sarcasms.

Other means of reaching an audience through prose were the reading of papers to literary and philosophical societies and the giving of a series of lectures. An incalculable influence on the style and form of the political speech was, of course, the sermon, where indeed the two were separate. In the hands of the young Coleridge, for instance, the sermon was no excercise in classical tedium. We have from Hazlitt a marvellous description of Coleridge's preaching in 1798:

> The preacher then launched into his subject, like an eagle dallying with the wind. The sermon was upon peace and war; upon church and state — not their alliance, but their separation — on the spirit of the world and the spirit of Christianity, not as the same, but as opposed to one another. He talked of those who had 'inscribed the cross of Christ on banners drifting with human gore'. He made a poetical and pastoral excursion — and to show the fatal effects of war, drew a striking contrast between the simple shepherd boy, driving his team afield, or sitting under the hawthorn, piping to his flock, 'as though he should never be old', and the same

poor country-lad, crimped, kidnapped, brought into town, made drunk at an alehouse, turned into a wretched drummer-boy, with his hair sticking on end with powder and pomatum, a long cue at his back, and tricked out in the loathsome finery of the profession of blood.

Such were the notes our once-lov'd poet sung. And for myself I could not have been more delighted if I had heard the music of the spheres. Poetry and Philosophy had met together, Truth and Genius had embraced, under the eye and with the sanction of Religion. This was even beyond my hopes.

It is doubtful which is the more attractive here, the original sermon or the report which it inspired, but again the two have become inseparable. Even while dwelling on a theme of sustained seriousness, Hazlitt manipulates a tone which is flexible and expressive of personal excitement. By the 1820's the periodical press had taken over much of the reporting, criticism and reminiscence which the post used to receive, and now the reading public felt itself to be the confidant of everybody. In 1824 Mary Russell Mitford explained the new conditions to her old-fashioned friend Sir William Elford, who had questioned the propriety of the style of her books;

We are free and easy in these days, and talk to the public as a friend. Read 'Elia' or the 'Sketch Book', or Hazlitt's 'Table Talk', or any popular book of the new school, and you will find that we have turned over the Johnsonian periods and the Blairian formality to keep company with the wigs and hoops.

Obviously the dominant virtues of prose were now to be informality and freedom. The Victorian period, however, brought other changes, most notably an increase in the self-importance of prose-writers who felt the need to stake a claim to greatness and to design works on an appropriate scale. This Victorian achievement in discursive prose is very impressive indeed, but the freshness and brightness of the Romantic age were by then evidently lost.

Alan W. Bellringer.
C.B. Jones.

Richard Price (1723-1791), a prominent Dissenting clergyman, had established a reputation with works on economics and moral philosophy and had produced influential pamphlets in support of American independence. We open the anthology with extracts from a sermon in which Price echoes the widespread satisfaction with events in France: an address from the same meeting of the Revolution Society was transmitted to the French Assembly, looking forward to a union of France and Britain to spread the principles of liberty. Edmund Burke (1729-1797) was one of the first writers to anticipate the dangers of 'French principles' in England, and as a former critic of the American War, his attack on libertarian ideas surprised and shocked his parliamentary colleagues, Fox and Sheridan, and split the Whig party. His long-held distrust of metaphysical reason in favour of what can now be termed pragmatic evolutionary expediency, and his opposition to the extension of the franchise, made the *Reflections* the culmination of a development of conservative thought. The work was held by many to provide a philosophy of counter-revolution and moral responsibility. In looking back to moral ideas associated with medieval times to combat modern economic individualism, Burke was followed by a line of Romantic and Victorian thinkers like Coleridge, Carlyle and Morris. The main radical attack on the *Reflections* was made by Thomas Paine (1737-1809), son of a Quaker staymaker of Thetford. After a period in the excise-service, Paine emigrated to America in 1774 with a letter of introduction from Benjamin Franklin and played an important role in the literary battles of the American War through his journalism and pamphlets. In the *Rights of Man*, Part I, he states his doctrine that man forfeits none of his natural rights when entering the compact of society. He also mounts violent satiric attacks upon Burke, British institutions and that 'necessary evil', government. In Part II a more constructive approach envisages government as playing a beneficial role in social administration. Another critic of Burke, James Mackintosh (1765-1832), then reading for the bar, seized on the logical weakness of Burke's limitation of rights. In his *Vindiciae Gallicae* his generally moderate reformist view includes a disconcerting acceptance of the necessity for violence in revolutionary change. Mackintosh recanted his revolutionary views in 1799. Mary Wollstonecraft (1759-1797), whose life as lady's companion, governess, school-teacher and abandoned mistress gave a note of bitter personal experience to her writings, extended the debate on liberty to the position of women. In her *Vindication of the Rights of Woman* she ascribes the acknowledged failings of women to their dependence on men, and advocates for them a more responsible, less sheltered role, where their talents could gain recognition in an equal society. William Godwin (1756-1836), a lapsed Dissenting minister, whom she married in 1797, took libertarian ideas to an anarchistic extreme, denying the legitimacy of any constraint upon the individual save the principle of justice evident to his reason. In *Political Justice* Godwin's fulminations against property and his utopian speculations made him a main target for satirists but an inspiring prophet for the young Romantic poets.

RICHARD PRICE

From *A Discourse on the Love of our Country, delivered on November 4, 1789*
(The extract is from the first edition, 1790).

We are met to thank God for that event in this country to which the name of THE REVOLUTION has been given; and which, for more than a century, it has been usual for the friends of freedom, and more especially Protestant Dissenters, under the title of the REVOLUTION SOCIETY,[1] to celebrate with expressions of joy and exultation. ...By a bloodless victory, the fetters which despotism had been long preparing for us were broken; the rights of the people were asserted, a tyrant expelled, and a Sovereign of our own choice appointed in his room. Security was given to our property, and our consciences were emancipated. The bounds of free enquiry were enlarged; the volume in which are the words of eternal life, was laid more open to our examination; and that *aera* of light and liberty was introduced among us, by which we have been made an example to other kingdoms, and became the instructors of the world. Had it not been for this deliverance, the probability is, that, instead of being thus distinguished, we should now have been a base people, groaning under the infamy and misery of popery and slavery.

---

1. the REVOLUTION SOCIETY: The Society for Commemorating the Revolution in Great Britain met annually on November 4, birthday of William of Orange, to celebrate the 'Glorious Revolution' of 1688 by listening to a sermon and holding a meeting at a nearby tavern.

...We have, therefore, on this occasion, peculiar reasons for thanksgiving — But let us remember that we ought not to satisfy ourselves with thanksgivings. Our gratitude, if genuine, will be accompanied with endeavours to give stability to the deliverance our country has obtained, and to extend and improve the happiness with which the Revolution has blest us — Let us, in particular, take care not to forget the principles of the Revolution. This Society has, very properly, in its Reports, held out these principles, as an instruction to the public. I will only take notice of the three following:

First; The right to liberty of conscience in religious matters.
Secondly; The right to resist power when abused. And,
Thirdly; The right to chuse our own governors; to cashier them for misconduct; and to frame a government for ourselves.

On these three principles, and more especially the last, was the Revolution founded. Were it not true that liberty of conscience is a sacred right; that power abused justifies resistance; and that civil authority is a delegation from the people — Were not, I say, all this true; the Revolution would have been not an ASSERTION, but an INVASION of rights; not a REVOLUTION, but a REBELLION. Cherish in your breasts this conviction, and act under its influence; detesting the odious doctrines of passive obedience, non-resistance, and the divine right of kings — doctrines which, had they been acted upon in this country, would have left us at this time wretched slaves — doctrines which imply, that God made mankind to be oppressed and plundered; and which are no less a blasphemy against him, than an insult on common sense.
...What an eventful period is this! I am thankful that I have lived to see it; and I could almost say, *Lord, now lettest thou thy servant depart in peace, for mine eyes have seen thy salvation.*[2] I have lived to see a diffusion of knowledge, which has undermined superstition and error — I have lived to see the rights of men better understood than ever; and nations panting for liberty, which seemed to have lost the idea of it. — I have lived to see THIRTY MILLIONS of people, indignant and resolute, spurning at slavery, and demanding liberty with an irresistible voice; their king led in triumph, and an arbitrary monarch surrendering himself to his subjects. — After sharing in the benefits of one Revolution, I have been spared to be a witness to two other Revolutions, both glorious. — And now, methinks, I see the ardour for liberty catching and spreading; a general amendment beginning in human affairs; the do-

2. Luke 2.29, 30.

minion of kings changed for the dominion of laws, and the dominion of priests giving way to the dominion of reason and conscience.

Be encouraged, all ye friends of freedom, and writers in its defence! The times are auspicious. Your labours have not been in vain. Behold kingdoms, admonished by you, starting from sleep, breaking their fetters, and claiming justice from their oppressors! Behold, the light you have struck out, after setting America free, reflected to FRANCE, and there kindled into a blaze that lays despotism in ashes, and warms and illuminates EUROPE!!

Tremble all ye oppressors of the world! Take warning all ye supporters of slavish governments, and slavish hierarchies! Call no more (absurdly and wickedly) REFORMATION, innovation. You cannot now hold the world in darkness. Struggle no longer against increasing light and liberality. Restore to mankind their rights; and consent to the correction of abuses, before they and you are destroyed together.

EDMUND BURKE

From *Reflections on the Revolution in France, and on the Proceedings in Certain Societies in London relative to that Event. In a Letter intended to have been sent to a Gentleman in Paris*
(The extracts are from the first edition, 1790. The Reflections are addressed to Chames-Jean-François de Pont, who had corresponded with Burke from Paris on the French Revolution).

...It is far from impossible to reconcile, if we do not suffer ourselves to be entangled in the mazes of metaphysic sophistry, the use both of a fixed rule and an occasional deviation: the sacredness of an hereditary principle of succession in our government with a power of change in its application in cases of extreme emergency. Even in that extremity (if we take the measure of our rights by our exercise of them at the Revolution) the change is to be confined to the peccant part only; to the part which produced the necessary deviation; and even then it is to be effected without a decomposition of the whole civil and political mass for the purpose of originating a new civil order out of the first elements of society.

A state without the means of some change is without the means of its conservation. Without such means it might even risk the loss of that part of the constitution which it wished the most religiously to preserve. The two principles of conservation and correction operated strongly at the two critical periods of the Restoration and Revolution, when England found itself without a king. At both those periods the nation had lost the bond of union in their ancient edifice; they did not, however, dissolve the whole fabric. On the contrary, in both cases they regenerated the deficient part of the old constitution through the parts which were not impaired. They kept these old parts exactly as they were, that the part recovered might be suited to them. They acted by the ancient organized states in the shape of their old organization, and not by the organic *moleculae* of a disbanded people. At no time, perhaps, did the sovereign legislature manifest a more tender regard to that fundamental principle of British constitutional policy than at the time of the Revolution, when it deviated from the direct line of hereditary succession. The crown was carried somewhat out of the line in which it had before moved, but the new line was derived from the same stock. it was still a line of hereditary descent, still an hereditary descent in the same blood, though an hereditary descent qualified with Protestantism. When the legislature altered the direction, but kept the principle, they showed that they held it inviolable.

...You will observe that from Magna Charta to the Declaration of Right it has been the uniform policy of our constitution to claim and assert our liberties as an *entailed inheritance* derived to us from our forefathers, and to be transmitted to our posterity; as an estate specially belonging to the people of this kingdom, without any reference whatsoever to any other more general or prior right. By this means our constitution preserves an unity in so great a diversity of its parts. We have an inheritable crown, an inheritable peerage, and an House of Commons and a people inheriting privileges, franchises, and liberties from a long line of ancestors.

This policy appears to me to be the result of profound reflection; or rather the happy effect of following nature, which is wisdom without reflection, and above it. A spirit of innovation is generally the result of a selfish temper and confined views. People will not look forward to posterity, who never look backward to their ancestors. Besides, the people of England well know that the idea of inheritance furnishes a sure principle of conservation, and a sure principle of transmission; without at all excluding a principle of improvement. It leaves acquisiton free; but it secures what it acquires. Whatever advantages are obtained by a state proceeding on these maxims are locked fast as in a sort of family settlement; grasped as in a kind of mortmain forever. By a constitutional policy, working after the pattern of nature, we receive, we hold, we transmit our governments and our privileges in the same manner in which we enjoy and transmit our property and our lives. The institution of policy, the goods of fortune, the gifts of Providence are handed down, to us and from us, in the same course and order. Our political system is placed in a just correspondence and symmetry with the order of the world, and with the mode of existence decreed to a permanent body composed of transitory parts: wherein, by the disposition of a stupendous wisdom, molding together the great mysterious incorporation of the human race, the whole, at one time, is never old, or middle-aged, or young, but in a condition of unchangeable constancy, moves on through the varied tenor of perpetual decay, fall, renovation, and progression. Thus, by preserving the method of nature in the conduct of the state, in what we improve we are never wholly new; in what we retain we are never wholly obsolete. By adhering in this manner and on those principles to our forefathers, we are guided not by the superstition of antiquarians, but by the spirit of philosophic analogy. In this choice of inheritance we have given to our frame of polity the image of a relation in blood, binding up the constitution of our country with our dearest domestic ties, adopting our fundamental laws into the bosom of our family affections; keeping inseparable and cherishing with the warmth of all their combined and mutually reflected charities, our state, our hearths, our sepulchres, and our altars.

Through the same plan of a conformity to nature in our artificial institutions, and by calling in the aid of her unerring and powerful instincts to fortify the fallible and feeble contrivances of our reason, we have derived several other, and those no small benefits, from considering our liberties in the light of an inheritance. Always acting as if in the presence of canonized forefathers, the spirit of freedom, leading in itself to misrule and excess, is tempered with an awful gravity. This idea of a liberal descent inspires us with a sense of habitual native dignity, which prevents that upstart insolence almost inevitably adhering to and dis-gracing those who are the first acquirers of any distinction. By this means our liberty becomes a noble freedom. It carries an imposing and majestic aspect. It has a pedigree and illustrious ancestors. It has its bearings, and its ensigns armorial. It has its gallery of portraits; its monumental inscriptions; its records, evidences, and titles. We procure reverence to our civil institutions on the principle upon which nature teaches us to revere individual men; on account of their age; and on account of those from whom they are descended. All your sophisters cannot produce anything better adapted to preserve a rational and manly freedom than the course that we have pursued, who have chosen our nature rather than our speculations, our breasts rather than our inventions, for the great conservatories and magazines of our rights and privileges.

...If civil society be the offspring of convention, that convention must be its law. That convention must limit and modify all the descriptions of constitution which are formed under it. Every sort of legislative, judicial, or executory power are its creatures. They can have no being in any other state of things; and how can any man claim, under the conventions of civil society, rights which do not so much as suppose of its existence? Rights which are absolutely repugnant to it? One of the first motives to civil society, and which becomes one of its fundamental rules, is *that no man should be judge in his own cause*. By this each person has at once divested himself of the first fundamental right of uncovenanted man, that is, to judge for himself and to assert his own cause. He abicates all right to be his own governor. He inclusively, in a great measure, abandons the right of self-defense, the first law of nature. Man cannot enjoy the rights of an uncivil and of a civil state together. That he may obtain justice, he gives up his right of determining what it is in points the most essential to him. That he may secure some liberty, he makes a surrender in trust of the whole of it.

Government is not made in virtue of natural rights, which may and do exist in total independence of it; and exist in much greater clearness and in a much greater degree of abstract perfection; but their abstract perfection is their practical defect. By having a right to everything they want everything. Government is a contrivance of human wisdom to provide for human *wants*. Men have a right that these wants should be provided for by this wisdom. Among these wants is to be reckoned the want, out of civil society, of a sufficient restraint upon their passions. Society requires not only that the passions of individuals should be subjected, but that even in the mass and body, as well as in the individuals, the inclinations of men should frequently be thwarted, their will controlled, and their passions brought into subjection. This can only be done *by a power out of themselves*; and not, in the exercise ot its function, subject to that will and those passions which it is its office to bridle and subdue. In this sense the restraints on men, as well as their liberties, are to be reckoned among their rights. But as the liberties and the restrictions vary with times and circumstances, and admit to infinite modifications, they cannot be settled upon any abstract rule, and nothing is so foolish as to discuss them upon that principle.

...It is now sixteen or eighteen years since I saw the queen of France,[3] then the Dauphiness, at Versailles, and surely never lighted on this orb, which she hardly seemed to touch, a more delightful vision. I saw her just above the horizon, decorating and cheering the elevated sphere she just began to move in, — glittering like the morning star, full of life, and splendour, and joy. Oh! what a revolution! and what an heart must I have, to contemplate without emotion that elevation and that fall! Little did I dream that, when she added titles of veneration to those

---

3. the queen of France: Marie-Antoinette, wife of Louis XVI. Burke is speaking of the confused events at Versailles in October, 1789, when a force from Paris arrived to escort the king and queen back to the capital.

of enthusiastic, distant, respectful love, that she should ever be obliged to carry the sharp antidote against disgrace concealed in that bosom; little did I dream that I should have lived to see such disasters fallen upon her in a nation of gallant men, in a nation of men of honour and of cavaliers. I thought ten thousand swords must have leaped from their scabbards to avenge even a look that threatened her with insult. — But the age of chivalry is gone. — That of sophisters, oeconomists, and calculators, has succeeded, and the glory of Europe is extinguished forever. Never, never more, shall we behold the generous loyalty to rank and sex, that proud submission, that dignified obedience, that subordination of the heart, which kept alive, even in servitude itself, the spirit of an exalted freedom. The unbought grace of life, the cheap defence of nations, the nurse of manly sentiment and heroic enterprize is gone! It is gone, that sensibility of principle, that chastity of honour, which felt a stain like a wound, which inspired courage whilst it mitigated ferocity, which ennobled whatever it touched, and under which vice itself lost half its evil, by losing all its grossness.

This mixed system of opinion and sentiment had its origin in the ancient chivalry; and the principle, though varied in its appearance by the varying state of human affairs, subsisted and influenced through a long succession of generations, even to the time we live in. If it should ever be totally extinguished, the loss I fear will be great. It is this which has given its character to modern Europe. It is this which has distinguished it under all its forms of government, and distinguished it to its advantage, from the states of Asia, and possibly from those states which flourished in the most brilliant periods of the antique world. It was this, which, without confounding ranks, had produced a noble equality and handed it down through all the gradations of social life. It was this opinion which mitigated kings into companions, and raised private men to be fellows with kings. Without force or opposition, it subdued the fierceness of pride and power; it obliged sovereigns to submit to the soft collar of social esteem, compelled stern authority to submit to elegance, and gave a domination vanquisher of laws, to be subdued by manners.

But now all is to be changed. All the pleasing illusions, which made power gentle and obedience liberal, which harmonized the different shades of life, and which, by a bland assimilation, incorporated into politics the sentiments which beautify and soften private society, are to be dissolved by this new conquering empire of light and reason. All the decent drapery of life is to be rudely torn off. All the superadded ideas, furnished from the wardrobe of a moral imagination, which the heart owns and the understanding ratifies as necessary to cover the defects of our naked, shivering nature, and to raise it to dignity in our own estimation, are to be exploded as a ridiculous, absurd, and antiquated fashion.

...I almost venture to affirm, that not one in a hundred amongst us participates in the "triumph" of the Revolution Society. If the king and queen of France, and their children, were to fall into our hands by the chance of war, in the most acrimonious of all hostilities (I deprecate such an event, I deprecate such hostility) they would be treated with another sort of triumphal entry into London. We formerly have had a king of France in that situation;[4] you have read how he was treated by the victor in the field; and in what manner he was afterwards received in England. Four hundred years have gone over us, but I believe we are not materially changed since that period. Thanks to our sullen resistance to innovation, thanks to the cold sluggishness of our national character, we still bear the stamp of our forefathers. We have not (as I conceive) lost the generosity and dignity of thinking of the fourteenth century; nor as yet have we subtilized ourselves into savages. We are not the converts of Rousseau; we are not the disciples of Voltaire; Helvetius has made no progress amongst us.[5] Atheists are not our preachers; madmen are not our lawgivers. We know that *we* have made no discoveries, and we think that no discoveries are to be made, in morality; nor many in the great principles of government, nor in the ideas of liberty, which were understood long before we were born, altogether as well as they will be after the grave has heaped its mould upon our presumption, and the silent tomb shall have imposed its law on our pert loquacity. In England we have not yet been completely embowelled of our natural entrails; we still feel within us, and we cherish and cultivate, those inbred sentiments which are the faithful guardians, the active monitors of our duty, the true supporters of all liberal and manly morals. We have not been drawn and trussed, in order that we may be filled, like stuffed birds in a museum, with chaff and rags, and paltry, blurred shreds of paper about the rights of man. We preserve the whole of our feelings still native and entire, unsophisticated by pedantry and infidelity. We have real hearts of flesh and blood beating in our bosoms. We fear God; we look up with awe to kings; with affection to parliaments; with duty to magistrates; with reverence to priests; and with respect to nobility. Why? Because when such ideas are brought before our minds, it is *natural* to be so affected; because all other feelings are false and spurious, and tend to corrupt our minds, to

4. a king of France in that situation: John the Good was captured by the Black Prince in 1356. He was entertained chivalrously by Edward III for 4 years before a treaty for his return to France was concluded. Later, when this treaty was held to have been broken, he returned to England voluntarily and on his death was given a sumptuous funeral in St. Paul's Cathedral.
5. Jean Jacques Rousseau (1712-1777), François-Marie Arouet (1694-1778), and Claude Adrian Helvetius (1715-1771); three celebrated contributors to the intellectual movement which preceded the French Revolution.

vitiate our primary morals, to render us unfit for rational liberty; and, by teaching us a servile, licentious, and abandoned insolence, to be our low sport for a few holidays, to make us perfectly fit for, and justly deserving of slavery, through the whole course of our lives.

You see, Sir, that in this enlightened age I am bold enough to confess, that we are generally men of untaught feelings; that, instead of casting away all our old prejudices, we cherish them to a very considerable degree, and, to take more shame to ourselves, we cherish them because they are prejudices; and the longer they have lasted, and the more generally they have prevailed, the more we cherish them. We are afraid to put men to live and trade each on his own private stock of reason; because we suspect that this stock in each man is small, and that the individuals would do better to avail themselves of the general bank and capital of nations, and of ages. Many of our men of speculation, instead of exploding general prejudices, employ their sagacity to discover the latent wisdom which prevails in them. If they find what they seek, and they seldom fail, they think it more wise to continue the prejudice, with the reason involved, than to cast away the coat of prejudice, and to leave nothing but the naked reason; because prejudice, with its reason, has a motive to give action to that reason, and an affection which will give it permanence. Prejudice is of ready application in the emergency; it previously engages the mind in a steady course of wisdom and virtue, and does not leave the man hesitating in the moment of decision sceptical, puzzled, and unresolved. Prejudice renders a man's virtue his habit; and not a series of unconnected acts. Through just prejudice, his duty becomes a part of his nature.

THOMAS PAINE
From *Rights of Man*

(The extracts are from Part I, first edition, 1791, and from Part II, first edition, 1792).

...The error of those who reason by precedents drawn from antiquity, respecting the rights of man, is, that they do not go far enough into antiquity. They do not go the whole way. They stop in some of the intermediate stages of an hundred or a thousand years, and produce what was then done, as a rule for the present day. This is no authority at all. If we travel still farther into antiquity, we shall find a direct contrary opinion and practice prevailing; and if antiquity is to be authority, a thousand such authorities may be produced, successively contradicting each other: But if we proceed on, we shall at last come out right; we shall come to the time when man came from the hand of his Maker. What was he then? Man. Man was his high and only title, and a higher cannot be given him. — But of titles I shall speak hereafter.

We are now got at the origin of man, and at the origin of his rights. As to the manner in which the world has been governed from that day to this, it is no further any concern of ours than to make a proper use of the errors or the improvements which the history of it presents. Those who lived a hundred or a thousand years ago, were then moderns, as we are now. They had their ancients, and those ancients had others, and we also shall be ancients in our turn. If the mere name of antiquity is to govern in the affairs of life, the people who are to live a hundred or a thousand years hence, may as well take us for a precedent, as we make a precedent of those who lived an hundred or a thousand years ago. The fact is, that portions of antiquity, by proving everything, establish nothing. It is authority against authority all the way, till we come to the divine origin of the rights of man at the creation. Here our inquiries find a resting-place, and our reason finds a home. If a dispute about the rights of man had arisen at the distance of an hundred years from the creation, it is to this source of authority they must have referred, and it is to the same source of authority that we must now refer.

...The Mosaic account of the creation, whether taken as divine authority, or merely historical, is full to this point, *the unity or equality of man*. The expressions admit of no controversy. 'And God said, Let us make man in our own image. In the image of God created he him; male and female created he them.'[6] The distinction of sexes is pointed out, but no other distinction is even implied. If this be not divine authority, it is at least historical authority, and shows that the equality of man, so far from being a modern doctrine, is the oldest upon record.

It is also to be observed, that all the religions known in the world are founded, so far as they relate to man, on the *unity of man*, as being all of one degree. Whether in heaven or in hell, or in whatever state man may be supposed to exist hereafter, the good and the bad are the only distinctions. Nay, even the laws of governments are obliged to slide into this principle, by making degrees to consist in crimes, and not in persons.

It is one of the greatest of all truths, and of the highest advantage to cultivate. By considering man in this light, and by instructing him to consider himself in this light, it places him in a close connexion with all his duties, whether to his Creator, or to the creation, of which he is a part; and it is only when he forgets his origin, or, to use a more fashionable

6. Genesis 1. 26, 27.

phrase, his *birth and family*, that he becomes dissolute. It is not among the least of the evils of the present existing governments in all parts of Europe, that man, considered as man, is thrown back to a vast distance from his Maker, and the artificial chasm filled up by a succession of barriers, or sort of turnpike gates, through which he has to pass. I will quote Mr. Burke's catalogue of barriers that he has set up between man and his Maker. Putting himself in the character of a herald, he says — "We fear God — we look with *awe* to kings — with affection to parliaments — with duty to magistrates — with reverence to priests, and with respect to nobility".[7] Mr. Burke has forgotten to put in "*chivalry*". He has also forgotten to put in Peter.[8]

The duty of man is not a wilderness of turnpike gates, through which he is to pass by tickets from one to the other. It is plain and simple, and consists but of two points. His duty to God, which every man must feel; and with respect to his neighbour, to do as he would be done by. If those to whom power is delegated do well, they will be respected; if not, they will be despised: and with regard to those to whom no power is delegated, but who assume it, the rational world can know nothing of them.

Hitherto we have spoken only (and that but in part) of the natural rights of man. We have now to consider the civil rights of man, and to show how the one originates from the other. Man did not enter into society to become *worse* than he was before, nor to have fewer rights than he had before, but to have those rights better secured. His natural rights are the foundations of all his civil rights. But in order to pursue this distinction with more precision, it will be necessary to mark the different qualities of natural and civil rights.

A few words will explain this. Natural rights are those which appertain to man in right of his existence. Of this kind are all the intellectual rights, or rights of the mind, and also all those rights of acting as an individual for his own comfort and happiness, which are not injurious to the natural rights of others. Civil rights are those which appertain to man in right of his being a member of society. Every civil right has for its foundation, some natural right pre-existing in the individual, but to the enjoyment of which his individual power is not, in all cases, sufficiently competent. Of this kind are all those which relate to security and protection.

...When a set of artful men pretended, through the medium of oracles, to hold intercourse with the Deity, as familiarly as they now march up the back-stairs in European courts, the world was completely under the government of superstition. The oracles were consulted, and whatever

---

7. 'We fear God...' *etc.*: see Burke, *Reflections*, above p. 25.
8. Peter: because of his Irish background Burke had to withstand accusations of Catholic tendencies throughout his career.

they were made to say, became the law; and this sort of government lasted as long as this sort of superstition lasted.

After these a race of conquerors arose, whose government, like that of William the Conqueror, was founded in power, and the sword assumed the name of the sceptre. Governments thus established, last as long as the power to support them lasts; but that they might avail themselves of every engine in their favour, they united fraud to force, and set up an idol which they called *Divine Right*, and which, in imitation of the Pope, who affects to be spiritual and temporal, and in contradiction to the Founder of the Christian religion, twisted itself afterwards into an idol of another shape, called *Church and State*. They key of St. Peter, and the key of the Treasury, became quartered on one another and the wondering cheated multitude worshiped the invention.

When I contemplate the natural dignity of man, when I feel (for Nature has not been kind enough to me to blunt my feelings) for the honour and happiness of its character, I become irritated at the attempt to govern mankind by force and fraud, as if they were all knaves and fools, and can scarcely avoid disgust at those who are thus imposed upon.

...It has been thought a considerable advantage towards establishing the principles of Freedom, to say, that government is a compact between those who govern and those who are governed: but this cannot be true, because it is putting the effect before the cause; for as man must have existed before governments existed, there necessarily was a time when governments did not exist, and consequently there could originally exist no governors to form such a compact with. The fact therefore must be, that the *individuals themselves,* each in his own personal and sovereign right, *entered into a compact with each other* to produce a government: and this is the only mode in which governments have a right to arise, and the only principle on which they have a right to exist.

...Not a thirtieth, scarcely a fortieth, part of the taxes which are raised in England are either occasioned by, or applied to, the purposes of civil government. It is not difficult to see, that the whole which the actual government does in this respect, is to enact laws, and that the country administers and executes them, at its own expence, by means of magistrates, juries, sessions, and assize, over and above the taxes which it pays.

In this view of the case, we have two distinct characters of government; the one the civil government, or the government of laws, which operates at home, the other the court or cabinet government, which operates abroad, on the rude plan of uncivilized life; the one attended with little charge, the other with boundless extravagance; and so distinct are the two, that if the latter were to sink as it were by a sudden opening of the earth, and totally disappear, the former would not be deranged. It would still proceed, because it is the common interest of the nation that it should, and all the means are in practice.

Revolutions, then, have for their object, a change in the moral condition of governments, and with this change the burthen of public taxes will lessen, and civilization will be left to the enjoyment of that abundance, of which it is now deprived.

In contemplating the whole of this subject, I extend my views into the department of commerce. In all my publications, where the matter would admit, I have been an advocate for commerce because I am a friend to its effects. It is a pacific system, operating to cordialize mankind, by rendering nations, as well as individuals, useful to each other. As to mere theoretical reformation, I have never preached it up. The most effectual process is that of improving the condition of man by means of his interest; and it is on this ground that I take my stand.

If commerce were permitted to act to the universal extent it is capable, it would extirpate the system of war, and produce a revolution in the uncivilized state of governments. The invention of commerce has arisen since those governments began, and is the greatest approach towards universal civilization, that has yet been made by any means not immediately flowing from moral principles.

...No question has arisen within the records of history that pressed with the importance of the present. It is not whether this or that party shall be in or out, or whig, or tory, or high or low shall prevail; but whether man shall inherit his rights, and universal civilization take place? Whether the fruits of his labours shall be enjoyed by himself, or consumed by the profligacy of governments? Whether robbery shall be banished from courts, and wretchedness from countries?

When, in countries that are called civilized, we see age going to the workhouse and youth to the gallows, something must be wrong in the system of government. It would seem, by the exterior appearance of such countries, that all was happiness; but there lies hidden from the eye of the common observation, a mass of wretchedness that has scarcely any other chance, than to expire in poverty or infamy. Its entrance into life is marked with the presage of its fate; and until this is remedied, it is in vain to punish.

[Paine proceeds to enumerate the particulars of his plan to remedy social evils]

...First, Abolition of two million poor-rates.

Secondly, Provision for two hundred and fifty-two thousand poor families.

Thirdly, Education for one million and thirty thousand children.

Fourthly, Comfortable provision for one hundred and forty thousand aged persons.

Fifthly, Donation of twenty shillings each for fifty thousand births.

Sixthly, Donation of twenty shillings each for twenty thousand marriages.

Seventhly, Allowance of twenty thousand pounds for the funeral expenses of persons travelling for work, and dying at a distance from their friends.
Eighthly, Employment, at all times, for the casual poor in the cities of London and Westminster.

By the operation of this plan, the poor laws, those instruments of civil torture, will be superseded, and the wasteful expense of litigation prevented. The hearts of the humane will not be shocked by ragged and hungry children, and persons of seventy and eighty years of age begging for bread. The dying poor will not be dragged from place to place to breathe their last, as a reprisal of parish upon parish. Widows will have maintenance for their children, and not be carted away, on the death of their husbands, like culprits and criminals; and children will no longer be considered as increasing the distresses of their parents. The haunts of the wretched will be known, because it will be to their advantage; and the number of petty crimes, the offspring of distress and poverty, will be lessened. The poor, as well as the rich, will then be interested in the support of government, and the cause and apprehension of riots and tumults will cease. — Ye who sit in ease, and solace yourselves in plenty, and such there are in Turkey and Russia, as well as in England, and who say to yourselves, "Are we not well off", have ye thought of these things? When ye do, ye will cease to speak and feel for yourselves alone.

...Never did so great an opportunity offer itself to England , and to all Europe, as is produced by the two Revolutions of America and France. By the former, freedom has a national champion in the Western world; and by the latter, in Europe. When another nation shall join France, despotism and bad government will scarcely dare to appear. To use a trite expression, the iron is becoming hot all over Europe. The insulted German and the enslaved Spaniard, the Russ and the Pole, are beginning to think. The present age will hereafter merit to be called the Age of reason, and the present generation will appear to the future as the Adam of a new world.

JAMES MACKINTOSH
From *Vindiciae Gallicae*
(The extracts, from Sections III and IV, are taken from the first edition, 1791, omitting one footnote).

That no great revolutions can be accomplished without excesses and miseries at which humanity revolts, is a truth which cannot be denied. This unfortunately is true, in a peculiar manner, of those revolutions, which, like that of France, are strictly *popular*. Where the people are led by a faction, its leaders find no difficulty in the reestablishment of that order which must be the object of their wishes, because it is the sole security of their power. But when a general movement of the popular mind levels a despotism with the ground, it is far less easy to restrain excess. There is more resentment to satiate and less authority to control. The passion which produced an effect so tremendous, is too violent to subside in a moment into serenity and submission. The spirit of revolt breaks out with fatal violence after its object is destroyed, and turns against the order of freedom those arms by which it had subdued the strength of tyranny. The attempt to *punish* the spirit that actuates a *people*, if it were just, would be in vain, and if it were possible, would be cruel. They are too *many* to be punished in a view of justice, and too *strong* to be punished in a view of policy. The ostentation of vigour would in such a case prove the display of impotence, and the rigor of justice conduct to the cruelty of extirpation. No remedy is therefore left but the progress of instruction, the force of persuasion, the mild authority of opinion. These remedies, though infallible, are of slow operation; and in the interval which elapses before a calm succeeds the boisterous moments of a Revolution, it is vain to expect that a people inured to barbarism by their oppressors, and which has ages of oppression to avenge, will be punctiliously generous in their triumph, nicely discriminative in their vengence, or cautiously mild in their mode of retaliation. "They will break their chains on the heads of their oppressors".*

Such was the state of France, and such were the obvious causes that gave birth to scenes which the friends of freedom deplore as tarnishing her triumphs. They *feel* these evils as men of humanity. But they will not bestow the name on that womanish and complexional sensibility, towards which, even in the still intercourse of private life, *indulgence* is mingled with love. The only humanity which, in the great affairs of men, claims their respect, is that manly and expanded humanity, which fixes its steady eye on the object of general happiness. The sensibility which shrinks at a present evil, without extending its views to future good, is not a virtue, for it is not a quality beneficial to mankind: It would arrest the

---

*The eloquent expression of Mr. Curran[9] in the Parliament of Ireland, respecting the Revolution.

9. John Philpot Curran (1750-1817), Irish barrister, statesman and patriot. His speeches were not written and were badly reported. The quotation bears some resemblance to his remark about the French in 1790: 'In this struggle they have burst their chains, and, on the altar erected by despotism to public slavery, they have enthroned the image of public liberty' (*The Speeches of the Right Honourable John Philpot Curran*, ed. T. Davis, Dublin, 1853, p. 99). References to France in Irish debates are few: the bare mention of France was considered intimidatory in the Irish Parliament.

arm of a Surgeon in amputating a gangrened limb, or the hand of a Judge in signing the sentence of a parricide. I do not say (God forbid!) that a crime may be committed for the prospect of good. Such a doctrine would shake morals to their centre. But the case of the French Revolutionists is totally different. Has any moralist ever pretended, *that we are to decline the pursuit of a good which our duty prescribed to us, because we foresaw that some partial and incidental evil would arise from it*? This is the true view of the question, and it is only by this principle that we are to estimate the responsibility of the leaders of the Revolution for the excesses which attend it.

...That system of manners which arose among the Gothic nations of Europe, of which chivalry was more properly the effusion than the source, is without doubt one of most peculiar and interesting appearances in human affairs. The moral causes which formed its character have not, perhaps, been hitherto investigated with the happiest success. But to confine ourselves to the subject before us. Chivalry was certainly one of the most prominent features and remarkable effects of this system of manners. Candor must confess, that this singular institution is not *alone* admirable as a corrector of the ferocious ages in which it flourished. It contributed to polish and soften Europe. It paved the way for that diffusion of knowledge and extension of commerce which afterwards, in some measure, supplanted it, and gave a new character to manners.

Society is inevitably progressive. — In Government, commerce has overthrown that "feudal and chivalrous system" under whose shade it first grew. In religion, learning has subverted that superstition whose opulent endowments had first fostered it. Peculiar circumstances softened the barbarism of the middle ages to a degree which favoured the admission of commerce and the growth of knowledge. These circumstances were connected with the manners of chivalry; but the sentiments peculiar to that institution could only be preserved by the situation which gave them birth. They were, therefore, enfeebled in the progress from ferocity and turbulence, and almost obliterated by tranquillity and refinement. But the auxiliaries which the manners of chivalry had in rude ages reared, gathered strength from its weakness, and flourished in its decay. Commerce and diffused knowledge have, in fact, so completely assumed the ascendant in polished nations, that it will be difficult to discover any relics of *Gothic manners*, but in a fantastic exterior, which has survived the generous illusions that made these manners splendid and seductive. Their *direct* influence has long ceased in Europe, but their *indirect* influence, through the medium of those causes, which would not perhaps have existed, but for the mildness which chivalry created in the midst of a barbarous age, still operates with increasing vigor. The manners of the middle ages were, in the most singular sense, compulsory. Enterprizing benevolence was produced by general fierceness, gallant courtesy by ferocious rudeness, and artificial gentleness resisted the torrent of natural barbarism. But a less incongruous system has succeeded, in which commerce, which unites men's interests, and knowledge, which excludes those prejudices that tend to embroil them, present a broader basis for the stability of civilized and beneficient manners.

...Now, the *object* for which a man resigns any portion of his natural sovereignty over his own actions is, that he may be protected from the *abuse* of the same dominion in other men. No greater sacrifice is therefore necessary than is prescribed by this object, the resignation of *powers* that in their exercise might be injurious to ANOTHER. Nothing, therefore, can be more fallacious than to pretend that we are precluded in the social state from *any* appeal to natural right. It remains in its full integrity and vigour, if we except that *portion* of it which men mutually sacrifice for protection against each other. They do not surrender *all*; that is not exacted by the object they have in view; and whatever Government, under pretence of that surrender of natural right which is made for mutual security, assumes more than that object *rigorously* prescribes, is an usurpation supported by sophistry, a despotism varnished by illusion. It follows from this principle, that the surrender of right must be *equal* in all the members of society, as the object is to all precisely the same. In effect, society, instead of destroying, realizes and substantiates equality. In a state of *nature*, the equality of right is an impotent theory, which inequalities of strength and skill every moment violate. It is called into energy and effect only by society. As natural equality is not contested, and that the sum of right surrendered by every individual is equal, it cannot be denied that the remnant spared by the social compact must be equal also. *Civil* inequalities, or, more correctly, civil distinction, must exist in the social body, because it must possess organs destined for different functions. But political inequality is equally inconsistent with the principles of natural right, and the object of civil institution.

...If the only criterion of Governments be the supposed *convention* which forms them, ALL are equally legitimate, for the only interpreter of the convention is the usage of the Government, which is thus pre-posterously made its own standard. Governors must, indeed, abide by the maxims of the Constitution they administer; but what the Constitution is, must be on this system immaterial. The King of France it does not, indeed, permit to put out the eyes of the Princes of the blood, nor the Sophi of Persia to have recourse to *lettres de cachet*.[10] They must

---

10. *lettres de cachet*: orders under the seal of the king for imprisonment or exile without trial.

tyrannize by precedent, and oppress in reverend imitation of the models consecrated by the usage of despotic predecessors. But if they adhere to these, there is no remedy for the oppressed, since an appeal to the rights of Nature were treason against the principles of the social union. If, indeed, any offence against *precedent*, in the kind or degree of oppression, be omitted, this theory may (though most inconsistently) permit resistance. But as long as the *forms* of any government are preserved, it possesses, in a view of *justice*, (whatever be its nature), equal claims to obedience. This inference is irresistible, and it is *thus* evident that the doctrines of Mr. Burke are doubly refuted by the fallacy of the logic which supports them, and the absurdity of the conclusions to which they lead.

MARY WOLLSTONECRAFT
From *A Vindication of the Rights of Woman*
(The extracts, from Chs. 4, 5, 9, 12 and 13, are reprinted from the second edition, 1792, which was corrected by the author).

...Mankind, including every description, wish to be loved and respected by *something*; and the common herd will always take the nearest road to the completion of their wishes. The respect paid to wealth and beauty is the most certain and unequivocal; and, of course, will always attract the vulgar eye of common minds. Abilities and virtues are absolutely necessary to raise men form the middle rank of life into notice; and the natural consequence is notorious, the middle rank contains most virtue and abilities. Men have thus, in one station, at least an opportunity of exerting themselves with dignity, and of rising by the exertions which really improve a rational creature; but the whole female sex are, till their character is formed, in the same condition as the rich: for they are born, I now speak of a state of civilization, with certain sexual privileges, and whilst they are gratuitously granted them, few will ever think of works of supererogation, to obtain the esteem of a small number of superior people.

...In short, women, in general, as well as the rich of both sexes, have acquired all the follies and vices of civilization, and missed the useful fruit. It is not necessary for me always to premise, that I speak of the condition of the whole sex, leaving exceptions out of the question. Their senses are inflamed, and their understandings neglected, consequently they become the prey of their senses, delicately termed sensibility, and are blown about by every momentary gust of feeling. Civilized women are, therefore, so weakened by false refinement, that, respecting their morals, their condition is much below what it would be were they left in a state nearer to nature. Ever restless and anxious, their over exercised sensibility not only renders them uncomfortable themselves, but troublesome, to use a soft phrase, to others. All their thoughts turn on things calculated to excite emotion; and feeling, when they should reason, their conduct is unstable, and their opinions are wavering — not the wavering produced by deliberation or progressive views, but by contradictory emotions. By fits and starts they are warm in many pursuits; yet this warmth, never concentrated into perseverance, soon exhausts itself; exhaled by its own heat, or meeting some other fleeting passion, to which reason has never given any specific gravity, neutrality ensues. Miserable, indeed, must be that being whose cultivation of mind has only tended to inflame its passions! A distinction should be made between inflaming and strengthening them. The passions thus pampered, whilst the judgement is left unformed, what can be expected to ensue? — Undoubtedly, a mixture of madness and folly!

This observation should not be confined to the *fair* sex; however, at the present, I only mean to apply it to them.

Novels, music, poetry, and gallantry, all tend to make women the creatures of sensation, and their character is thus formed in the mould of folly during the time they are acquiring accomplishments, the only improvement they are excited, by their station in society, to acquire. This overstretched sensibility naturally relaxes the other powers of the mind, and prevents intellect from attaining that sovereignty which it ought to attain to render a rational creature useful to others and content with its own station: for the exercise of the understanding, as life advances, is the only method pointed out by nature to calm the passions.

...If you mean to secure ease and prosperity on earth as the first consideration, and leave futurity to provide for itself; you act prudently in giving your child an early insight into the weaknesses of his nature. You may not, it is true, make an Inkle[11] of him; but do not imagine that he will stick to more than the letter of the law, who has very early imbibed a mean opinion of human nature; nor will he think it necessary to rise much above the common standard. He may avoid gross vices, because

---

11. Inkle: young English merchant in a tale by Steele (*Spectator, No. 11*). Inkle had been brought up to resist the 'natural Impulses of his Passions, by Prepossession towards his interests'. Having landed in America, he excapes an Indian raid by the assistance of Yarico, an Indian maiden, with whom he falls in love. After being rescued and taken to Barbados, Inkle regrets his loss of time and money and sells Yarico into slavery. The story, based on fact, became popular in England and Europe. A dramatised version of the tale is *Inkle and Yarico* (1787), a romantic comedy by George Colman the Younger.

honesty is the best policy; but he will never aim at attaining great virtues. The example of writers and artists will illustrate this remark.

I must therefore venture to doubt whether what has been thought an axiom in morals may not have been a dogmatical assertion made by men who have coolly seen mankind through the medium of books, and say, in direct contradiction to them, that the regulation of the passions is not, always, wisdom. — On the contrary, it would seem, that one reason why men have superior judgement, and more fortitude than women, is undoubtedly this, that they give a freer scope to the grand passions, and by more frequently going astray enlarge their minds. If then by the exercise of their own reason they fix on some stable principle, they have probably to thank the force of their passions, nourished by *false* views of life, and permitted to overleap the boundary that secures content. But if, in the dawn of life, we could soberly survey the scenes before us in perspective, and see everything in its true colours, how could the passions gain sufficient strength to unfold the faculties?

...The youth should *act*; for had he the experience of a grey head he would be fitter for death than life, though his virtues, rather residing in his head than his heart, could produce nothing great, and his understanding, prepared for this world, would not, by its noble flights, prove that it had a title to a better.

Besides, it is not possible to give a young person a just view of life; he must have struggled with his own passions before he can estimate the force of the temptation which betrayed his brother into vice. Those who are entering life, and those who are departing, see the world from such very different points of view, that they can seldom think alike, unless the unfledged reason of the former never attempted a solitary flight.

When we hear of some daring crime — it comes full on us in the deepest shade of turpitude, and raises indignation; but the eye that gradually saw the darkness thicken, must observe it with more compassionate forbearance. The world cannot be seen by an unmoved spectator, we must mix in the throng, and feel as men feel before we can judge of their feelings. If we mean, in short, to live in the world to grow wiser and better, and not merely to enjoy the good things of life, we must attain a knowledge of others at the same time that we become acquainted with ourselves — knowledge acquired any other way only hardens the heart, and perplexes the understanding.

I may be told, that the knowledge thus acquired is sometimes purchased at too dear a rate. I can only answer that I very much doubt whether any knowledge can be attained without labour and sorrow; and those who wish to spare their children both, should not complain, if they are neither wise nor virtuous. They only aimed at making them prudent; and prudence, early in life, is but the cautious craft of ignorant self-love.

...There is a homely proverb, which speaks a shrewd truth, that whoever the devil finds idle he will employ. And what but habitual idleness can hereditary wealth and titles produce? For man is so constituted that he can only attain a proper use of his faculties by exercising them, and will not excercise them unless necessity, of some kind, first set the wheels in motion. Virtue likewise can only be acquired by the discharge of relative duties; but the importance of these sacred duties will scarcely be felt by the being who is cajoled out of his humanity by the flattery of sycophants. There must be more equality established in society, or morality will never gain ground, and this virtuous equality will not rest firmly even when founded on a rock, if one-half of mankind be chained to its bottom by fate, for they will be continually undermining it through ignorance or pride.

It is vain to expect virtue from women till they are in some degree independent of men; nay, it is vain to expect that strength of natural affection which would make them good wives and mothers. Whilst they are absolutely dependent on their husbands they will be cunning, mean, and selfish, and the men who can be gratified by the fawning fondness of spaniel-like affection, have not much delicacy, for love is not to be bought, in any sense of the words, its silken wings are instantly shrivelled up when anything beside a return in kind is sought. Yet whilst wealth enervates men; and women live, as it were, by their personal charms, how can we expect them to discharge those ennobling duties which equally require exertion and self-denial? Hereditary property sophisticates the mind, and the unfortunate victims to it, if I may express myself, swathed from their birth, seldom exert the locomotive faculty of body or mind; and thus viewing everything through one medium, and that a false one, they are unable to discern in what true merit and happiness consist. False, indeed, must be the light when the drapery of situation hides the man, and makes him stalk in masquerade, dragging from one scene of dissipation to another the nerveless limbs that hang with stupid list-lessness, and rolling round the vacant eye, which plainly tells us that there is no mind at home.

I mean, therefore, to infer that the society is not properly organized which does not compel men and women to discharge their respective duties by making it the only way to acquire that countenance from their fellow-creatures, which every human being wishes some way to attain. The respect, consequently, which is paid to wealth and mere personal charms, is a true north-east blast, that blights the tender blossoms of affection and virtue. Nature has wisely attached affections to duties, to sweeten toil, and to give that vigour to the exertions of reason which only the heart can give. But the affection which is put on merely because it is the appropriate insignia of a certain character, when its duties are not fulfilled, is one of the empty compliments which vice and folly are obliged to pay to virtue and the real nature of things.

...It is a melancholy truth; yet such is the blessed effect of civilization! the most respectable women are the most oppressed; and, unless they have understandings far superior to the common run of understandings, taking in both sexes, they must, from being treated like contemptible beings, become contemptible. How many women thus waste life away the prey of discontent, who might have practised as physicians, regulated a farm, managed a shop, and stood erect, supported by their own industry, instead of hanging their heads surcharged with the dew of sensibility, that consumes the beauty to which it at first gave lustre; nay, I doubt whether pity and love are so near akin as poets feign, for I have seldom seen much compassion excited by the helplessness of females, unless they were fair; then, perhaps, pity was the soft handmaid of love, or the harbinger of lust.

...If marriage be the cement of society, mankind should all be educated after the same model, or the intercourse of the sexes will never deserve the name of fellowship, nor will women ever fulfil the peculiar duties of their sex, till they become enlightened citizens, till they become free by being enabled to earn their own subsistence, independent of men; in the same manner, I mean, to prevent misconstruction, as one man is independent of another. Nay, marriage will never be sacred till women, by being brought up with men, are prepared to be their companions rather than their mistresses; for the mean doublings of cunning will ever render them contemptible, whilst oppression renders them timid. So convinced am I of this truth, that I will venture to predict that virtue will never prevail in society till the virtues of both sexes are founded on reason; and, till the affections common to both are allowed to gain their strength by the discharge of mutual duties.

Were boys and girls permitted to pursue the same studies together, those graceful decencies might early be inculcated which produce modesty without those sexual distinctions that taint the mind. Lessons of politeness, and that formulary of decorum, which treads on the heels of falsehood, would be rendered useless by habitual propriety of behaviour. Not, indeed, put on for visitors, like the courtly robe of politeness, but the sober effect of cleanliness of mind. Would not this simple elegance of sincerity be a chaste homage paid to domestic affections, far surpassing the meretricious compliments that shine with false lustre in the heartless intercourse of fashionable life? But, till more understanding preponderates in society, there will ever be a want of heart and taste, and the harlot's *rouge* will supply the place of that celestial suffusion which only virtuous affections can give to the face. Gallantry, and what is called love, may subsist without simplicity of character; but the main pillars of friendship are respect and confidence — esteem is never founded on it cannot tell what!

...From the tyranny of man, I firmly believe, the greater number of female follies proceed; and the cunning, which I allow makes at present a part of their character, I likewise have repeatedly endeavoured to prove, is produced by oppression.

Were not dissenters, for instance, a class of people, with strict truth, characterized as cunning? And may I not lay some stress on this fact to prove, that when any power but reason curbs the free spirit of man, dissimulation is practised, and the various shifts of art are naturally called forth? Great attention to decorum, which was carried to a degree of scrupulosity, and all that puerile bustle about trifles and consequential solemnity, which Butler's caricature of a dissenter, brings before the imagination, shaped their persons as well as their minds in the mould of prim littleness. I speak collectively, for I know how many ornaments in human nature have been enrolled amongst sectaries; yet, I assert, that the same narrow prejudice for their sect, which women have for their families, prevailed in the dissenting part of the community, however worthy in other respects; and also that the same timid prudence, or headstrong efforts, often disgraced the exertions of both. Oppression thus formed many of the features of their character perfectly to coincidence with that of the oppressed half of mankind; for is it not notorious that dissenters were, like women, fond of deliberating together, and asking advice of each other, till by a complication of little contrivances, some little end was brought about? A similar attention to preserve their reputation was conspicuous in the dissenting and female world, and was produced by a similar cause.

Asserting the rights which women in common with men ought to contend for, I have not attempted to extenuate their faults; but to prove them to be the natural consequence of their education and station in society. If so, it is reasonable to suppose that they will change their character, and correct their vices and follies, when they are allowed to be free in a physical, moral, and civil sense.

WILLIAM GODWIN
From *Enquiry Concerning Political Justice*
(The extracts, from Book II, ch. 2, Book III, Ch. 7, Book IV, Ch. 2, and Book VIII, Chs. 1, 2 and 6, are reprinted from the first edition, 1793).

Considerable light will probably be thrown upon our investigation, if, quitting for the present the political view, we examine justice merely as it exists among individuals. Justice is a rule of conduct originating in the connection of one percipient being with another. A comprehensive maxim which has been laid down upon the subject is, "that we should love our neighbour as ourselves". But this maxim, though possessing considerable merit as a popular principle, is not modelled with the strictness of philosophical accuracy.

In a loose and general view I and my neighbour are both of us men; and of consequence entitled to equal attention. But in reality it is probable that one of us is a being of more worth and importance than the other. A man is of more worth than a beast, because, being possessed of higher faculties, he is capable of a more refined genuine happiness. In the same manner the illustrious archbishop of Cambray[12] was of more worth than his chambermaid,[13] and there are few of us that would hesitate to pronounce, if his palace were in flames and the life of only one of them could be preserved, which of the two ought to be preferred.

But there is another ground of preference, beside the private consideration of one of them being farther removed from the state of a mere animal. We are not connected with one or two percipient beings, but with a society, a nation, and in some sense with the whole family of mankind. Of consequence that life ought to be preferred which will be most conducive to the general good. In saving the life of Fenelon, suppose at the moment when he was conceiving the project of his immortal Telemachus, I should be promoting the benefit of thousands, who have been cured by the perusal of it of some error, vice and consequent unhappiness. Nay, my benefit would extend farther than this, for every individual thus cured has become a better member of society, and has contributed in his turn to the happiness, the information and improvement of others.

Supposing I had been myself the chambermaid, I ought to have chosen to die, rather than that Fenelon should have died. The life of Fenelon was really preferable to that of the chambermaid. But understanding is the faculty that perceives the truth of this and similar propositions; and justice is the principle that regulates my conduct accordingly. It would have been just in the chambermaid to have preferred the archbishop to herself. To have done otherwise would have been a breach of justice.

Supposing the chambermaid had been my wife, my mother or my benefactor. This would not alter the truth of the proposition. The life of

---

12. archbishop of Cambray: François de Salignac de la Motte (1651-1715), 'Fénelon'. Fénelon achieved the philosopher's ambition of becoming tutor to a prince under Louis XIV. His *Télémaque* (1699) was seen as critical of Louis' politics. Fénelon's palace was seriously damaged by fire at the same time that he was dismissed from his post.

13. chambermaid: in the second edition, 1796, Godwin tempered this assault upon filial sentiment by substituting a valet/father for the chambermaid/mother.

Fenelon would still be more valuable than that of the chambermaid; and justice, pure, unadulterated justice, would still have preferred that which was most valuable. Justice would have taught me to save the life of Fenelon at the expense of the other. What magic is there in the pronoun "my", to overturn the decisions of everlasting truth? My wife or my mother may be a fool or a prostitute, malicious, lying or dishonest. If they be, of what consequence is it that they are mine?

"But my mother endured for me the pains of child bearing, and nourished me in the helplessness of infancy". When she first subjected herself to the necessity of these cares, she was probably influenced by no particular motives of benevolence to her future offspring. Every voluntary benefit however entitles the bestower to some kindness and retribution. But why so? Because a voluntary benefit is an evidence of benevolent intention, that is, of virtue. It is the disposition of the mind, not the external action, that entitles to respect. But the merit of this disposition is equal, whether the benefit was conferred upon me or upon another.

I and another man cannot both be right in preferring our own individual benefactor, for no man can be at the same time both better and worse than his neighbour. My benefactor ought to be esteemed, not because he bestowed a benefit upon me, but because he bestowed it upon a human being. His desert will be in exact proportion to the degree in which that human being was worthy of the distinction conferred. Thus every view of the subject brings us back to the consideration of my neighbour's moral worth and his importance to the general weal, as the only standard to determine the treatment to which he is entitled. Gratitude therefore, a principle which has so often been the theme of the moralist and the poet, is no part of either of justice or virtue. By gratitude I understand a sentiment, which would lead me to prefer one man to another, from some other consideration than that of his superior usefulness or worth: that is which would make something true to me (for example this preferableness), which cannot be true to another man, and is not true in itself.

...Man is in a state of perpetual progress. He must grow either better or worse, either correct his habits or confirm them. The government proposed must either increase our passions and prejudices by fanning the flame, or by gradually discouraging tend to extirpate them. In reality, it is sufficiently difficult to imagine a government that shall have the latter tendency. By its very nature political institution has a tendency to suspend the elasticity, and put an end to the advancement of mind. Every scheme for embodying imperfection must be injurious. That which is today a considerable melioration, will at some future period, if preserved unaltered, appear a defect and disease in the body politic. It were earnestly to be desired that each man was wise enough to govern himself without the intervention of any compulsory restraint; and, since government even in its best state is an evil, the object principally to be aimed at is, that we should have as little of it as the general peace of human society will permit.

...The true principle of social improvement lies in the correcting public opinion. Whatever reform is stolen upon the community unregarded, and does not spontaneously flow from the energy of the general mind, is unworthy of congratulation. It is in this respect with nations as with individuals. He that quits a vicious habit, not from reason and conviction, but because his appetites no longer solicit him to its indulgence, does not deserve the epithet of virtuous. The object it becomes us to pursue is, to give vigour to public opinion, not to sink it into listlessness and indifference.

When partial reformation proceeds from its legitimate cause, the progress society has made in the acquisition of truth, it may frequently be entitled to our applause. Man is the creature of habits. Gradual improvement is a most conspicuous law of his nature. When therefore some considerable advantage is sufficiently understood by the community to induce them to desire its establishment, that establishment will afterwards react to the enlightening of intellect and the generating of virtue. It is natural for us to take our stand upon some leading truth, and from thence explore the regions we have still to traverse.

There is indeed a sense in which gradual improvement is the only alternative between reformation and no reformation. All human intellects are at sea upon the great ocean of infinite truth, and their voyage though attended with hourly advantage will never be at an end. If therefore we will stay till we shall have devised a reformation so complete, as shall need no farther reformation to render it more complete, we shall eternally remain in inaction. Whatever is fairly understood upon general principles by a considerable part of the community, and opposed by none or by a very few, may be considered as sufficiently ripe for execution.

To recapitulate the principal object of this chapter, I would once again repeat, that violence may suit the plan of any political partisan, rather than of him that pleads the cause of simple justice. There is even a sense in which the reform aimed at by the true politician may be affirmed to be less a gradual than an entire one, without contradicting the former position. The complete reformation that is wanted, is not instant but future reformation. It can in reality scarcely be considered as of the nature of action. It consists in an universal illumination. Men feel their situation, and the restraints, that shackled them before, vanish like a mere deception. When the true crisis shall come, not a sword will need to be drawn, not a finger to be lifted up. The adversaries will be too few and too feeble to dare to make a stand against the universal sense of mankind.

...What is the criterion that must determine whether this or that substance, capable of contributing to the benefit of a human being, ought to be considered as your property or mine? To this question there can be but one answer — Justice. Let us then recur to the principles of justice.

To whom does any article of property, suppose a loaf of bread, justly belong? To him who most wants it, or to whom the possession of it will be most beneficial. Here are six men famished with hunger, and the loaf is, absolutely considered, capable of satisfying the cravings of them all. Who is it that has a reasonable claim to benefit by the qualities with which this loaf is endowed? They are all brothers perhaps, and the law of primogeniture bestows it exclusively on the eldest. But does justice confirm this award? The laws of different countries dispose of property in a thousand different ways; but there can be but one way which is most conformable to reason.

It would have been easy to put a case much stronger than that which has just been stated. I have an hundred loaves in my possession, and in the next street there is a poor man expiring with hunger, to whom one of these loaves would be the means of preserving his life. If I withhold this loaf from him, am I not unjust? If I impart it, am I not complying with what justice demands? To whom does the loaf justly belong?

I suppose myself in other respects to be in easy circumstances, and that I do not want this bread as an object of barter or sale, to procure me any of the other necessaries of a human being. Our animal wants have long since been defined, and are stated to consist of food, clothing and shelter. If justice have any meaning, nothing can be more iniquitous, than for one man to possess superfluities, while there is a human being in existence that is not adequately supplied with these.

Justice does not stop here. Every man is entitled, so far as the general stock will suffice, not only to the means of being, but of well being. It is unjust, if one man labour to the destruction of his health or his life, that another man may abound in luxuries. It is unjust, if one man be deprived of leisure to cultivate his rational powers, while another man contributes not a single effort to add to the common stock. The faculties of one man are like the faculties of another man. Justice directs that each man, unless perhaps he be employed more beneficially to the public, should contribute to the cultivation of the common harvest, of which each man consumes a share.

...Hereditary wealth is in reality a premium paid to idleness, an immense annuity expended to retain mankind in brutality and ignorance. The poor are kept in ignorance by the want of leisure. The rich are furnished indeed with the means of cultivation and literature, but they are paid for being dissipated and indolent. The most powerful means that malignity could have invented, are employed to prevent them from improving their talents, and becoming useful to the public.

This leads us to observe that the established system of property, is the true levelling system with respect to the human species, by as much as the cultivation of intellect and truth, is more valuable and more characteristic of man, than the gratifications of vanity or appetite. Accumulated property treads the powers of thought in the dust, extinguishes the sparks of genious, and reduces the great mass of mankind to be immersed in sordid cares; beside depriving the rich, as we have already said, of the most salubrious and effectual motives to activity. If superfluity were banished, the necessity for the greater part of the manual industry of mankind would be superseded; and the rest, being amicably shared among all the active and vigorous members of the community, would be burthensome to none. Every man would have a frugal, yet wholesome diet; every man would go forth to that moderate exercise of his corporal functions that would give hilarity to the spirits; none would be made torpid with fatigue, but all would have leisure to cultivate the kindly and philanthropical affections of the soul, and to let loose his faculties in the search of intellectual improvement. What a contrast does this scene present us with the present state of human society, where the peasant and the labourer work, till their understandings are benumbed with toil, their sinews contracted and made callous by being for ever on the stretch, and their bodies invaded with infirmities and surrendered to an untimely grave? What is the fruit of this disproportioned and unceasing toil? At evening they return to a family, famished with hunger, exposed half naked to the inclemencies of the sky, hardly sheltered, and denied the slenderest instruction, unless in a few instances, where it is dispensed by the hands of ostentatious charity, and the first lesson communicated is unprincipled servility.

...It is absurd to expect that the inclinations and wishes of two human beings should coincide through any long period of time. To oblige them to act and to live together, is to subject them to some inevitable portion of thwarting, bickering and unhappiness. This cannot be otherwise, so long as man has failed to reach the standard of absolute perfection. The supposition that I must have a companion for life, is the result of a complication of vices. It is the dictate of cowardice, and not of fortitude. It flows from the desire of being loved and esteemed for something that is not desert.

But the evil of marriage as it practised in European countries lies deeper than this. The habit is, for a thoughtless and romantic youth of each sex to come together, to see each other for a few times and under circumstances full of delusion, and then to vow to each other eternal attachment. What is the consequence of this? In almost every instance they find themselves deceived. They are reduced to make the best of an irretrievable mistake. They are presented with the strongest imaginable temptation to become the dupes of falsehood. They are led to conceive it their wisest policy to shut their eyes upon realities, happy if by any perversion of intellect they can persuade themselves that they were right in their first crude opinion of their companion. The institution of marriage is a system of fraud; and men who carefully mislead their judgments in the daily affair of their life, must always have a crippled judgment in every other concern. We ought to dismiss our mistake as soon as it is detected; but we are taught to cherish it. We ought to be incessant in our search after virtue and worth; but we are taught to check our enquiry, and shut our eyes upon the most attractive and admirable objects. Marriage is law, and the worst of all laws. Whatever our understandings may tell us of the person from whose connexion we should derive the greatest improvement, of the worth of one woman and the demerits of another, we are obliged to consider what is law, and not what is justice.

Add to this, that marriage is an affair of property, and the worst of all properties. So long as two human beings are forbidden by positive institution to follow the dictates of their own mind, prejudice is alive and vigorous. So long as I seek to engross one woman to myself, and to prohibit my neighbour from proving his superior desert and reaping the fruits of it, I am guilty of the most odious of all monopolies. Over this imaginary prize men watch with perpetual jealousy, and one man will find his desires and his capacity to circumvent as much excited, as the other is excited to traverse his projects and frustrate his hopes. As long as this state of society continues, philanthropy will be crossed and checked in a thousand ways, and the still augmenting stream of abuse will continue to flow.

The abolition of marriage will be attended with no evils. We are apt to represent it to ourselves as the harbinger of brutal lust and depravity. But it really happens in this as in other cases, that the positive laws which are made to restrain our vices, irritate and multiply them. Not to say, that the same sentiments of justice and happiness which in a state of equal property would destroy the relish for luxury, would decrease our inordinate appetites of every kind, and lead us universally to prefer the pleasures of intellect to the pleasures of sense.

Imagination

Our first extracts under this heading are from the prose works of William Wordsworth (1770-1850). The Preface affixed to the second edition of *Lyrical Ballads* was the outcome of discussions between Wordsworth and Coleridge over a long period of poetic co-operation, although Coleridge later dissented from some of Wordsworth's more polemic positions. Wordsworth attempted to restore the true mimetic basis of poetry in its fidelity both to the objects represented and to the responses of the experiencing mind. Wordsworth's theory of imagination is general: a Poet is 'a Man speaking to Men' yet this, like other of his epigrammatic statements, is heavily qualified, and the poet is seen to require 'organic sensibility' and a sense of the joyous activity of the universe. Although Wordsworth's praise of Poetry is exuberant, his 'Poet' is never an unregarded nightingale exerting an ideal influence on his hearers, but a celebrator of the visible common life around him. In his stress on the naturally developed passions and his contention that low and rustic life provided material and language for the depiction of the most valuable characteristics of human nature, Wordsworth antagonised reviewers such as Francis Jeffrey (1773-1850), editor of the *Edinburgh Review*. Jeffrey demanded a mature and public poetry which could show its face in the drawing-room without embarrassment; in his review of *The Excursion*, he prizes good sense above imagination. Wordsworth's analysis of the imagination in the 1815 Preface distinguishes it as an active power and departs from the eighteenth-century definition of it as a store-house of fixed picture-images. But he does not approach Coleridge's more comprehensive account of the imagination as a faculty of perception and the organising principle of a whole work of art. Thomas Love Peacock (1785-1866), himself a poet and friend of Percy Bysshe Shelley (1792-1822), produced his 'The Four Ages of Poetry' in the satiric spirit of his own witty novels, which were themselves far from espousing the cause of political economists. Shelley, however, responded not only to Peacock, but also to the more serious attack on poetry and imagination made by the utilitarians. His 'A Defence of Poetry' attempts to link the mimetic theories of Wordsworth and Coleridge with a Platonic theory of inspiration, but it also claims imagination as *the* distinctive humanising force, bringing human order, political, moral or aesthetic, to the otherwise soulless world of calculation and statistics. In his letters, John Keats (1795-1821) also sought in beauty and the imagination a force to confront the ills of life, while recognising the imagination's impatience of philosophical and even moral consistency. In his praise of 'gusto', in his criticism of the Wordsworthian 'egotistical sublime', Keats is echoing the words of William Hazlitt (1778-1830), whose attitude towards Poets and Poetry betrays the complex response of a disappointed radical who had seen the first Romantic poets desert the cause of freedom. In Hazlitt's essay, 'My first Acquaintance with Poets', the account of his youthful hero-worship is qualified by many shrewd critical remarks. His romantic temperament is also shown in his evocative description of landscape. Among those who had contributed to the reasoned appreciation of landscape was Uvedale Price (1747-1829), who attempted to establish the principles of the picturesque, a category marked by its effect on the emotions, from the peaceful intricacies of a natural woodland to the awe-inspiring ruggedness of mountains. In his *An Essay on the Picturesque* he argues for a natural irregularity rather than the smooth outlines and artful dispositions of elements practised by fashionable landscape gardeners like Humphrey Repton. Picturesque landscape provides an emotional backcloth for the high passions of the Gothic novel. There is also a striking intellectual interest in the contribution of Mary Wollstonecraft Shelley (1777-1851) to this *genre*. She wrote many novels after *Frankenstein*, most of them inspired by the personalities and speculations of Shelley and Byron. Though *Frankenstein* has been interpreted as a psychological *exposé* of her tortured feelings towards Shelley, it is also a Gothic novel of ideas in the tradition of Godwin's *St. Leon* (1797), a tragedy of the misuse of great abilities and the perversion of misguided benevolence. It is also the first example of something else. Her Preface throws an interesting light on a new field for the imagination, science-fiction.

WILLIAM WORDSWORTH
From Preface to *Lyrical Ballads, With Pastoral and Other Poems*

(The extracts are from the expanded version of the Preface, published in 1802).

...The principal object then which I proposed to myself in these Poems was to chuse incidents and situations from common life, and to relate or describe them, throughout, as far as was possible, in a selection of language really used by men, and, at the same time, to throw over them a certain colouring of imagination, whereby ordinary things should be presented to the mind in an unusual way; and, further, and above all, to make these incidents and situations interesting by tracing in them, truly though not ostentatiously, the primary laws of our nature: chiefly, as far as regards the manner in which we associate ideas in a state of excitement. Low and rustic life was generally chosen, because in that condition, the essential passions of the heart find a better soil in which they can attain their maturity, are less under restraint and speak a plainer and more emphatic language; because in that condition of life our elementary feelings co-exist in a state of greater simplicity, and, consequently, may be more accurately contemplated, and more forcibly communicated; because the manners of rural life germinate from those elementary feelings, and from the necessary character of rural occupations, are more easily comprehended, and are more durable; and, lastly, because in that condition the passions of men are incorporated with the beautiful and permanent forms of nature. The language, too, of these men is adopted (purified indeed from what appear to be its real defects, from all lasting and rational causes of dislike or disgust) because such men hourly communicate with the best objects from which the best part of language is originally derived; and because, from their rank in society and the sameness and narrow circle of their intercourse, being less under the influence of social vanity, they convey their feelings and notions in simple and unelaborated expressions. Accordingly, such a language, arising out of repeated experience and regular feelings, is a more permanent, and a far more philosophical language, than that which is frequently substituted for it by Poets, who think that they are conferring honour upon themselves and their art, in proportion as they separate themselves from the sympathies of men, and indulge in arbitrary and capricious habits of expression, in order to furnish food for fickle tastes, and fickle appetites, of their own creation.*

I cannot, however, be insensible of the present outcry against the triviality and meanness both of thought and language, which some of my contemporaries have occasionally introduced into their metrical compositions; and I acknowledge, that this defect, where it exists, is more dishonorable to the Writer's own character than false refinement or arbitrary innovation, though I should contend at the same time that it is far less pernicious in the sum of its consequences. From such verses the Poems in these volumes will be found distinguished at least by one mark

---

*It is worth while here to observe that the affecting parts of Chaucer are almost always expressed in language pure and universally intelligible even to this day.

of difference, that each of them has a worthy *purpose*. Not that I mean to say, that I always began to write with a distinct purpose formally conceived; but I believe that my habits of meditation have so formed my feelings, as that my descriptions of such objects as strongly excite those feelings, will be found to carry along with them a *purpose*. If in this opinion I am mistaken, I can have little right to the name of a Poet. For all good poetry is the spontaneous overflow of powerful feelings: but though this be true, Poems to which any value can be attached, were never produced on any variety of subjects but by a man, who being possessed of more than usual organic sensibility, had also thought long and deeply. For our continued influxes of feeling are modified and directed by our thoughts, which are indeed the representatives of all our past feelings; and, as by contemplating the relation of these general representatives to each other we discover what is really important to men, so, by the repetition and continuance of this act, our feelings will be connected with important subjects, till at length, if we be originally possessed of much sensibility, such habits of mind will be produced, that, by obeying blindly and mechanically the impulses of those habits, we shall describe objects, and utter sentiments, of such a nature and in such connection with each other, that the understanding of the being to whom we address ourselves, if he be in a healthful state of association, must necessarily be in some degree enlightened, and his affections ameliorated.

...The subject is indeed important! For the human mind is capable of being excited without the application of gross and violent stimulants; and he must have a very faint perception of its beauty and dignity who does not know this, and who does not further know, that one being is elevated above another, in proportion as he possesses this capability. It has therefore appeared to me, that to endeavour to produce or enlarge this capability is one of the best services in which, at any period, a Writer can be engaged; but this service, excellent at all times, is especially so at the present day. For a multitude of causes, unknown to former times, are now acting with a combined force to blunt the discriminating powers of the mind, and unfitting it for all voluntary exertion to reduce it to a state of almost savage torpor. The most effective of these causes are the great national events which are daily taking place, and the encreasing accumulation of men in cities, where the uniformity of their occupations produces a craving for extraordinary incident, which the rapid communication of intelligence hourly gratifies. To this tendency of life and manners the literature and theatrical exhibitions of the country have conformed themselves. The invaluable works of our elder writers, I had almost said the works of Shakespeare and Milton, are driven into neglect by frantic novels, sickly and stupid German Tragedies, and deluges of idle and extravagant stories in verse. — When I think upon this degrading thirst after outrageous stimulation, I am almost ashamed to have spoken of the feeble effort with which I have endeavoured to counteract it; and, reflecting upon the magnitude of the general evil, I should be oppressed with no dishonorable melancholy, had I not a deep impression of certain inherent and indestructible qualities of the human mind, and likewise of certain powers in the great and permanent objects that act upon it which are equally inherent and indestructible; and did I not further add to this impression a belief, that the time is approaching when the evil will be systematically opposed, by men of greater powers, and with far more distinguished success.

...a large portion of the language of every good poem can in no respect differ from that of good Prose. I will go further. I do not doubt that it may be safely affirmed, that there neither is, nor can be, any essential difference between the language of prose and metrical composition.

...What is a Poet? To whom does he address himself? And what language is to be expected from him. He is a man speaking to men: a man, it is true, endowed with more lively sensibility, more enthusiasm and tenderness, who has a greater knowledge of human nature, and a more comprehensive soul, than are supposed to be common among mankind; a man pleased with his own passions and volitions, and who rejoices more than other men in the spirit of life that is in him; delighting to contemplate similar volitions and passions as manifested in the goings-on of the Universe, and habitually impelled to create them where he does not find them. To these qualities he has added a disposition to be affected more than other men by absent things as if they were present; an ability of conjuring up in himself passions, which are indeed far from being the same as those produced by real events, yet (especially in those parts of the general sympathy which are pleasing and delightful) do more nearly resemble the passions produced by real events, than anything which, from the motions of their own minds merely, other men are accustomed to feel in themselves: whence, and from practice, he has acquired a greater readiness and power in expressing what he thinks and feels, and especially those thoughts and feelings which, by his own choice, or from the structure of his own mind, arise in him without immediate external excitement.

But whatever portion of this faculty we may suppose even the greatest Poet to possess, there cannot be a doubt but that the language which it will suggest to him, must, in liveliness and truth, fall far short of that which is uttered by men in real life, under the actual pressure of those passions, certain shadows of which the Poet thus produces, or feels to be produced, in himself. However exalted a notion we would wish to cherish of the character of a Poet, it is obvious, that while he describes and imitates passions, his employment is altogether slavish and mechanical, compared with the freedom and power of real and substantial action and suffering. So that it will be with the wish of the Poet to bring his feelings near to those of the persons whose feelings he describes, nay, for short spaces of time perhaps, to let himself slip into an entire delusion, and even confound and identify his own feelings with theirs; modifying only the language which is thus suggested to him, by a consideration that he describes for a particular purpose, that of giving pleasure.

...What then does the Poet? He considers man and the objects that surround him as acting and re-acting upon each other, so as to produce an infinite complexity of pain and pleasure; he considers man in his own nature and in his ordinary life as contemplating this with a certain quantity of immediate knowledge, with certain convictions, intuitions, and deductions, which by habit become of the nature of intuitions; he considers him as looking upon this complex scene of ideas and sensations, and finding everywhere objects that immediately excite in him sympathies which, from the necessities of his nature, are accompanied by an overbalance of enjoyment.

To this knowledge which all men carry about with them, and to these sympathies in which without any other discipline than that of our daily life we are fitted to take delight, the Poet principally directs his attention. He considers man and nature as essentially adapted to each other, and the mind of man as naturally the mirror of the fairest and most interesting qualities of nature. And thus the Poet, prompted by this feeling of pleasure, which accompanies him through the whole course of his studies, converses with general nature with affections akin to those, which, through labour and length of time, the Man of Science has raised up in himself, by conversing with those particular parts of nature which are the objects of his studies. The knowledge both of the Poet and the Man of Science is pleasure; but the knowledge of the one cleaves to us as a necessary part of our existence, our natural and unalienable inheritance; the other is a personal and individual acquisition, slow to come to us, and by no habitual and direct sympathy connecting us with our fellow-beings. The Man of Science seeks truth as a remote and unknown benefactor; he cherishes and loves it in his solitude: the Poet, singing a song in which all human beings join with him, rejoices in the presence of truth as our visible friend and hourly companion. Poetry is the breath and finer spirit of all knowledge; it is the impassioned expression which is in the countenance of all Science. Emphatically may it be said of the Poet, as Shakespeare hath said of man, "that he looks before and after"[1].He is the rock of defence of human nature; an upholder and preserver, carrying everywhere with him relationship and love. In spite of difference of soil

1. *Hamlet*, IV, 4, 37.

and climate, of language and manners, of laws and customs, in spite of things silently gone out of mind and things violently destroyed, the Poet binds together by passion and knowledge the vast empire of human society, as it is spread over the whole earth, and over all time. The objects of the Poet's thoughts are everywhere; though the eyes and senses of man are, it is true, his favorite guides, yet he will follow wheresoever he can find an atmosphere of sensation in which to move his wings. Poetry is the first and last of all knowledge — it is as immortal as the heart of man. If the labours of men of Science should ever create any material revolution, direct or indirect, in our condition, and in the impressions which we habitually receive, the Poet will sleep then no more than at present, but he will be ready to follow the steps of the Man of Science, not only in those general indirect effects, but he will be at his side, carrying sensation into the midst of the objects of the Science itself. The remotest discoveries of the Chemist, the Botanist, or Mineralogist, will be as proper objects of the Poet's art as any upon which it can be employed, if the time should ever come when these things shall be familiar to us, and the relations under which they are contemplated by the followers of these respective Sciences shall be manifestly and palpably material to us as enjoying and suffering beings.

...If I had undertaken a systematic defence of the theory upon which these poems are written, it would have been my duty to develope the various causes upon which the pleasure received from metrical language depends. Among the chief of these causes is to be reckoned a principle which must be well known to those who have made any of the Arts the object of accurate reflection; I mean the pleasure which the mind derives from the perception of similitude in dissimilitude. This principle is the great spring of the activity of our minds, and their chief feeder. From this principle the direction of the sexual appetite, and all the passions connected with it take their origin: It is the life of our ordinary conversation; and upon the accuracy with which similitude in dis-similitude, and dissimilitude in similitude are perceived, depend our taste and our moral feelings. It would not have been a useless employment to have applied this principle to the consideration of metre, and to have shewn that metre is hence enabled to afford much pleasure, and to have pointed out in what manner that pleasure is produced. But my limits will not permit me to enter upon this subject, and I must content myself with a general summary.

I have said that Poetry is the spontaneous overflow of powerful feelings: it takes its origin from emotion recollected in tranquillity: the emotion is contemplated till by a species of reaction the tranquillity gradually disappears, and an emotion, kindred to that which was before the subject of contemplation, is gradually produced, and does itself actually exist in the mind. In this mood successful composition generally begins, and in a mood similar to this it is carried on; but the emotion, of whatever kind, and in whatever degree, from various causes is qualified by various pleasures, so that in describing any passions whatsoever, which are voluntarily described, the mind will upon the whole be in a state of enjoyment. Now, if Nature be thus cautious in preserving in a state of enjoyment a being so employed, the Poet ought to profit by the lesson held forth to him, and ought especially to take care, that, whatever passions he communicates to his Reader, those passions, if his Reader's mind be sound and vigorous, should always be accompanied with an overbalance of pleasure. Now the music of harmonious metrical language, the sense of difficulty overcome, and the blind association of pleasure which has been previously received from works of rhyme or metre of the same or similar construction, an indistinct perception perpetually renewed of language closely resembling that of real life, and yet, in the circumstance of metre, differing from it so widely, all these imperceptibly make up a complex feeling of delight, which is of the most important use in tempering the painful feeling which will always be found intermingled with powerful descriptions of the deeper passions. This effect is always produced in pathetic and impassioned poetry; while, in lighter compositions, the ease and gracefulness with which the Poet manages his numbers are themselves confessedly a principal source of the gratification of the Reader.

From Preface to *Poems, including Lyrical Ballads*
(The extracts are from the first edition, 1815, with two errors in the quotations corrected).

...Imagination, in the sense of the word as giving title to a class of the following Poems, has no reference to images that are merely a faithful copy, existing in the mind, of absent external objects; but is a word of higher import, denoting operations of the mind upon those objects, and processes of creation or of composition, governed by certain fixed laws. I proceed to illustrate my meaning by instances. A parrot *hangs* from the wires of his cage by his beak or by his claws; or a monkey from the bough of a tree by his paws or his tail. Each creature does so literally and actually. In the first Eclogue of Virgil, the shepherd, thinking of the time when he is to take leave of his farm, thus addresses his goats:-

'Non ego vos posthac viridi projectus in antro
Dumosa *pendere* procul de rupe videbo'.

— 'half way down
Hangs one who gathers samphire',[2]

is the well-known expression of Shakespeare, delineating an ordinary
image upon the cliffs of Dover. In these two instances is a slight exertion
of the faculty which I denominate imagination, in the use of one word:
neither the goats nor the samphire-gatherer do literally hang, as does the
parrot or the monkey; but, presenting to the senses something of such an
appearance, the mind in its activity, for its own gratification, con-
templates them as hanging.

'As when far off at sea a fleet descried
Hangs in the clouds, by equinoctial winds
Close sailing from Bengala, or the isles
Of Ternate or Tidore, whence merchants bring
Their spicy drugs; they on the trading flood
Through the wide Ethiopian to the Cape
Ply, stemming nightly toward the Pole: so seemed
Far off the flying Fiend'.[3]

Here is the full strength of the imagination involved in the word
hangs, and exerted upon the whole image: First, the fleet, an aggregate of
many ships, is represented as one mighty person, whose track, we know
and feel, is upon the waters; but, taking advantage of its appearance to
the senses, the Poet dares to represent it as *hanging in the clouds*, both for
the gratification of the mind in contemplating the image itself, and in
reference to the motion and appearance of the sublime object to which it
is compared.

From images of sight we will pass to those of sound:

...'Shall I call thee Bird
Or but a wandering Voice?'[4]

This concise interrogation characterises the seeming ubiquity of the
voice of the cuckoo, and dispossesses the creature almost of a corporeal
existence; the Imagination being tempted to this exertion of her power by
a consciousness in the memory that the cuckoo is almost perpetually
heard throughout the season of spring, but seldom becomes an object of
sight.

Thus far of images independent of each other, and immediately
endowed by the mind with properties that do not inhere in them, upon an
incitement from properties and qualities the existence of which is
inherent and obvious. These processes of imagination are carried on

2. Virgil, *Eclogues*, I, 75-76, and *King Lear*, IV, 6, 14-15.
3. Milton, *Paradise Lost*, II, 636-643.
4. Wordsworth's 'To the Cuckoo', ll. 3-4, composed 1802 and first published in
Poems in Two Volumes (1807).

either by conferring additional properties upon an object, or abstracting from it some of those which it actually possesses, and thus enabling it to re-act upon the mind which hath performed the process, like a new existence.

I pass from the Imagination acting upon an individual image to a consideration of the same faculty employed upon images in a conjunction by which they modify each other. The Reader has already had a fine instance before him in the passage quoted from Virgil, where the apparently perilous situation of the goat, hanging upon the shaggy precipice, is contrasted with that of the shepherd contemplating it from the seclusion of the cavern in which he lies stretched at ease and in security. Take these images separately, and how unaffecting the picture compared with that produced by their being thus connected with, and opposed to, each other!—

'As a huge stone is sometimes seen to lie
Couched on the bald top of an eminence,
Wonder to all who do the same espy
By what means it could thither come, and whence
So that it seems a thing endued with sense,
Like a sea-beast crawled forth, which on a shelf
Of rock or sand reposeth, there to sun himself.

Such seemed this man; not all alive or dead
Nor all asleep, in his extreme old age.

. . . .

Motionless as a cloud the old Man stood,
That heareth not the loud winds when they call,
And moveth altogether if it move at all'.[5]

In these images, the conferring, the abstracting, and the modifying powers of the Imagination, immediately and mediately acting, are all brought into conjunction. The stone is endowed with something of the power of life to approximate it to the sea-beast; and the sea-beast stripped of some of its vital qualities to assimilate it to the stone; which intermediate image is thus treated for the purpose of bringing the original image, that of the stone, to a nearer resemblance to the figure and condition of the aged Man; who is divested of so much of the indications of life and motion as to bring him to the point where the two objects unite and coalesce in just comparison. After what has been said, the image of the cloud need not be commented upon.

Thus far of an endowing or modifying power: but the Imagination also shapes and *creates*; and how? By innumerable processes; and in none does it more delight than in that of consolidating numbers into unity, and

5. Wordsworth's 'Resolution and Independence', ll. 57-65 and 75-77, composed 1802 and first published in 1807.

dissolving and separating unity into number, — alternations proceeding from, and governed by, a sublime consciousness of the soul in her own mighty and almost divine powers.

FRANCIS JEFFREY
From review of Wordsworth's *The Excursion*
(The extracts are from *Edinburgh Review*, XXIV, November, 1814).

This will never do. It bears no doubt the stamp of the author's heart and fancy; but unfortunately not half so visibly as that of his peculiar system. His former poems were intended to recommend that system, and to bespeak favour for it by their individual merit; –- but this, we suspect, must be recommended by the system — and can only expect to succeed where it has been previously established. It is longer, weaker, and tamer, than any of Mr. Wordsworth's other productions; with less boldness of originality, and less even of that extreme simplicity and lowliness of tone which wavered so prettily, in the Lyrical Ballads, between silliness and pathos. We have imitations of Cowper, and even of Milton here, engrafted on the natural drawl of the Lakers — and all diluted into harmony by that profuse and irrepressible wordiness which deluges all the blank verse of this school of poetry, and lubricates and weakens the whole structure of their style.

...Long habits of seclusion, and an excessive ambition of originality, can alone account for the disproportion which seems to exist between this author's taste and his genius; or for the devotion with which he has sacrificed so many precious gifts at the shrine of those paltry idols which he has set up for himself among his lakes and his mountains. Solitary musings, amidst such scenes, might no doubt be expected to nurse up the mind to the majesty of poetical conception, — (though it is remarkable, that all the greater poets lived, or had lived, in the full current of society): — But the collision of equal minds, — the admonition of prevailing impressions — seems necessary to reduce its redundancies, and repress that tendency to extravagance or puerility, into which the self-indulgence and self-admiration of genius is so apt to be betrayed, when it is allowed to wanton, without awe or restraint, in the triumph and delight of its own intoxication. That its flights should be graceful and glorious in the eyes of men, it seems almost to be necessary that they should be made in the consciousness that men's eyes are to behold them, — and that the inward transport and vigour by which they are inspired, should be tempered by an occasional reference to what will be thought of them by those ultimate dispensers of glory. An habitual and general knowledge of the few settled and permanent maxims, which form the canon of general taste in all large and polished societies — a certain tact, which informs us at once that many things, which we still love and are moved by in secret, must necessarily be despised as childish, or derided as absurd, in all such societies — though it will not stand in the place of genius, seems necessary to the success of its exertions; and though it will never enable any one to produce the higher beauties of art, can alone secure the talent which does produce them, from errors that must render it useless. Those who have most of the talent, however, commonly acquire this knowledge with the greatest facility; — and if Mr. Wordsworth, instead of confining himself almost entirely to the society of the dalesmen and cottagers, and little children, who form the subjects of his book, had condescended to mingle a little more with the people that were to read and judge of it, we cannot help thinking, that its texture would have been considerably improved: At least it appears to us to be absolutely impossible, that any one who had lived or mixed familiarly with men of literature and ordinary judgment in poetry, (of course we exclude the coadjutors and disciples of his own school), could ever have fallen into such gross faults, or so long mistaken them for beauties. His first essays we looked upon in a good degree as poetical paradoxes, — maintained experimentally, in order to display talent, and court notoriety; — and so maintained, with no more serious belief in their truth, than is usually generated by an ingenious and animated defence of other paradoxes. But when we find, that he has been for twenty years exclusively employed upon articles of this very fabric, and that he has still enough of raw material on hand to keep him so employed for twenty years to come, we cannot refuse him the justice of believing that he is a sincere convert to his own system, and must ascribe the peculiarities of his composition, not to any transient affectation, or accidental caprice of imagination, but to a settled perversity of taste or understanding, which has been fostered, if not altogether created, by the circumstances to which we have already alluded.

...The character of the work is decidedly didactic; and more than nine tenths of it are occupied with a species of dialogue, or rather a series of long sermons or harangues which pass between the pedlar, the author, the old chaplain, and a worthy vicar, who entertains the whole party at dinner on the last day of their excursion. The incidents which occur in the course of it are as few and trifling as can be imagined; — and those which the different speakers narrate in the course of their discourses, are introduced rather to illustrate their arguments or opinions, than for any interest they are supposed to possess of their own. — The doctrine which the work is intended to enforce, we are by no means certain that we have discovered. In so far as we can collect, however, it seems to be neither more nor less than the old familiar one, that a firm belief in the providence of a wise and beneficent Being, must be our great stay and support under all afflictions and perplexities upon earth — and that there are indications of his power and goodness in all the aspects of the visible universe, whether living or inanimate — every part of which should therefore be regarded with love and reverence, as exponents of those great attributes. We can testify, at least, that these salutary and important truths are inculcated at far greater length, and with more repetitions, than in any ten volumes of sermons that we ever perused. It is also maintained with equal conciseness and originality, that there is frequently much good sense, as well as much enjoyment, in the humbler conditions of life; and that, in spite of great vices and abuses, there is a reasonable allowance both of happiness and goodness in society at large. If there be any deeper or more recondite doctrines in Mr. Wordsworth's book, we must confess that they have escaped us; — and, convinced as we are of the truth and soundness of those to which we have alluded, we cannot help thinking that they might have been better enforced with less parade and prolixity. His effusions on what may be called the physiognomy of external nature, or its moral and theological expression, are eminently fantastic, obscure, and affected.

UVEDALE PRICE

From *An Essay on the Picturesque as compared with the Sublime and the Beautiful; and, on the use of studying pictures, for the purpose of improving real landscape*
(The extracts are from part I, Ch. 2 and part II, Ch. 1 of volume I of the expanded version of Price's *Essay*, published in three volumes in 1810; volume I had been first published in 1794, and volume II in 1798).

It seems to me that the neglect, which prevails in the works of modern improvers, of all that is picturesque, is owing to their exclusive attention to high polish and flowing lines: the charms of which they are so engaged in contemplating, that they overlook two of the most fruitful sources of human pleasure: the first, that great and universal source of pleasure, *variety*---the power of which is independent of beauty, but without which even beauty itself soon ceases to please, the second, *intricacy*---a quality which, though distinct from variety, is so connected and blended with it, that the one can hardly exist without the other.

According to the idea I have formed of it, intricacy in landscape might be defined, *that disposition of objects, which, by a partial and uncertain concealment, excites and nourishes curiosity*. Variety can hardly require a definition, though from the practice of many layers-out of ground, one might suppose it did. Upon the whole, it appears to me, that as intricacy in the disposition, and variety in the forms, the tints, and the lights and shadows of objects, are the great characteristics of picturesque scenery; so monotony and baldness, are the great defects of improved places.

Nothing would place this in so distinct a point of view, as a comparison between some familiar scene in its natural and picturesque state, and in that which would be its improved state according to the present mode of gardening. All painters who have imitated the more confined scenes of nature, have been fond of making studies from old neglected bye roads and hollow ways; and perhaps there are few spots that in so small a compass, have a greater variety of that sort of beauty called picturesque; but, I believe, the instances are very rare of painters, who have turned out volunteers into a gentleman's walk or drive, either when made between artificial banks, or when the natural sides or banks have been improved. I shall endeavour to examine whence it happens, that a painter looks coldly on what is very generally admired, and discovers a thousand interesting objects, where an improver passes on with indifference, if not with disgust.

Perhaps what is most immediately striking in a lane of this kind is its intricacy. Any winding road, indeed, especially where there are banks, must necessarily have some degree of intricacy; but in a dressed lane every effort of art seems directed against that disposition of the ground: the sides are so regularly sloped, so regularly planted, and the space, when there is any, between them and the road, so uniformly levelled; the sweeps of the road so plainly artificial, the verges of grass that bound it so nicely edged; the whole, in short, has such an appearance of having been made by a receipt, that curiosity, that most active principle of pleasure, is almost extinguished.

But in hollow lanes and bye roads, all the leading features, and a thousand circumstances of detail, promote the natural intricacy of the ground: the turns are sudden and unprepared; the banks sometimes broken and abrupt; sometimes smooth, and gently, but not uniformly sloping; now wildly overhung with thickets of trees and bushes; now loosely skirted with wood: no regular verge of grass, no cut edges, no distinct lines of separation; all is mixed and blended together, and the border of the road itself, shaped by the mere tread of passengers and animals, is as unconstrained as the footsteps that formed it. Even the tracks of the wheels (for no circumstance is indifferent) contribute to the picturesque effect of the whole: the varied lines they describe just mark the way among trees and bushes; often some obstacle, a cluster of low thorns, a furze-bush, a tussuck, a large stone, forces the wheels into sudden and intricate turns; often a group of trees or a thicket, occasions the road to separate into two parts, leaving a sort of island in the middle.

These are a few of the picturesque accidents, which in lanes and bye roads attract the notice of painters. In many scenes of that kind, the varieties of form, of colour, and of light and shade, which present themselves at every step, are numberless; and it is a singular circumstance that some of the most striking among them should be owing to the indiscriminate hacking of the peasant, nay, to the very decay that is occasioned by it. When opposed to the tameness of the poor pinioned trees (whatever their age) of a gentleman's plantation drawn up strait and even together, there is often a sort of spirit and animation, in the manner in which old neglected pollards stretch out their limbs quite across these hollow roads, in every wild and irregular direction: on some, the large knots and protuberances, add to the ruggedness of their twisted trunks; in others, the deep hollow of the inside, the mosses on the bark, the rich yellow of the touch-wood, with the blackness of the more decayed substance, afford such variety of tints, of brilliant and mellow lights, with deep and peculiar shades, as the finest timber tree, however beautiful in other respects, with all its health and vigour cannot exhibit.

...We have, indeed, made but a poor progress, by changing the formal, but simple and majestic avenue, for the thin circular verge called a belt; and the unpretending ugliness of the strait, for the affected sameness of the serpentine canal:

...The avenue has a most striking effect, from the very circumstance of its being strait; no other figure can give that image of a grand gothic aisle with its natural columns and vaulted roof, the general mass of which fills the eye, while the particular parts insensibly steal from it in a long gradation of perspective. The broad solemn shade adds a twilight calm to the whole, and makes it above all other places, most suited to meditation. To that also its straitness contributes; for when the mind is disposed to turn inwardly on itself, any serpentine line would distract the attention.

All the characteristic beauties of the avenue, its solemn stillness, the religious awe it inspires, are greatly heightened by moon-light. This I once very strongly experienced in approaching a venerable, castle-like mansion, built in the beginning of the 15th century: a few gleams had pierced the deep gloom of the avenue; a large massive tower at the end of it, seen through a long perspective, and half lighted by the uncertain beams of the moon, had a grand mysterious effect. Suddenly a light appeared in this tower — then as suddenly its twinkling vanished — and only the quiet, silvery rays of the moon prevailed; again, more lights quickly shifted to different parts of the building, and the whole scene most forcibly brought to my fancy the times of fairies and chivalry. I was much hurt to learn from the master of the place, that I might take my leave of the avenue and its romantic effects, for that a death warrant was signed.

The destruction of so many of these venerable approaches, is a fatal consequence of the present excessive horror of strait lines.... When from the avenue you turn either to the right or to the left, the whole country, with all its intricacies and varieties, is open before you: but from the belt there is no escaping; it hems you in on all sides; and if you please yourself with having discovered some wild sequestered part (if such there ever be where a belt-maker has been admitted) or some new pathway, and are in the pleasing uncertainty whereabouts you are, and whither it will lead you, the belt soon appears, and the charm of expectation is over. If you turn to either side, it keeps winding round you: if you break through it, it catches you at your return; and the idea of this distinct, unavoidable line of separation, damps all search after novelty.

THOMAS LOVE PEACOCK
From 'The Four Ages of Poetry'

(Peacock's 'The Four Ages of Poetry' first appeared in *Ollier's Literary Miscellany*, No. 1, 1820. Our text is from H.F.B. Brett-Smith's *The Four Ages of Poetry, etc.*, 1921, which contains a *verbatim* reproduction of the essay).

While the historian and the philosopher are advancing in, and accelerating, the progress of knowledge, the poet is wallowing in the rubbish of departed ignorance, and raking up the ashes of dead savages to find gewgaws and rattles for the grown babies of the age. Mr. Scott digs up the poachers and cattle-stealers of the ancient border. Lord Byron cruizes for thieves and pirates on the shores of the Morea and among the Greek Islands. Mr. Southey wades through ponderous volumes of travels and old chronicles, from which he carefully selects all that is false, useless, and absurd, as being essentially poetical; and when he has a commonplace book full of monstrosities, strings them into an epic. Mr. Wordsworth picks up village legends from old women and sextons; and Mr. Coleridge to the valuable information acquired from similar sources, superadds the dreams of crazy theologians and the mysticisms of German metaphysics, and favours the world with visions in verse, in which the quadruple elements of sexton, old woman, Jeremy Taylor,[6] and Emanuel

6. Jeremy Taylor: see n.16 to *S.T. Coleridge* section below, p. 92.

Kant, are harmonized into a delicious poetical compound. Mr. Moore presents us with a Persian, and Mr. Campbell with a Pennsylvanian tale,[7] both formed on the same principle as Mr. Southey's epics, by extracting from a perfunctory and desultory perusal of a collection of voyages and travels, all that useful investigation would not seek for and that common sense would reject.

A poet in our times is a semi-barbarian in a civilized community. He lives in the days that are past. His ideas, thoughts, feelings, associations, are all with barbarous manners, obsolete customs, and exploded superstitions. The march of his intellect is like that of a crab, backward. The brighter the light diffused around him by the progress of reason, the thicker is the darkness of antiquated barbarism, in which he buries himself like a mole, to throw up the barren hillocks of his Cimmerian[8] labours. The philosophic mental tranquillity which looks round with an equal eye on all external things, collects a store of ideas, discriminates their relative value, assigns to all their proper place, and from the materials of useful knowledge thus collected, appreciated, and arranged, forms new combinations that impress the stamp of their power and utility on the real business of life, is diametrically the reverse of that frame of mind which poetry inspires, or from which poetry can emanate. The highest inspirations of poetry are resolvable into three ingredients: the rant of unregulated passion, the whining of exaggerated feeling, and the cant of factitious sentiment: and can therefore serve only to ripen a splendid lunatic like Alexander,[9] a puling driveller like Werter,[10] or a morbid dreamer like Wordsworth. It can never make a philosopher, nor a statesman, nor in any class of life an useful or rational man. It cannot claim the slightest share in any one of the comforts and utilities of life of which we have witnessed so many and so rapid advances.

7. Thomas Moore (1779-1852) published *Lalla Rookh* in 1817, and Thomas Campbell (1777-1844) published *Gertrude of Wyoming* in 1809.

8. Cimmerian: totally dark, alluding to the Cimmerii, a race supposed to live in permanent darkness.

9. Alexander III of Macedon (356-323 B.C.), Alexander the Great, is the subject of an extensive Mediaeval romance literature.

10. Werter: see n.9 to *S.T. Coleridge* below, p. 85.

PERCY BYSSHE SHELLEY
From 'A Defence of Poetry'

(Shelley's 'A Defence of Poetry' was written in 1821. Our text is from the first published version, in P.B. Shelley, *Essays, Letters from Abroad, Translations and Fragments*, ed. Mary Shelley, 1840, I).

...Poetry, in a general sense, may be defined to be "the expression of the imagination:" and poetry is connate with the origin of man. Man is an instrument over which a series of external and internal impressions are driven, like the alternations of an everchanging wind over an Æolian lyre,[11] which move it by their motion to ever-changing melody. But there is a principle within the human, and perhaps within all sentient beings, which acts otherwise than in a lyre, and produces not melody alone, but harmony, by an internal adjustment of the sounds and motions thus excited to the impressions which excite them. It is as if the lyre could accommodate its chords to the motions of that which strikes them, in a determined proportion of sound; even as the musician can accommodate his voice to the sound of the lyre. A child at play by itself will express its delight by its voice and motions, and every inflexion of tone and gesture will bear exact relation to a corresponding antitype in the pleasurable impressions which had awakened it; it will be the reflected image of that impression; and as the lyre trembles and sounds after the wind has died away, so the child seeks, by prolonging in its voice and motions the duration of the effect, to prolong also a consciousness of the cause. In relation to the objects which delight a child, these expressions are what poetry is to higher objects. The savage (for the savage is to ages what the child is to years) expresses the emotions produced in him by surrounding objects in a similar manner; and language and gesture, together with plastic or pictorial imitation, become the image of the combined effect of those objects and his apprehension of them. Man in society, with all his passions and his pleasures, next becomes the object of the passions and pleasures of man; an additional class of emotions produces an augmented treasure of expression; and language, gesture, and the imitative arts, become at once the representation and the medium, the pencil and the picture, the chisel and the statue, the chord and the harmony. The social sympathies, or those laws from which as from its elements society results, begin to develop themselves from the moment that two human beings coexist; the future is contained within the present as the plant within the

11. Æolian lyre: stringed instrument played automatically by the wind; after Aeolus, god of the winds.

seed; and equality, diversity, unity, contrast, mutual dependence, become
the principles alone capable of affording the motives according to which
the will of a social being is determined to action, inasmuch as he is social;
and constitute pleasure in sensation, virtue in sentiment, beauty in art,
truth in reasoning, and love in the intercourse of kind. Hence men, even
in the infancy of society, observe a certain order in their words and
actions, distinct from that of the objects and the impressions represented
by them, all expression being subject to the laws of that from which it
proceeds. But let us dismiss those more general considerations which
might involve an inquiry into the principles of society itself, and restrict
our view to the manner in which the imagination is expressed upon its
forms.

In the youth of the world, men dance and sing and imitate natural
objects observing in these actions, as in all others, a certain rhythm or
order. And, although all men observe a similar, they observe not the same
order, in the motions of the dance, in the melody of the song, in the
combinations of language, in the series of their imitations of natural
objects. For there is a certain order or rhythm belonging to each of these
classes of mimetic representation, from which the hearer and the
spectator receive an intenser and purer pleasure than from any other: the
sense of an approximation to this order has been called taste by modern
writers. Every man in the infancy of art, observes an order which
approximates more or less closely to that from which this highest delight
results: but the diversity is not sufficiently marked, as that its gradations
should be sensible, except in those instances where the predominance of this
faculty of approximation to the beautiful (for so we may be permitted to
name the relation between this highest pleasure and its cause) is very
great. Those in whom it exists to excess are poets, in the most universal
sense of the word; and the pleasure resulting from the manner in which
they express the influence of society or nature upon their own minds,
communicates itself to others, and gathers a sort of reduplication from
the community. Their language is vitally metaphorical; that is, it marks
the before unapprehended relations of things and perpetuates their
apprehension, until words, which represent them, become, through time,
signs for portions or classes of thought, instead of pictures of integral
thoughts; and then, if no new poets should arise to create afresh the
associations which have been thus disorganised, language will be dead to
all the nobler purposes of human intercourse. These similitudes or
relations are finely said by Lord Bacon to be "the same footsteps of
nature impressed upon the various subjects of the world"[12] — and he

12. See Francis Bacon, *De Augment Scient.*, cap. I, lib. iii. Compare his *The Advancement of Learning*, II, v, 3.

considers the faculty which perceives them as the storehouse of axioms common to all knowledge. In the infancy of society every author is necessarily a poet, because language itself is poetry; and to be a poet is to apprehend the true and the beautiful, in a word, the good which exists in the relation, subsisting, first between existence and perception, and secondly between perception and expression. Every original language near to its source is in itself the chaos of a cyclic poem: the copiousness of lexicography and the distinctions of grammar are the works of a later age, and are merely the catalogue and the form of the creations of poetry.

But poets, or those who imagine and express this indestructible order, are not only the authors of language and of music, of the dance, and architecture, and statuary, and painting; they are the institutors of laws and the founders of civil society, and the inventors of the arts of life, and the teachers who draw into a certain propinquity with the beautiful and the true, that partial apprehension of the agencies of the invisible world which is called religion. Hence all original religions are allegorical or susceptible of allegory, and, like Janus, have a double face of false and true. Poets, according to the circumstances of the age and nation in which they appeared, were called, in the earlier epochs of the world, legislators or prophets: a poet essentially comprises and unites both these characters. For he not only beholds intensely the present as it is, and discovers those laws according to which present things ought to be ordered, but he beholds the future in the present, and his thoughts are the germs of the flower and the fruit of latest time. Not that I assert poets to be prophets in the gross sense of the word, or that they can foretell the form as surely as they foreknow the spirit of events: such is the pretence of superstition, which would make poetry an attribute of prophecy, rather than prophecy an attribute of poetry. A poet participates in the eternal, the infinite, and the one; as far as relates to his conceptions, time and place and number are not.

...Poetry is ever accompanied with pleasure: all spirits upon which it falls open themselves to receive the wisdom which is mingled with its delight. In the infancy of the world, neither poets themselves nor their auditors are fully aware of the excellence of poetry: for it acts in a divine and unapprehended manner, beyond and above consciousness; and it is reserved for future generations to contemplate and measure the mighty cause and effect in all the strength and splendour of their union. Even in modern times, no living poet ever arrived at the fullness of his fame; the jury which sits in judgment upon a poet, belonging as he does to all time, must be composed of his peers: it must be empanelled by time from the selectest of the wise of many generations. A poet is a nightingale, who sits in darkness and sings to cheer its own solitude with sweet sounds; his auditors are as men entranced by the melody of an unseen musician, who feel that they are moved and softened, yet know not whence or why. The poems of Homer and his contemporaries were the delight of infant Greece; they were the elements of that social system which is the column upon which all succeeding civilisation has reposed. Homer embodied the ideal perfection of his age in human character; nor can we doubt that those who read his verses were awakened to an ambition of becoming like to Achilles, Hector, and Ulysses: the truth and beauty of friendship, patriotism, and persevering devotion to an object, were unveiled to their depths in these immortal creations: the sentiments of the auditors must have been refined and enlarged by a sympathy with such great and lovely impersonations, until from admiring they imitated and from imitation they identified themselves with the objects of their admiration.

...Ethical science arranges the elements which poetry has created, and propounds schemes and proposes examples of civil and domestic life: nor is it for want of admirable doctrines that men hate, and despise, and censure, and deceive, and subjugate one another. But poetry acts in another and diviner manner. It awakens and enlarges the mind itself by rendering it the receptacle of a thousand unapprehended combinations of thought. Poetry lifts the veil from the hidden beauty of the world, and makes familiar objects be as if they were not familiar; it reproduces all that it represents, and the impersonations clothed in its Elysian light stand thenceforward in the minds of those who have once contemplated them, as memorials of that gentle and exalted content which extends itself over all thoughts and actions with which it coexists. The great secret of morals is love; or a going out of our own nature, and an identification of ourselves with the beautiful which exists in thought, action, or person, not our own. A man, to be greatly good, must imagine intensely and comprehensively; he must put himself in the place of another and of many others; the pains and pleasures of his species must become his own. The great instrument of moral good is the imagination; and poetry administers to the effect by acting upon the cause. Poetry enlarges the circumference of the imagination by replenishing it with thoughts of ever new delight, which have the power of attracting and assimilating to their own nature all other thoughts, and which form new intervals and interstices whose void for ever craves fresh food. Poetry strengthens the faculty which is the organ of the moral nature of man, in the same manner as exercise strengthens a limb. A poet therefore would do ill to embody his own conceptions of right and wrong, which are usually those of his place and time, in his poetical creations, which participate in neither. By this assumption of the inferior office of interpreting the effect, in which perhaps after all he might acquit himself but imperfectly, he would resign a glory in the participation of the cause.

...The exertions of Locke, Hume, Gibbon, Voltaire, Rousseau, and their disciples, in favour of oppressed and deluded humanity, are entitled to the gratitude of mankind. Yet it is easy to calculate the degree of moral and intellectual improvement which the world would have exhibited, had they never lived. A little more nonsense would have been talked for a century or two; and perhaps a few more men, women, and children, burnt as heretics. We might not at this moment have been congratulating each other on the abolition of the Inquisition in Spain. But it exceeds all imagination to conceive what would have been the moral condition of the world if neither Dante, Petrarch, Boccaccio, Chaucer, Shakespeare, Calderon, Lord Bacon, nor Milton, had ever existed; if Raphael and Michael Angelo had never been born; if the Hebrew poetry had never been translated; if a revival of the study of Greek literature had never taken place; if no monuments of ancient sculpture had been handed down to us; and if the poetry of the religion of the ancient world had been extinguished together with its belief. The human mind could never, except by the intervention of these excitements, have been awakened to the invention of the grosser sciences, and that application of analytical reasoning to the aberrations of society, which it is now attempted to exalt over the direct expression of the inventive and creative faculty itself.

We have more moral, political, and historical wisdom, than we know how to reduce into practice; we have more scientific and economical knowledge than can be accommodated to the just distribution of the produce which it multiplies. The poetry, in these systems of thought, is concealed by the accumulation of facts and calculating processes. There is no want of knowledge respecting what is wisest and best in morals, government, and political economy, or at least what is wiser and better than what men now practise and endure. But we let "*I dare not* wait upon *I would*, like the poor cat in the adage".[13] We want the creative faculty to imagine that which we know; we want the generous impulse to act that which we imagine; we want the poetry of life; our calculations have outrun conception; we have eaten more than we can digest. The cultivation of those sciences which have enlarged the limits of the empire of man over the external world, has, for want of the poetical faculty, proportionally circumscribed those of the internal world; and man, having enslaved the elements, remains himself a slave. To what but a cultivation of the mechanical arts in a degree disproportioned to the presence of the creative faculty, which is the basis of all knowledge, is to be attributed the abuse of all invention for abridging and combining labour, to the exasperation of the inequality of mankind? From what other cause has it arisen that the discoveries which should have lightened, have added a weight to the curse imposed on Adam?

13. *Macbeth*, I, 7, 43-44.

Poetry, and the principle of Self, of which money is the visible incarnation, are the God and Mammon of the world.

The functions of the poetical faculty are twofold; by one it creates new materials of knowledge, and power, and pleasure; by the other it engenders in the mind a desire to reproduce and arrange them according to a certain rhythm and order, which may be called the beautiful and the good. The cultivation of poetry is never more to be desired than at periods when, from an excess of the selfish and calculating principle, the accumulation of the materials of external life exceed the quantity of the power of assimilating them to the internal laws of human nature. The body has then become too unwieldy for that which animates it.

Poetry is indeed something divine. It is at once the centre and circumference of knowledge; it is that which comprehends all science, and that to which all science must be referred. It is at the same time the root and blossom of all other systems of thought; it is that from which all spring, and that which adorns all; and that which, if blighted, denies the fruit and the seed, and withholds from the barren world the nourishment and the succession of the scions of the tree of life. It is the perfect and consummate surface and bloom of all things; it is as the odour and the colour of the rose to the texture of the elements which compose it, as the form, and splendour of unfaded beauty to the secrets of anatomy and corruption. What were virtue, love, patriotism, friendship, — what were the scenery of this beautiful universe which we inhabit; what were our consolations on this side of the grave — and what were our aspirations beyond it, if poetry did not ascend to bring light and fire from those eternal regions where the owl-winged faculty of calculation dare not ever soar? Poetry is not like reasoning, a power to be exerted according to the determination of the will. A man cannot say, "I will compose poetry". The greatest poet even cannot say it; for the mind in creation is as a fading coal, which some invisible influence, like an inconstant wind, awakens to transitory brightness; this power arises from within, like the colour of a flower which fades and changes as it is developed, and the conscious portions of our nature are unprophetic either of its approach or its departure. Could this influence be durable in its original purity and force, it is impossible to predict the greatness of the results; but when composition begins, inspiration is already on the decline, and the most glorious poetry that has ever been communicated to the world is probably a feeble shadow of the original conceptions of the poet. I appeal to the greatest poets of the present day, whether it is not an error to assert that the finest passages of poetry are produced by labour and study. The toil and the delay recommended by critics, can be justly interpreted to mean no more than a careful observation of the inspired moments and an artificial connection of the spaces between their suggestions, by the intertexture of conventional expressions; a necessity only imposed by the limitedness of the poetical faculty itself:... .

...In spite of the low-thoughted envy which would undervalue contemporary merit, our own will be a memorable age in intellectual achievements, and we live among such philosophers and poets as surpass beyond comparison any who have appeared since the last national struggle for civil and religious liberty. The most unfailing herald, companion, and follower of the awakening of a great people to work a beneficial change in opinion or institution, is poetry. At such periods there is an accumulation of the power of communicating and receiving intense and impassioned conceptions respecting man and nature. The persons in whom this power resides, may often, as far as regards many portions of their nature, have little apparent correspondence with that spirit of good of which they are the ministers. But even whilst they deny and abjure, they are yet compelled to serve, the power which is seated on the throne of their own soul. It is impossible to read the compositions of the most celebrated writers of the present day without being startled with the electric life which burns within their words. They measure the circumference and sound the depths of human nature with a comprehensive and all-penetrating spirit, and they are themselves perhaps the most sincerely astonished at its manifestations; for it is less their spirit than the spirit of the age. Poets are the hierophants of an unapprehended inspiration; the mirrors of the gigantic shadows which futurity casts upon the present; the words which express what they understand not; the trumpets which sing to battle and feel not what they inspire; the influence which is moved not, but moves. Poets are the unacknowledged legislators of the world.

JOHN KEATS

From letters to Benjamin Bailey, 22 November 1817, to George and Thomas Keats, 21 December, 1817, To John Hamilton Reynolds, 3 May, 1818, and to Richard Woodhouse, 27 October, 1818

(The extracts are from *The Letters of John Keats*, edited by H.B. Forman, 1895).

I am certain of nothing but of the holiness of the Heart's affections and the truth of Imagination — What the imagination seizes as Beauty must be Truth — whether it existed before or not, — for I have the same Idea of all our Passions as of Love: they are all, in their sublime, creative of essential Beauty. In a Word, you may know my favourite speculation by my first Book, and the little Song I sent in my last, which is a representation from the fancy of the probable mode of operating in these Matters. The Imagination may be compared to Adam's dream,[14] — he awoke and found it truth: — I am the more zealous in this affair, because I have never yet been able to perceive how any thing can be known for truth by consecutive reasoning — and yet it must be. Can it be that even the greatest Philosopher ever arrived at his Goal without putting aside numerous objections? However it may be, O for a Life of Sensations rather than of Thoughts! It is 'a Vision in the form of Youth' a Shadow of reality to come — and this consideration has further convinced me, — for it has come as auxiliary to another favourite speculation of mine, — that we shall enjoy ourselves here after by having what we called happiness on Earth repeated in a finer tone. And yet such a fate can only befall those who delight in Sensation, rather than hunger as you do after Truth. Adam's dream will do here, and seems to be a Conviction that Imagination and its empyreal reflection is the same as human life and its spiritual repetition.

...I had not a dispute, but a disquisition, with Dilke,[15] upon various subjects; several things dovetailed in my mind, and at once it struck me what quality went to form a man of achievement, especially in Literature, and which Shakespeare possessed so enormously — I mean *Negative Capability*, that is when a man is capable of being in uncertainties, Mysteries, doubts, without any irritable reaching after fact and reason. Coleridge, for instance, would let go by a fine isolated verisimilitude caught from the Penetralium of mystery, from being incapable of remaining content with half knowledge. This pursued through volumes would perhaps take us no further than this, that with a great poet the sense of Beauty overcomes every other consideration, or rather obliterates all consideration.

...I compare human life to a large Mansion of Many Apartments, two of which I can only describe, the doors of the rest being as yet shut upon me. The first we step into we call the Infant or Thoughtless Chamber, in which we remain as long as we do not think. We remain there a long while, and notwithstanding the doors of the second Chamber remain wide open, showing a bright appearance, we care not to hasten to it; but are at length imperceptibly impelled by the awakening of the thinking principle within us — we no sooner get into the second Chamber, which I shall call the Chamber of Maiden-Thought, than we become intoxicated with the light and the atmosphere, we see nothing but pleasant wonders,

14. See Genesis 2. 21-23.
15. Charles Wentworth Dilke (1789-1864), civil servant and editor of old plays.

and think of delaying there for ever in delight: However among the effects this breathing is father of is that tremendous one of sharpening one's vision into the heart and nature of Man — of convincing one's nerves that the world is full of Misery and Heartbreak, Pain, Sickness and oppression — whereby this Chamber of Maiden Thought becomes gradually darken'd, and at the same time, on all sides of it many doors are set open — but all dark — all leading to dark passages. We see not the ballance of good and evil; we are in a Mist, *we* are now in that state, we feel the "Burden of the Mystery", To this Point was Wordsworth come, as far as I can conceive, when he wrote "Tintern Abbey" and it seems to me that his genius is explorative of those dark Passages. Now if we live, and go on thinking, we too shall explore them. He is a Genius and superior [to] us, in so far as he can, more than we, make discoveries, and shed a light in them. Here I must think Wordsworth is deeper than Milton.

...As to the poetical character itself (I mean that sort of which, if I am anything, I am a member; that sort distinguished from the Wordsworthian or egotistical Sublime; which is a thing per se, and stands alone) it is not itself — it has no self — it is every thing and nothing — It has no character — it enjoys light and shade; it lives in gusto, be it foul or fair, high or low, rich or poor, mean or elevated. — It has as much delight in conceiving an Iago as an Imogen. What shocks the virtuous philospher, delights the camelion Poet. It does no harm from its relish of the dark side of things any more than from its taste for the bright one; because they both end in speculation. A Poet is the most unpoetical of any thing in existence, because he has no Identity — he is continually in for — [?informing] and filling some other Body. — The Sun, the Moon, the Sea, and men and women who are creatures of impulse are poetical and have about them an unchangeable attribute; the poet has none; no identity — he is certainly the most unpoetical of all God's Creatures.

WILLIAM HAZLITT
From 'My first Acquaintance with Poets'
(The extracts are from *The Liberal*, No. 3, April, 1823).

My father was a Dissenting Minister at Wem in Shropshire; and in the year 1798 (the figures that compose the date are to me like the 'dreaded name of Demogorgon'[16]) Mr. Coleridge came to Shrewsbury, to succeed

16. *Paradise Lost,* II, 964-965.

Mr. Rowe in the spiritual charge of a Unitarian congregation there... .
Coleridge had agreed to come over to see my father, according to the
courtesy of the country, as Mr. Rowe's probable successor;...No two
individuals were ever more unlike than were the host and his guest. A
poet was to my father a sort of nondescript: yet whatever added grace to
the Unitarian cause was to him welcome. He could hardly have been
more surprised or pleased, if our visitor had worn wings. Indeed, his
thoughts had wings; and as the silken sounds rustled round our little
wainscoted parlour, my father threw back his spectacles over his
forehead, his white hairs mixing with its sanguine hue; and a smile of
delight beamed across his rugged cordial face, to think that Truth had
found a new ally in Fancy! Besides, Coleridge seemed to take considerable notice of me, and that of itself was enough. He talked very
familiarly, but agreeably, and glanced over a variety of subjects. At
dinner time he grew more animated, and dilated in a very edifying
manner on Mary Wollstonecraft and Mackintosh. The last, he said, he
considered (on my father's speaking of his *Vindiciae Gallicae* as a capital
performance) as a clever scholastic man — a master of the topics, — or as
the ready warehouseman of letters, who knew exactly where to lay his
hand on what he wanted, though the goods were not his own. He thought
him no match for Burke, either in style or matter. Burke was a
metaphysician, Mackintosh a mere logician. Burke was an orator (almost
a poet) who reasoned in figures, because he had an eye for nature:
Mackintosh, on the other hand, was a rhetorician, who had only an eye
to commonplaces. On this I ventured to say that I had always entertained
a great opinion of Burke, and that (as far as I could find) the speaking of
him with contempt might be made the test of a vulgar democratical mind.
This was the first observation I ever made to Coleridge, and he said it
was a very just and striking one. I remember the leg of Welsh mutton and
the turnips on the table that day had the finest flavour imaginable.
Coleridge added that Mackintosh and Tom Wedgwood[17] (of whom,
however, he spoke highly) had expressed a very indifferent opinion of his
friend Mr. Wordsworth, on which he remarked to them — "He strides on
so far before you, that he dwindles in the distance!" Godwin had once
boasted to him of having carried on an argument with Mackintosh for
three hours with dubious success; Coleridge told him — "If there had
been a man of genius in the room he would have settled the question in
five minutes". He asked me if I had ever seen Mary Wollstonecraft, and I
said, I had once for a few moments, and that she seemed to me to turn off
Godwin's objections to something she advanced with quite a playful, easy

17. Thomas Wedgwood (1771-1805), son of Josiah Wedgwood the potter, and
patron of Coleridge.

air. He replied, that "this was only one instance of the ascendancy which people of imagination exercised over those of mere intellect". He did not rate Godwin very high (this was caprice or prejudice, real or affected) but he had a great idea of Mrs. Wollstonecraft's powers of conversation, none at all of her talent for book-making. We talked a little about Holcroft.[18] He had been asked if he was not much struck *with* him, and he said, he thought himself in more danger of being struck *by* him. I complained that he would not let me get on at all, for he required a definition of every the commonest word, exclaiming, "What do you mean by a *sensation*, Sir? What do you mean by an *idea*?" This, Coleridge said, was barricadoing the road to truth: — it was setting up a turnpike-gate at every step we took. I forget a great number of things, many more than I remember; but the day passed off pleasantly, and the next morning Mr. Coleridge was to return to Shrewsbury. When I came down to breakfast, I found that he had just received a letter from his friend T. Wedgwood, making him an offer of £150 a year if he chose to waive his present pursuit, and devote himself entirely to the study of poetry and philosophy. Coleridge seemed to make up his mind to close with this proposal in the act of tying on one of his shoes. It threw an additional damp on his departure. It took the wayward enthusiast quite from us to cast him into Deva's winding vales,[19] or by the shores of old romance. Instead of living at ten miles' distance, of being the pastor of a Dissenting congregation at Shrewsbury, he was henceforth to inhabit the Hill of Parnassus,[20] to be a Shepherd on the Delectable Mountains.[21] Alas! I knew not the way thither, and felt very little gratitude for Mr. Wedgwood's bounty. I was presently relieved from this dilemma; for Mr. Coleridge, asking for a pen and ink, and going to a table to write something on a bit of card, advanced towards me with undulating step, and giving me the precious document, said that that was his address, *Mr. Coleridge, Nether-Stowey, Somersetshire*; and that he should be glad to see me there in a few weeks' time, and, if I chose, would come half-way to meet me. I was not less surprised than the shepherd-boy (this simile is to be found in *Cassandra*[22]) when he sees a thunderbolt fall close at his feet. I stammered out my acknowledgements and acceptance of this offer (I

18. Thomas Holcroft (1745-1809), Radical, novelist and playwright.
19. Deva's winding vales: the valley of the Dee in North Wales.
20. Hill of Parnassus: mountain, north of Delphi, sacred to the Muses.
21. Shepherd on the Delectable Mountains: in John Bunyan's *The Pilgrim's Progress* (1678), the Shepherds (named Knowledge, Experience, Watchful and Sincere) welcome Christian and Hopeful to the Delectable Mountains and show them Error, Caution, the way to the Doubting Castle and the gates of the Celestial City.
22. *Cassandre* (10 vols., 1644-1650), a romance by Gautier de Costes de la Calprenède. The simile is found in Part II, Book 5.

thought Mr. Wedgwood's annuity a trifle to it) as well as I could; and this mighty business being settled, the poet-preacher took leave, and I accompanied him six miles on the road. It was a fine morning in the middle of winter, and he talked the whole way. The scholar in Chaucer is described as going

— "Sounding on his way".[23]

So Coleridge went on his. In digressing, in dilating, in passing from subject to subject, he appeared to me to float in the air, to slide on ice. ...On my way back, I had a sound in my ears, it was the voice of Fancy: I had a light before me, it was the face of Poetry. The one still lingers there, the other has not quitted my side! Coleridge in truth met me half-way on the ground of philosophy, or I should not have been won over to his imaginative creed. I had an uneasy, pleasurable sensation all the time, till I was to visit him. During those months the chill breath of winter gave me a welcoming; the vernal air was balm and inspiration to me. The golden sunsets, the silver star of evening, lighted me on my way to new hopes and prospects. *I was to visit Coleridge in the Spring.* This circumstance was never absent from my thoughts, and mingled with all my feelings. I wrote to him at the time proposed, and received an answer postponing my intended visit for a week or two, but very cordially urging me to complete my promise then. This delay did not damp, but rather increase my ardour.
    ...I arrived and was well received. The country about Nether-Stowey is beautiful, green and hilly, and near the sea-shore. I saw it but the other day, after an interval of twenty years, from a hill near Taunton. How was the map of my life spread out before me, as the map of the country lay at my feet! In the afternoon, Coleridge took me over to All-Foxden, a romantic old family mansion of the St. Aubins, where Wordsworth lived. It was then in the possession of a friend of the poet's, who gave him the free use of it. Somehow that period (the time just after the French Revolution) was not a time when *nothing was given for nothing.* The mind opened, and a softness might be perceived coming over the heart of individuals, beneath "the scales that fence"[24] our self-interest. Wordsworth himself was from home, but his sister kept house, and set before us a frugal repast; and we had free access to her brother's poems, the *Lyrical Ballads,* which were still in manuscript, or in the form of *Sibylline Leaves.* I dipped into a few of these with great satisfaction, and with the

23. Compare Chaucer's *Prologue to the Canterbury Tales,* 1.307.
    24. Source untraced. However, it was Thomas Poole of Nether Stowey, Coleridge's friend, who persuaded the tenant of Alfoxden House to let it to Wordsworth.

faith of a novice. I slept that night in an old room with blue hangings, and covered with the round-faced family-portraits of the age of George I and II, and from the wooded declivity of the adjoining park that overlooked my window, at the dawn of day, could

— "hear the loud stag speak!".[25]

In the outset of life (and particularly at this time I felt it so) our imagination has a body to it. We are in a state between sleeping and waking, and have indistinct but glorious glimpses of strange shapes, and there is always something to come better than what we see. As in our dreams the fullness of the blood gives warmth and reality to the coinage of the brain, so in youth our ideas are clothed, and fed, and pampered with our good spirits; we breathe thick with thoughtless happiness, the weight of future years presses on the strong pulses of the heart, and we repose with undisturbed faith in truth and good. As we advance, we exhaust our fund of enjoyment and hope. We are no longer wrapped in *lamb's-wool*, lulled in Elysium. As we taste the pleasures of life, their spirit evaporates, the sense palls; and nothing is left but the phantoms, the lifeless shadows of what *has been*!

...The next day Wordsworth arrived from Bristol at Coleridge's cottage. I think I see him now. He answered in some degree to his friend's description of him, but was more gaunt and Don Quixote-like. He was quaintly dressed (according to the *costume* of that unconstrained period) in a brown fustian jacket and striped pantaloons, There was something of a roll, a lounge in his gait, not unlike his own Peter Bell. There was a severe, worn pressure of thought about his temples, a fire in his eye (as if he saw something in objects more than the outward appearance), an intense high narrow forehead, a Roman nose, cheeks furrowed by strong purpose and feeling, and a convulsive inclination to laughter about the mouth, a good deal at variance with the solemn, stately expression of the rest of his face. Chantrey's bust wants the marking traits; but he was teased into making it regular and heavy:[26] Haydon's[27] head of him, introduced into the *Entrance of Christ into Jerusalem*, is the most like his drooping weight of thought and expression. He sat down and talked very naturally and freely, with a mixture of clear gushing accents in his voice, a deep gutteral intonation, and a strong tincture of the northern *burr*, like the crust on wine. He instantly began to make havoc of the half of a Cheshire cheese on the table, and said triumphantly that "his marriage

25. Ben Jonson, 'To Sir Robert Worth', 1.22 (No. 3 of *The Forrest*, 1616).
26. Sir Francis Chantry (1781-1841), sculptor.
27. Benjamin Robert Haydon (1786-1846) historical painter.

with experience had not been so productive as Mr. Southey's in teaching him a knowledge of the good things of this life". He had been to see the *Castle Spectre* by Monk Lewis,[28] while at Bristol, and described it very well. He said "it fitted the taste of the audience like a glove". This *ad captandum* merit was, however, by no means a recommendation of it, according to the severe principles of the new school, which reject rather than court popular effect. Wordsworth, looking out of the low, latticed window, said, 'How beautifully the sun sets on that yellow bank!" I thought within myself, 'With what eyes these poets see nature!" and ever after, when I saw the sunset stream upon the objects facing it, conceived I had made a discovery, or thanked Mr. Wordsworth for having made one for me! We went over to All-Foxden again the day following, and Wordsworth read us the story of Peter Bell in the open air; and the comment made upon it by his face and voice was very different from that of some later critics! Whatever might be thought of the poem, "his face was as a book where men might read strange matters,"[29] and he announced the fate of his hero in prophetic tones. There is a *chaunt* in the recitation both of Coleridge and Wordsworth, which acts as a spell upon the hearer, and disarms the judgement. Perhaps they have deceived themselves by making habitual use of this ambiguous accompaniment. Coleridge's manner is more full, animated, and varied; Wordsworth's more equable, sustained, and internal. The one might be termed more *dramatic*, the other more *lyrical*. Coleridge has told me that he himself liked to compose in walking over uneven ground, or breaking through the straggling branches of a copsewood; whereas Wordsworth always wrote (if he could) walking up and down a straight gravel-walk, or in some spot where the continuity of his verse met with no collateral interruptions. Returning that same evening, I got into a metaphysical argument with Wordsworth, while Coleridge was explaining the different notes of the nightingale to his sister, in which we neither of us succeeded in making ourselves perfectly clear and intelligible. Thus I passed three weeks at Nether Stowey and in the neighbourhood, generally devoting the afternoons to a delightful chat in an arbour made of bark by the poet's friend Tom Poole, sitting under two fine elm-trees, and listening to the bees humming round us, while we quaffed our *flip*.[30] It was agreed, among other things, that we should make a jaunt down the Bristol Channel, as far as Lynton...In the morning of the second day, we breakfasted luxuriously in an old-fashioned parlour on tea, toast, eggs,

28. Matthew G. Lewis (1775-1818), author of *The Monk* (1796) and *The Castle Spectre* (1796), a Gothic music-drama.
29. *Macbeth*, I, 5, 62-63.
30. *flip*: beer and spirit mixed and heated with a hot iron.

and honey, in the very sight of the beehives from which it had been taken, and a garden full of thyme and wild flowers that had produced it. On this occasion Coleridge spoke of Virgil's Georgics, but not well. I do not think he had much feeling for the classical or elegant. It was in this room that we found a little worn-out copy of the *Seasons*, lying in a window-seat, on which Coleridge exclaimed, "*That* is true fame!" He said Thomson was a great poet, rather than a good one; his style was as meretricious as his thoughts were natural. He spoke of Cowper as the best modern poet. He said the *Lyrical Ballads* were an experiment about to be tried by him and Wordsworth, to see how far the public would endure poetry written in a more natural and simple style than had hitherto been attempted; totally discarding the artifices of poetical diction, and making use only of such words as had probably been common in the most ordinary language since the days of Henry II.

...I saw no more of him for a year or two, during which period he had been wandering in the Hartz Forest in Germany; and his return was cometary, meteorous, unlike his setting out. It was not till some time after that I knew his friends Lamb and Southey. The last always appears to me (as I first saw him) with a commonplace book under his arm, and the first with a *bon-mot* in his mouth. It was at Godwin's that I met with Holcroft and Coleridge, where they were disputing fiercely which was the best — *Man as he was, or man as he is to be.* "Give me", says Lamb, "man as he is *not* to be". This saying was the beginning of a friendship between us, which I believe still continues.

MARY WOLLSTONECRAFT SHELLEY
From Author's Introduction to *Frankenstein*

(Mary Shelley's *Frankenstein; or, The Modern Prometheus* was first published in 1818. Her introduction was written for the re-issue of the novel in 1831 as the ninth of the Standard Novels series published by Colburn and Bentley).

...I busied myself *to think of a story*, — a story to rival those which had excited us to this task. One which would speak to the mysterious fears of our nature and awaken thrilling horror — one to make the reader dread to look round, to curdle the blood, and quicken the beatings of the heart. If I did not accomplish these things, my ghost story would be unworthy of its name. I thought and pondered — vainly. I felt that blank incapability of invention which is the greatest misery of authorship, when dull Nothing replies to our anxious invocations. *Have you thought of a story?* I was asked each morning, and each morning I was forced to reply with a mortifying negative.

Everything must have a beginning, to speak in Sanchean[31] phrase; and that beginning must be linked to something that went before, The Hindus give the world an elephant to support it, but they make the elephant stand upon a tortoise. Invention, it must be humbly admitted, does not consist in creating out of void, but out of chaos; the materials must, in the first place, be afforded: it can give form to dark, shapeless substances, but cannot bring into being the substance itself. In all matters of discovery and invention, even of those that appertain to the imagination, we are continually reminded of the story of Columbus and his egg. Invention consists on the capacity of seizing on the capabilities of a subject; and in the power of moulding and fashioning ideas suggested to it.

Many and long were the conversations between Lord Byron and Shelley, to which I was a devout but nearly silent listener. During one of these, various philosophical doctrines were discussed, and among others the nature of the principle of life, and whether there was any probability of its ever being discovered and communicated. They talked of the experiments of Dr. Darwin[32] (I speak not of what the doctor really did, or said that he did, but , as more to my purpose, of what was then spoken of having been done by him), who preserved a piece of vermicelli in a glass till by some extraordinary means it began to move with voluntary motion. Not thus, after all, would life be given. Perhaps a corpse would be re-animated; galvanism[33] had given token of such things; perhaps the component parts of a creature might be manufactured, brought together, and endued with vital warmth.

Night waned upon this talk, and even the witching hour had gone by before we retired to rest. When I placed my head on my pillow, I did not sleep, nor could I be said to think. My imagination, unbidden, possessed and guided me, gifting the successive images that arose in my mind with a vividness far beyond the usual bounds of reverie. I saw — with shut eyes, but acute mental vision — I saw the pale student of unhallowed arts kneeling beside the thing he had put together. I saw the hideous phantasm of a man stretched out, and then, on the working of some powerful engine, show signs of life, and stir with an uneasy, half vital

---

31. Sanchean: alluding to Sancho Panza, peasant companion of Don Quixote in Cervantes' novel.

32. Erasmus Darwin (1731-1802), grandfather of Charles Darwin. A physician at Lichfield, he wrote poems on botany and a treatise, *Zoonomia* (1794-1796), in which he traced all living animals to an original living filament.

33. galvanism: theory of animal electricity named after Luigi Galvani (1737-1798), who attributed electric power to the muscles of frogs.

motion. Frightful must it be; for supremely frightful would be the effect of any human endeavour to mock the stupendous mechanism of the Creator of the world. His success would terrify the artist; he would rush away from his odious handiwork, horror-stricken. He would hope that, left to itself, the slight spark of life which he had communicated would fade; that this thing which had received such imperfect animation would subside into dead matter, and he might sleep in the belief that the silence of the grave would quench forever the transient existence of the hideous corpse which he had looked upon as the cradle of life. He sleeps; but he is awakened; he opens his eyes; behold, the horrid thing stands at his bedside, opening his curtains and looking on him with yellow, watery, but speculative eyes.

I opened mine in terror. The idea so possessed my mind that a thrill of fear ran through me, and I wished to exchange the ghastly image of my fancy for the realities around. I see them still; the very room, the dark *parquet*, the closed shutters with the moonlight struggling through, and the sense I had that the glassy lake and white high Alps were beyond. I could not so easily get rid of my hideous phantom; still it haunted me. I must try to think of something else. I recurred to my ghost story — my tiresome, unlucky ghost story! Oh! if I could only contrive one which would frighten my reader as I myself had been frightened that night!

Swift as light and as cheering was the idea that broke in upon me. "I have found it! What terrified me will terrify others; and I need only describe the spectre which had haunted my midnight pillow". On the morrow I announced that I had *thought of a story*. I began that day with the words, *It was on a dreary night of November*, making only a transcript of the grim terrors of my waking dream.

S.T. Coleridge

Samuel Taylor Coleridge (1772-1834) shares with Wordsworth the leading literary position of the English Romantic Movement. The son of a Devon vicar, he was educated at Christ's Hospital and at Jesus College, Cambridge. During abortive preparations for an egalitarian settlement in America with Southey and others, Coleridge became engaged to and married Sara Fricker in 1795. The marriage was unequal and unhappy. Coleridge established his own Radical periodical, *The Watchman*, again Bristol-based and backed by a thousand subscribers, but it ran for only ten numbers. The essay on the Slave-Trade, from the fourth number, is particularly interesting for its analysis of romantic concepts like imagination and sensibility in the context of humanitarian politics. Coleridge's friendship with Wordsworth, begun shortly after this period, led to their residence with or near each other in the West Country, the Lake District and, briefly, in Germany, as they collaborated in ambitious poetic projects which were to achieve the major shift in English poetic style and subject-matter from the Augustan to the Romantic modes. A deepening religious and political conservatism accompanied these joint efforts and, as Coleridge went more his own way, gave his London lectures on past writers and gathered his admirers around himself at Highgate, his unified intuitionist conviction formed the basis of thought in his numerous prose works. The *Lay Sermon* of 1817 is a good example of the later Coleridge's style, showing his distrust of materialistic commerce and his fear of sudden social revolution. His main contribution to conservative ideology is his *On the Constitution of Church and State*, a work noted for its novel political terminology and its advocacy of gradualism. Coleridge's concern for the state's education and civilising role is also in evidence in his *Biographia Literaria*, the work in which he both defines those activities which constitute the writing and reading of poetry and also takes issue with Wordsworth over his having advocated too exclusive a role for simple diction in poetry and having neglected the expressive function of metre.

From *Conciones ad Populum, or Address to the People*

(The extracts, from the second lecture, 'On the Present War', are taken from the first edition, 1795).

...We will now take a rapid survey of the consequences of this unjust because unnecessary War. I mean not to describe the distressful stagnation of Trade and Commerce: I direct not your attention to the wretches that sadden every street in this City, the pale and Meagre Troop, who in the bitterness of reluctant Pride, are forced to beg the Morsel, for which they would be willing to "work their fingers to the bone" in honest Industry: I will not frighten you by relating the distresses of that brave Army, which has been melted away on the Continent,[1] nor picture to your imagination the loathsome pestilence that has mocked our Victories in the West-Indies: I bid you not hear the screams of the deluded Citizens of Toulon[2] — I will not press on your recollection the awful Truth, that in the course of this calamitous Contest more than a Million of men have perished — a MILLION[3] of men, of each one of whom the mangled corse terrifies the dreams of her that loved him, and makes some mother, some sister, some widow start from slumber with a shriek! These arguments have been urged even to satiety — a British Senator[4] has sneeringly styled them mere *common-place* against wars. I could weep for the criminal Patience of Humanity! These arguments are *hacknied;* yet *Wars* continue!

Horrors, the same in kind though perhaps not equal in degree, necessarily attend all wars: it was my intention to detail those only that are peculiar to the present. And first and least — the loss of our National Character. At the commencement of the War the Government solemnly disclaimed all intervention in the internal affairs of France: not six months passed, ere with matchless insincerity the Restitution of Monarchy became its avowed aim. This guilt however may perhaps rest on its first authors, and fly unclaimed by the People, unless it should be thought, that they, who permit, perpetrate. The depravation of private morals is a more serious and less transient evil. All our happiness and the

1. In Flanders during 1793-1795.
2. Royalists executed by republicans, who retook Toulon from British occupying forces in 1793.
3. By the internal disturbances of France in La Vendee and other places, disturbances incited by English agents, and rendered obstinate by our Ministers' promises, more than *Three Hundred Thousand* have been butchered (Coleridge's note).
4. Burke, in 1792.

greater part of our virtues depend on social confidence. This beautiful fabric of Love the system of Spies and Informers has shaken to the very foundation. There have been multiplied among us "Men who carry tales to shed blood!"[5] Men who resemble the familiar Spirits described by Isaiah, as "dark ones, that peep and that mutter!"[6] Men, who may seem to have been typically shadowed out in the Frogs that formed the second plague of Egypt: little low animals with chilly blood and staring eyes, that "come up into our houses and our bed-chambers!"[7] These men are plenteously scattered among us: our very looks are decyphered into disaffection, and we cannot move without treading on some political spring-gun. Nor here has the evil stopped. We have breathed so long the atmosphere of Imposture and Panic, that many honest minds have caught an aguish disorder; in their cold fits they shiver at Freedom, in their hot fits they turn savage against its advocates; and sacrifice to party Rage what they would have scornfully refused to Corruption. Traitors to friendship, that they may be faithful to the Constitution — Enemies of human nature, that they may prove themselves the Adorer of the God of Peace — they hide from themselves the sense of their crime by the merit of their motive. Thus every man begins to suspect his neighbour, the warm ebullience of our hearts is stagnating: and I dread, lest by long stifling the expressions of Patriotism, we may at last lose the Feeling. "Society is in every state a blessing; Government even in its best state but a necessary evil".[8] We are subverting this Blessing in order to support this Evil — or rather to support the desperate Quacks who are administering it with a Life-or-Death Temerity.

...Our national faith has been impaired; our social confidence hath been weakened, or made unsafe; our liberties have suffered a perilous breach, and even now are being (still more perilously) undermined; the Dearth, which would otherwise have been scarcely visible, hath enlarged its terrible features into the threatening face of Famine; and finally, of US will justice require a dreadful account of whatever guilt France has perpetrated, of whatever miseries France has endured. Are we men? Freemen? rational men? And shall we carry on this wild and priestly War against reason, against freedom, against human nature? If there be one among you, who departs from me without feeling it his immediate duty to petition or remonstrate against the continuance of it, I envy that man neither his head or his heart!

5. Compare Ezekial 22.9.
6. Compare Isaiah 8.19.
7. Compare Exodus 8.3.
8. Compare Thomas Paine, *Common Sense* (1791), 5.

From 'On the Slave Trade'

(The extracts are from *The Watchman*, No. IV, 25 March, 1796).

Whence arise our Miseries? Whence arise our Vices? From *imaginary* Wants. No man is wicked without temptation, no man is wretched without a cause. But if each among us confined his wishes to the actual necessaries and real comforts of Life, we should preclude all the causes of Complaint and all the motives to Iniquity. What Nature demands, she will supply, asking for it that portion only of *Toil*, which would otherwise have been necessary as *Exercise*. But Providence, which has distinguished Man from the lower orders of Being by the progressiveness of his nature, forbids him to be contented. It has given us the restless faculty of *Imagination*.

...I have dwelt anxiously on this subject, with a particular view, to the Slave-trade, which, I knew, has insinuated in the minds of many, uneasy doubts respecting the existence of a beneficent Deity. And indeed the evils arising from the formation of *imaginary* Wants, have in no instance been so dreadfully exemplified, as in this inhuman Traffic. We receive from the West-India Islands Sugars, Rum, Cotton, Logwood, Cocoa, Coffee, Pimento, Ginger, Indigo, Mahogany, and Conserves. Not one of these articles are necessary; indeed with the exception of Cotton and Mahogany we cannot truly call them even useful: and not one of them is at present attainable by the poor and labouring part of Society. In return we export vast quantities of necessary Tools, Raiment, and defensive Weapons, with great stores of Provision. So that in this Trade as in most others the Poor are employed with unceasing toil first to raise, and then to send away the Comforts, which they themselves absolutely want, in order to procure idle superfluities for their Masters. If this Trade had never existed, no one human being would have been less comfortably cloathed, housed, or nourished. Such is its value — they who would estimate the price which we pay for it, may consult the evidence delivered before the House of Commons. I will not mangle the feelings of my readers by detailing enormities, which the gloomy Imagination of Dante would scarcely have dared attribute to the Inhabitants of Hell. For the honour of our common nature, I would fain hope that these accounts have been exaggerated. But, by the confession of all, these enormities might have been perpetrated and with impunity: and when was power possessed and not exercised?

...Gracious God! enormities, at which a Caligula might have turned pale, are authorised by our laws, and jocosely defended by our Princes; and yet we have the impudence to call the French a Nation of *Atheists*!

They, who believe a God, believe him to be the loving Parent of all men — And is it possible that they who really believe and fear the Father, should fearlessly authorize the oppression of his Children? The Slavery and Tortures, and most horrible Murder of tens of thousands of his children!

Yes! the wicked and malignant can believe a God — they need not the solutions, which the enlarged views of the Optimist prompt; their own hearts teach them, that an intelligent being may be malevolent; and what they themselves are, they impiously imagine of the Deity. These men are not Atheists: they are the causes of Atheism.

...If only one tenth part among you who profess yourselves Christians; if one half only of the Petitioners; instead of bustling about with ostentatious sensibility, were to leave off — not *all* the West-India commodities - but only Sugar and Rum, the one useless and the other pernicious - all this misery might be stopped. Gracious Heaven! At your meals you rise up, and pressing your hand to your bosoms, you lift up your eyes to God, and say, "O Lord! bless the food which thou hast given us!" A part of that food among most of you, is sweetened with Brother's Blood. "Lord! bless the good which thou hast given us?" O Blasphemy! Did God give food mingled with the blood of the Murdered? will God bless the food which is polluted with the Blood of his own innocent children? Surely if the inspired Philanthropist of Galilee were to revisit Earth, and be among the Feasters as at Cana, he would not now change water into wine, but convert the produce into the things producing, the occasion into the things occasioned. Then with our fleshly eye should we behold what even now Imagination ought to paint to us; instead of conserves, tears and blood, and for music, groanings and the loud peals of the lash!

There is observable among the Many a false and bastard sensibility that prompts them to remove those evils and those evils alone, which by hideous spectacle or clamorous outcry are present to their senses, and disturb their selfish enjoyments. Other miseries, though equally certain and far more horrible, they not only do not endeavour to remedy — they support, they fatten on them. Provided the dunghill be not before their parlour window, they are well content to know that it exists, and that it is the hot-bed of their pestilent luxuries. — To this grievous failing we must attribute the frequency of wars, and the continuance of the Slave-trade. The merchant finds no argument against it in his ledger: the citizen at the crouded feast is not nauseated by the stench and filth of the slave-vessel — the fine lady's nerves are not shattered by the shrieks! She sips a beverage sweetened with human blood, even while she is weeping over the refined sorrows of Werter[9] or of Clementina.[10] Sensibility is not Bene-

9. Werter: the hero of Goethe's *Werther* (1774).

volence. Nay, by making us tremblingly alive to trifling misfortunes, it frequently prevents it, and induces effeminate and cowardly selfishness. Our own sorrows, like the Princes of Hell in Milton's Pandemonium, sit enthroned 'bulky and vast:"[11] while the miseries of our fellow-creatures dwindle into pigmy forms, and are crouded, an innumerable multitude, into some dark corner of the heart. There is one criterion by which we may always distinguish benevolence from mere sensibility - Benevolence impels to action, and is accompanied by self-denial.

From *A Lay Sermon, addressed to the Higher and Middle Classes, on the existing Distresses and Discontents*

(The extract is taken from the first edition, 1817).

...It was one among the many anomalies of the late War, that it acted, after a few years, as a universal stimulant. We almost monopolized the commerce of the world. The high wages of our artisans and the high prices of agricultural produce intercirculated. Leases of unusual length not seldom enabled the provident and thrifty farmer to purchase the estate he had rented. Every where might be seen roads, rail-ways, docks, canals, made, making, and projected; villages swelling into towns, while the metropolis surrounded itself, and became (as it were) *set* with new cities. Finally, in spite of all the waste and havock of a twenty years' war, the population of the empire was increased by more than two millions! The efforts and war-expenditure of the nation, and the yearly revenue, were augmented in the same proportion: and to all this we must add a fact of the utmost importance in the present question, that the war did not, as was usually the case in former wars, die away into a long expected peace by gradual exhaustion and weariness on both sides, but *plunged* to its conclusion by a concentration, we might almost say, by a *spasm* of energy, and consequently by an *anticipation* of our resources. We conquered by compelling *reversionary* power into alliance with our existing and natural strength. The first intoxication of triumph having passed over, this our "agony of glory", was succeeded, of course, by a general stiffness and relaxation. The antagonist passions came into play; financial solicitude was blended with constitutional and political jealousies, and both, alas! were exacerbated by personal imprudences, the

10. Clementina: a character in Samuel Richardson's *Sir Charles Grandison* (1753-1754)
11. Compare Milton, *Paradise Lost*, I, 196 and 780.

chief injury of which consisted in their own tendency to disgust and alienate the public feeling. And with all this, the financial errors and prejudices even of the more educated classes, in short, the general want or imperfection of clear views and a scientific insight into true effects and influences of Taxation, and the mode of its operation, became now a real misfortune, and opened an additional source of temporary embarrassment. Retrenchment could no longer proceed by cautious and calculated steps; but was compelled to hurry forward, like the one who crossing the sands at too late an hour finds himself threatened by the inrush of the tide. Nevertheless, it was a truth susceptible of little less than mathematical demonstration, that the more, and the more suddenly, the Revenue was diminished by the abandonment of the war-taxes, the greater would be the disturbance of the Balance: so that the agriculturalist, the manufacturer, or the tradesman, (all in short but annuitants and fixed stipendiaries) who during the war having paid as Five had Fifteen left behind, would shortly have less than Ten after having paid but Two and a Half.

But there is yet another circumstance, which we dare not pass by unnoticed. In the best of times — or what the world calls such — the spirit of commerce will occasion great fluctuations, some falling while others rise, and therefore in all times there will be a large sum of individual distress. Trades likewise have their seasons, and at all times there is a very considerable number of artificers who are not employed on the average more than seven or eight months in the year: and the distress from this cause is great or small in proportion to the greater or less degree of dissipation and improvidence prevailing among them. But besides this, that artificial life and vigor of Trade and Agriculture, which was produced or occasioned by the direct or indirect influence of the late War, proved by no means innoxious in its effects. Habit and familiarity with outward advantages, which takes off their *dazzle*; sense of character; and above all, the counterpoise of intellectual pursuits and resources; are all necessary preventives and antidotes to the dangerous properties of wealth and power with the great majority of mankind. It is a painful subject: and I leave to your own experience and recollection the assemblage of folly, presumption and extravagance, that followed in the procession of our late unprecedented prosperity; the blind practices and blending passions of speculation in the commercial world, with the shoal of ostentatious fooleries and sensual vices which the sudden influx of wealth let in on our farmers and yeomanry. Now though the whole mass of calamity consequent on these aberrations from prudence should in all fairness be attributed to the sufferer's own conduct; yet when there supervenes some one common cause or occasion of distress which pressing hard on many furnishes a pretext to all, this too will pass muster among its actual effects and assume the semblance and dignity of national calamity. Each unfortunate individual shares during *the hard times* in the immunities of a privileged order, as the most tottering and ruinous houses equally with those in best repair are included in the same brief after an extensive fire. The change of the moon will not produce a change of weather, except in places where the atmosphere has from local and particular causes been predisposed to its influence. But the former is one, placed aloft and conspicuous to all men; the latter are many and intricate, and known to few. Of course it is the moon that must bear the entire blame of wet summers and scanty crops. All these, however, whether they are distresses common to all times alike, or though *occasional* by the general revolution and stagnation, yet really *caused* by personal improvidence or misconduct, combine with its peculiar and inevitable effects in making the cup overflow. The latter class especially, as being in such cases always the most clamorous sufferers, increase the evil by swelling the alarm.

The principal part of the preceeding explication, the main causes of the present exigencies are so obvious, and lay so open to the common sense of mankind, that the labouring classes saw the connection of the change in the times with the suddenness of the peace, as clearly as their superiors, and being less heated with speculation, were in the first instance less surprized at the results. To a public event of universal concern there will often be more attributed than belongs to it; but never in the natural course of human feelings will there be less. That the depression began *with* the Peace would have been of itself a sufficient proof with the Many, that it arose *from* the Peace. But this opinion suited ill with the purposes of sedition. The truth, that could not be precluded, must be removed; and "when the needy speaketh aright" the more urgent occasion is there for the "*wicked device*" and the "*lying words*".[12] Where distress is felt, tales of wrong and oppression are readily believed, to the sufferer's own disquiet. Rage and Revenge make the cheek pale and the hand tremble, worse than even want itself: and the cup of sorrow overflows by being held unsteadily. On the other hand nothing calms the mind in the hour of bitterness as efficaciously as the conviction that it was not within the means of those above us, or around us, to have prevented it. An influence, mightier than fascination, dwells in the stern eye of Necessity, when it is fixed steadily on a man: for together with the *power* of resistance it takes away its agitations likewise. This is one mercy that always accompanies the visitions of the Almighty when they are received *as* such. If therefore the sufferings of the lower classes are to supply air and fuel to their passions, and are to be perverted into instruments of

12. Compare Isaiah 32.7.

mischief, they must be attributed to causes that can be represented as removeable; either to individuals who had been previously rendered unpopular, or to whole classes of men, according as the immediate object of their seducers may require. What,though nothing should be more remote from the true cause? What though the invidious charge would be not only without proof, but in the face of strong proof to the contrary? What though the pretended remedy should have no possible end but that of exasperating the disease? All will be of little or no avail, if these truths have not been administered beforehand.

From *Biographia Literaria; or Biographical Sketches of my Literary Life and Opinions*

(The extracts, from Vol. I, Chs. 4 and 13, and Vol. II, Chs. 14, 17, 18 and 22, are taken from the first edition, 1817, with a footnote omitted).

...Repeated meditations led me first to suspect, (and a more intimate analysis of the human faculties, their appropriate marks, functions, and effects matured my conjecture into full conviction) that fancy and imagination were two distinct and widely different faculties, instead of being, according to the general belief, either two names with one meaning, or at furthest, the lower and higher degrees of one and the same power. It is not, I own, easy, to conceive a more apposite translation of the Greek *Phantasia* than the Latin Imaginatio; but it is equally true that in all societies there exists an instinct of growth, a certain collective, unconscious good sense working progressively to desynonymize[13] those words originally of the same meaning, which the conflux of dialects had supplied to the more homogeneous languages, as the Greek and German: and which the same cause joined with accidents of translation from original works of different countries, occasion in mixt languages like our own. The first and most important point to be proved is, that two conceptions perfectly distinct are confused under one and the same word, and (this done) to appropriate that word exclusively to one meaning, and the synonyme (should there be one) to the other. But if (as will be often the case in the arts and sciences) no synonyme exists, we must either invent or borrow a word. In the present instance the appropriation had already begun, and been legitimated in the derivative adjective: Milton

13. desynonymize: give two words of the same meaning new, different, separate meanings.

had a highly *imaginative*, Cowley a very *fanciful* mind. If therefore I should succeed in establishing the actual existence of two faculties generally different, the nomenclature would be at once determined. To the faculty by which I had characterized Milton, we should confine the term *imagination*; while the other would be contra-distinguished as *fancy*. Now were it once fully ascertained, that this division is no less grounded in nature, than that of delirium from mania, or Otway's

"Lutes, lobsters, seas of milk, and ships of amber",[14]

from Shakespear's

"What! have his daughters brought him to this pass?"[15]

or from the preceding apostrophe to the elements; the theory of the fine arts, and of poetry in particular, could not, I thought, but derive some additional and important light. It would in its immediate effects furnish a torch of guidance to the philosophical critic; and ultimately to the poet himself. In energetic minds, truth soon changes by domestication into power; and from directing in the discrimination and appraisal of the product, becomes influencive in the production. To admire on principle, is the only way to imitate without loss of originaltiy.

...The IMAGINATION then I consider either as primary, or secondary. The primary IMAGINATION I hold to be the living Power and the prime Agent of all human perception, and as a repetition in the finite mind of the eternal act of creation in the infinite I AM. The secondary I consider as an echo of the former, co-existing with the conscious will, yet still as identical with the primary in the *kind* of its agency, and differing only in *degree*, and in the *mode* of its operation. It dissolves, diffuses, dissipates, in order to re-create; or where this process is rendered impossible, yet still at all events it struggles to idealize and to unify. It is essentially *vital*, even as all objects (*as* objects) are essentially fixed and dead.

Fancy, on the contrary, has no other counters to play with, but fixities and definites. The Fancy is indeed no other than a mode of Memory emancipated from the order of time and space; and blended with , and modified by that empirical phenomenon of the will, which we express by the word CHOICE. But equally with the ordinary memory it must receive all its materials ready made from the law of association.

...During the first year that Mr. Wordsworth and I were neighbours, our conversations turned frequently on the two cardinal points of poetry, the power of exciting the sympathy of the reader by a faithful adherence to the truth of nature, and the power of giving the interest of novelty by

14. *Venice Preserv'd*, V, 1, 369. Otway has 'laurels' for 'lobsters'.
15. *King Lear*, III, 4, 63.

the modifying colours of imagination. The sudden charm, which accidents of light and shade, which moon-light or sun-set diffused over a known and familiar landscape, appeared to represent the practicability of combining both. These are the poetry of nature. The thought suggested itself (to which of us I do not recollect) that a series of poems might be composed of two sorts. In the one, the incidents and agents were to be, in part at least, supernatural; and the excellence aimed at was to consist in the interesting of the affections by the dramatic truth of such emotions, as would naturally accompany such situations, supposing them real. And real in *this* sense they have been to every human being who, from whatever source of delusion, has at any time believed himself under supernatural agency. For the second class, subjects were chosen from ordinary life; the characters and incidents were to be such, as will be found in every village and its vicinity, where there is a meditative and feeling mind to seek after them, or to notice them, when they present themselves.

In this idea originated the plan of the "Lyrical Ballads"; in which it was agreed, that my endeavours should be directed to persons and characters supernatural, or at least romantic; yet so as to transfer from our inward nature a human interest and a semblance of truth sufficient to procure for these shadows of imagination that willing suspension of disbelief for the moment, which constitutes poetic faith. Mr. Wordsworth, on the other hand, was to propose to himself as his object, to give the charm of novelty to things of every day, and to excite a feeling analogous to the supernatural, by awakening the mind's attention from the lethargy of custom, and directing it to the loveliness and the wonders of the world before us; an inexhaustible treasure, but for which in consequence of the film of familiarity and selfish solicitude we have eyes, yet see not, ears that hear not, and hearts that neither feel nor understand.

...But the communication of pleasure may be the immediate object of a work not metrically composed; and that object may have been in a high degree attained, as in novels and romances. Would then the mere superaddition of metre, with or without rhyme, entitle *these* to the name of poems? The answer is, that nothing can permanently please, which does not contain in itself the reason why it is so, and not otherwise. If metre be superadded, all other parts must be made consonant with it. They must be such, as to justify the perpetual and distinct attention to each part, which an exact correspondent recurrence of accent and sound are calculated to excite. The final definition then, so deduced, may be thus worded. A poem is that species of composition, which is opposed to works of science, by proposing for its *immediate* object pleasure, not truth; and from all other species (having *this* object in common with it) it is discriminated by proposing to itself such delight from the *whole* as it is compatible with a distinct gratification from each component *part*.

Controversy is not seldom excited in consequence of the disputants attaching each a different meaning to the same word; and in few instances has this been more striking, than in disputes concerning the present subject. If a man chooses to call every composition a poem, which is rhyme, or measure, or both, I must leave his opinion uncontroverted. The distinction is at least competent to characterize the writer's intention. If it were subjoined, that the whole is likewise entertaining or affecting, as a tale, or as a series of interesting reflections, I of course admit this as another fit ingredient of a poem, and an additional merit. But if the definition sought for be that of a *legitimate* poem, I answer, it must be one, the parts of which mutually support and explain each other; all in their proportion harmonizing with, and supporting the purpose and known influences of metrical arrangement. The philosophic critics of all ages coincide with the ultimate judgement of all countries, in equally denying the praises of a just poem, on the one hand, to a series of striking lines or distichs, each of which absorbing the whole attention of the reader to itself disjoins it from its context, and makes it a separate whole, instead of an harmonizing part; and on the other hand, to an unsustained composition, from which the reader collects rapidly the general result unattracted by the component parts. The reader should be carried forward, not merely or chiefly by the mechanical impulse of curiosity, or by a restless desire to arrive at the final solution; but by the pleasurable activity of mind excited by the attractions of the journey itself.

...The writings of PLATO, and Bishop TAYLOR,[16] and the Theoria Sacra of Burnet,[17] furnish undeniable proofs that poetry of the highest kind may exist without metre, and even without the contradistinguishing objects of a poem. The first chapter of Isaiah (indeed a very large proportion of the whole book) is poetry in the most emphatic sense; yet it would be not less irrational than strange to assert, that pleasure, and not truth, was the immediate object of the prophet. In short, whatever *specific* import we attach to the word, poetry, there will be found involved in it, as a necessary consequence, that a poem of any length neither can be, nor ought to be, all poetry. Yet if an harmonious whole is to be produced, the remaining parts must be preserved *in keeping* with the poetry; and this can be no otherwise effected than by such a studied selection and artificial arrangement, as will partake of *one*, though not a *peculiar* property of poetry. And this again can be no other than the property of exciting a more continuous and equal attention, than the language of prose aims at, whether colloquial or written.

My own conclusions on the nature of poetry, in the strictest use of the

---

16. Jeremy Taylor, author of *Holy Living* and *Holy Dying* (1650-1651).
17. Thomas Burnet, *The Sacred Theory of the Earth* (1684-1690).

word, have been in part anticipated in the preceeding disquisition on the fancy and imagination. What is poetry? is so nearly the same question, with, what is a poet? that the answer to the one is involved in the solution of the other. For it is a distinction resulting from the poetic genius itself, which sustains and modifies the images, thoughts, and emotions of the poet's own mind. The poet, described in *ideal* perfection, brings the whole soul of man into activity, with the subordination of its faculties to each other, according to their relative worth and dignity. He diffuses a tone and spirit of unity, that blends and (as it were) *fuses*, each into each, by that synthetic and magical power, to which we have exclusively appropriated the name of imagination. This power, first put in action by the will and understanding, and retained under their irremissive, though gentle and unnoticed, controul (*laxis effertur habenis*)[18] reveals itself in the balance or reconciliation of opposite or discordant qualities: of sameness, with difference; of the general, with the concrete; the idea, with the image; the individual, with the representative; the sense of novelty and freshness, with old and familiar objects; a more than usual state of emotion, with more than usual order; judgement ever awake and steady self-possession, with enthusiasm and feeling profound or vehement; and while it blends and harmonizes the natural and the artificial, still subordinates art to nature; the manner to the matter; and our admiration of the poet to our sympathy with the poetry.

...My own differences from certain supposed parts of Mr. Wordsworth's theory ground themselves on the assumption, that his words had been rightly interpreted, as purporting that the proper diction for poetry in general consists altogether in a language taken, with due exceptions, from the mouths of men in real life, a language which actually constitutes the natural conversation of men under the influence of natural feelings. My objection is, first, that in *any* sense this rule is applicable only to *certain* classes of poetry; secondly, that even to these classes it is not applicable, except in such a sense, as hath never by any one (as far as I know or have read) been denied or doubted; and lastly, that as far as, and in that degree in which it is *practicable*, yet as a *rule* it is useless, if not injurious, and therefore either need not, or ought not to be practised. The poet informs his reader, that he had generally chosen *low and rustic* life, but not *as* low and rustic, or in order to repeat that pleasure of doubtful moral effect, which persons of elevated rank and of superior refinement oftentimes derive from a happy *imitation* of the rude unpolished manners and discourse of their inferiors. For the pleasure so derived may be traced to three exciting causes. The first is the natural-

18. *laxis effertur habenis*: is carried on with loose reins. Compare Virgil, *Georgics*, II, 364.

ness, in *fact*, of the things represented. The second is the apparent naturalness of the *representation*, as raised and qualified by an imperceptible infusion of the author's own knowledge and talent, which infusion does, indeed, constitute it an *imitation* as distinguished from a mere *copy*. The third cause may be found in the reader's conscious feeling of his superiority awakened by the contrast presented to him; even as for the same purpose the kings and great barons of yore retained, sometimes *actual* clowns and fools, but more frequently shrewd and witty fellows in that *character*.

...Now it is clear to me, that in the most interesting of the poems in which the author is more or less dramatic, as the "Brothers", "Michael", "Ruth", the "Mad Mother", etc. the persons introduced are by no means taken *from low or rustic life* in the common acceptation of those words; and it is not less clear, that the sentiments and language, as far as they can be conceived to have been really transferred from the minds and conversation of such persons, are attributable to causes and circumstances not necessarily connected with "their occupations and abode". The thoughts, feelings, language, and manners of the shepherd-farmers in the vales of Cumberland and Westmoreland, as far as they are actually adopted in those poems, may be accounted for from causes, which will and do produce the same results in *every* state of life, whether in town or country. As the two principal I rank that INDEPENDANCE, which raises a man above servitude, or daily toil for the profit of others, yet not above the necessity of industry and a frugal simplicity of domestic life; and the accompanying unambitious, but solid and religious EDUCATION, which has rendered few books familiar, but the bible, and the liturgy or hymn book. To this latter cause, indeed, which is so far *accidental*, that it is the blessing of particular countries and a particular age, not the product of particular places or employments, the poet owes the shew of probability, that his personages might really feel, think, and talk with any tolerable resemblance to his representation. It is an excellent remark of Dr. Henry More's (Enthusiasmus triumphatus, Sec. XXXV[19]) that "a man of confined education, but of good parts, by constant reading of the bible will naturally form a more winning and commanding rhetoric than those that are learned; the intermixture of tongues and of artificial phrases debasing *their* style".

It is, moreover, to be considered that to the formation of healthy feelings, and a reflecting mind, *negations* involve impediments not less formidable, than sophistication and vicious intermixture. I am convinced, that for the human soul to prosper in rustic life, a certain vantage-

---

19. Henry More, *Enthusiasmus Triumphatus*, Sec. 35 (1656).

ground is pre-requisite. It is not every man, that is likely to be improved by a country life or by country labours. Education, or original sensibility, or both, must pre-exist, if the changes, forms and incidents of nature are to prove a sufficient stimulant. And where these are not sufficient, the mind contracts and hardens by want of stimulants; and the man becomes selfish, sensual, gross, and hard-hearted. Let the management of the Poor Laws in Liverpool, Manchester, or Bristol be compared with the ordinary dispensation of the poor rates in agricultural villages, where the *farmers* are the overseers and guardians of the poor. If my own experience have not been particularly unfortunate, as well as that of the many respectable country clergymen with whom I have conversed on the subject, the result would engender more than scepticism concerning the desirable influence of low and rustic life in and for itself.

...a rustic's language, purified from all provincialism and grossness, and so far reconstructed as to be made consistent with the rules of grammar (which are in essence no other than the laws of universal logic, applied to Psychological materials) will not differ from the language of any other man of common-sense, however learned or refined he may be, except as far as the notions, which the rustic has to convey, are fewer and more indiscriminate. This will become still clearer, if we add the consideration (equally important though less obvious) that the rustic, from the more imperfect development of his faculties, and from the lower state of their cultivation, aims almost solely to convey *insulated facts*, either those of his scanty experience of his traditional belief; while the educated man chiefly seeks to discover and express those *connections* of things, or those relative *bearings* of fact to fact, from which some more or less general law is deducible. For *facts* are valuable to a wise man, chiefly as they lead to the discovery of the indwelling *law*, which is the true *being* of things, the sole solution of their modes of existence, and in the knowledge of which consists our dignity and our power.

As little can I agree with the assertion, that from the objects with which the rustic hourly communicates, the best part of language is formed. For first, if to communicate with an object implies such an acquaintance with it, as renders it capable of being discriminately reflected on; the distinct knowledge of an uneducated rustic would furnish a very scanty voccabulary. The few things, and modes of action, requisite for his bodily conveniences, would alone be individualized; while all the rest of nature would be expressed by a small number of confused, general terms. Secondly, I deny that the words and combinations of words derived from the objects, with which the rustic is familiar, whether with distinct or confused knowledge, can be justly said to form the *best* part of language. It is more than probable, that many classes of the brute creation possess discriminating sounds, by which they can convey to each other notices of such objects as concern their food, shelter, or safety. Yet we hesitate to call the aggregate of such sounds a language, otherwise than meta-phorically. The best part of human language, properly so called, is derived from reflections on the acts of the mind itself. It is formed by a voluntary appropriation of fixed symbols to internal acts, to processes and results of imagination, the greater part of which have no place in the consciousness of uneducated man; though in civilized society, by imitation and passive remembrance of what they hear from their religious instructors and other superiors, the most uneducated share in the harvest which they neither sowed or reaped. If the history of the phrases in hourly currency among our peasants were traced, a person not previously aware of the fact would be surprised at finding so large a number, which three or four centuries ago were the exclusive property of the universities and the schools; and at the commencement of the Reformation had been transferred from the school to the pulpit, and thus gradually passed into common life. The extreme difficulty, and often the impossibility, of finding words for the simplest moral and intellectual processes in the languages of uncivilized tribes has proved perhaps the weightiest obstacle to the progress of our most zealous and adroit missionaries. Yet these tribes are surrounded by the same nature, as our peasants are; but in still more impressive forms; and they are, moreover, obliged to *particularize* many more of them. When therefore Mr. Wordsworth adds, "accordingly such a language" (meaning, as before, the language of rustic life purified from provincialism), "arising out of repeated experience and regular feelings is a more permanent, and a far more philosophical language, than that which is frequently substituted for it by poets, who think they are conferring honor upon themselves and their art in proportion as they indulge in arbitrary and capricious habits of expression"; it may be answered, that the language, which he has in view, can be attributed to rustics with no greater right, than the style of Hooker or Bacon to Tom Brown[20] or Sir Robert L'Estrange.[21] Doubtless, if what is peculiar to each were omitted in each, the result must needs be the same. Further, that the poet, who uses an illogical diction, or a style fitted to excite only the low and changeable pleasure of wonder by means of groundless novelty, substitutes a language of *folly* and *vanity*, not for that of the *rustic*, but for that of *good sense* and *natural feeling*.

...The ultimate end of criticism is much more to establish the principles of writing, than to furnish *rules* how to pass judgement on what has been written by others; if indeed it were possible that the two could be separated. But if it be asked, by what principles the poet is to regulate his own style, if he do not adhere closely to the sort and order of words which

20. Thomas Brown (1663-1704), author of 'I do not love thee, Dr. Fell'.
21. Sir Roger L'Estrange (1616-1704), Royalist journalist.

he hears in the market, wake, high-road, or plough-field? I reply; by principles, the ignorance or neglect of which would convict him of being no *poet*, but a silly or presumptuous usurper of the name! By the principles of grammar, logic, psychology! In one word by such a knowledge of the facts, material and spiritual, that most appertain to his art, as if it have been governed and applied by *good sense*, and rendered instinctive by habit, becomes the representative and reward of our past conscious reasonings, insights, and conclusions, and acquires the name of TASTE. By what *rule* that does not leave the reader at the poet's mercy, and the poet at his own, is the latter to distinguish between the language suitable to *suppressed*, and the language, which is characteristic of *indulged*, anger? Or between that of rage and that of jealousy? Is it obtained by wandering about in search of angry or jealous people in uncultivated society, in order to copy their words? Or not far rather by the power of imagination proceeding upon the *all in each* of human nature? By *meditation*, rather than by *observation*? And by the latter in consequence only of the former? As eyes, for which the former has pre-determined their field of vision, and to which, as to *its* organ, it communicates a microscopic power? There is not, I firmly believe, a man now living, who has from his own inward experience a clearer intuition, than Mr. Wordsworth himself, that the last mentioned are the true sources of *genial* discrimination. Through the same process and by the same creative agency will the poet distinguish the degree and kind of the excitement produced by the very act of poetic composition. As intuitively will he know, what differences of style it at once inspires and justifies; what intermixture of conscious volition is natural to that state; and in what instances such figures and colours of speech degenerate into mere creatures of an arbitrary purpose, cold technical artifices of ornament or connection. For even as truth is its own light and evidence, discovering at once itself and falsehood, so it is the prerogative of poetic genius to distinguish by parental instinct its proper offspring from the changelings, which the gnomes of vanity or the fairies of fashion may have laid in its cradle or called by its names. Could a rule be given from *without*, poetry would cease to be poetry, and sink into a mechanical art.

...It is noticeable, how limited an acquaintance with the master-pieces of art will suffice to form a correct and even a sensitive taste, where none but master-pieces have been seen and admired: while on the other hand, the most correct notions, and the widest acquaintance with the works of excellence of all ages and countries, will not perfectly secure us against the contagious familiarity with the far more numerous offspring of tastelessness or of a perverted taste. If this be the case, as it notoriously is, with the arts of music and painting, much more difficult will it be, to avoid the infection of multiplied and daily examples as in the practice of an art, which uses words, and words only, as its instruements. In poetry, in which every line, every phrase, may pass the ordeal of deliberation and deliberate choice, it is possible, and barely possible, to attain that ultimatum which I have ventured to propose as the infallible test of a blameless style; namely; its *untranslatableness* in words of the same language without injury to the meaning. Be it observed, however, that I include in the *meaning* of a word not only its correspondent object, but likewise all the associations which it recalls. For language is framed to convey not the object alone, but likewise the character, mood and intentions of the person who is representing it. In poetry it *is* practicable to preserve the diction uncorrupted by the affectations and misappropriations, which promiscuous authorship, and reading not promiscuous only because it is disproportionally most conversant with the compositions of the day, have rendered general. Yet even to the poet, composing in his own province, it is an arduous work: and as the result and pledge of a watchful good sense, of fine and luminous distinction, and of complete self-possession, may justly claim all the honor which belongs to an attainment equally difficult and valuable, and the more valuable for being rare. It is at *all* times the proper food of the understanding; but in an age of corrupt eloquence it is both food and antidote.

In prose I doubt whether it be even possible to preserve our style wholly unalloyed by the vicious phraseology which meets us every where, from the sermon to the newspaper, from the harangue of the legislator to the speech from the convivial chair, announcing a *toast* or sentiment. Our chains rattle even while we are complaining of them. The poems of Boetius[22] rise high in our estimation when we compare them with those of his contemporaries, as Sidonius Apollinaris,[23] etc. They might even be referred to a purer age, but that the prose, in which they are set, as jewels in a crown of lead or iron, betrays the true age of the writer. Much however may be effected by education. I believe not only from grounds of reason, but from having in great measure assured myself of the fact by actual though limited experience, that to a youth led from his first boyhood to investigate the meaning of every word and the reason of its choice and position, Logic presents itself as an old acquaintance under new names.

On some future occasion, more especially demanding such disquisition, I shall attempt to prove the close connection between veracity and habits of mental accuracy; the beneficial after-effects of verbal precision in the preclusion of fanaticism, which masters the feelings more especially by indistinct watch-words; and to display the advantages which language alone, at least which language with incomparably greater ease and

22. Anicius Boethius (470-525), author of *De Consolatione Philosophiae*.
23. Sidonius Apollinaris (431-484), bishop of Auvergne.

certainty than any other means, presents to the instructor of impressing modes of intellectual energy so constantly, so imperceptibly, and as it were by such elements and atoms, as to secure in due time the formation of a second nature. When we reflect, that the cultivation of the judgment is a positive command of the moral law, since the reason can give the *principle* alone, and the conscience bears witness only to the *motive*, while the application and effects must depend on the judgement; when we consider, that the greater part of our success and comfort in life depends on distinguishing the similar from the same, that which is peculiar in each thing from that which it has in common with others, so as still to select the most probable, instead of the merely possible or positively unfit, we shall learn to value earnestly and with a practical seriousness a mean, already prepared for us by nature and society, of teaching the young mind to think well and wisely by the same unremembered process and with the same never forgotten results, as those by which it is taught to speak and converse. Now how much warmer the interest is, how much more genial the feelings of reality and practicability, and thence how much stronger the impulses to imitation are, which a *contemporary* writer, and especially a contemporary *poet*, excites in youth and commencing manhood, has been treated of in the earlier pages of these sketches. I have only to add, that all the praise which is due to the exertion of such influence for a purpose so important, joined with that which must be claimed for the infrequency of the same excellence in the same perfection, belongs in full right to Mr. Wordsworth. I am far however from denying that we have poets whose *general* style possesses the same excellence, as Mr. Moore, Lord Byron, Mr. Bowles, and in all his later and more important works our laurel-honoring Laureate.[24] But there are none, in whose works I do not appear to myself to find *more* exceptions, than in those of Wordsworth. Quotations or specimens would be wholly out of place, and must be left for the critic who doubts and would invalidate the justice of this eulogy so applied.

From *On the Constitution of Church and State, according to the Idea of Each*

(The extracts, from Chs. 1, 2, 5, 8 and 10, are from the first edition, 1830, which actually appeared in 1829. Paragraph headings from Chs. 5 and 8 are omitted, as are two notes, one to Ch. 2 and one to Ch. 5).

...to enable you fully to understand, and fairly to appreciate, my

24. Southey.

arguments, I must previously state (what I at least judge to be) the true Idea of A CONSTITUTION; and, likewise, of a NATIONAL CHURCH. And in giving the essential character of the latter, I shall briefly specify its distinction from the Church of Christ, and its contradistinction from a third form, which is neither national nor Christian, but irreconcileable with, and subversive of, both. By an *idea*, I mean (in this instance) that conception of a thing, which is not abstracted from any particular state, form, or mode, in which the thing may happen to exist at this or that time; nor yet generalized from any number or succession of such forms or modes; but which is given by the knowledge of *its ultimate aim.*

Only one observation I must be allowed to add, that this knowledge, or sense, may very well exist, aye, and powerfully influence a man's thoughts and actions, without his being distinctly conscious of the same, much more without his being competent to express it in definite words. This, indeed, is one of the points which distinguish *ideas* from *conceptions*, both terms being used in their strict and proper significations. The latter, *i.e.* a conception, *consists* in a conscious act of the understanding, bringing any given object or impression into the same class with any number of other objects, or impressions, by means of some character or characters common to them all. *Concipimus*, id est, capimus hoc *cum* illo,[25] — we take hold of both at once, we *comprehend* a thing, when we have learnt to comprise it in a known *class.* On the other hand, it is the privilege of the few to possess an idea: of the generality of men, it might be more truly affirmed, that they are possessed by it.

What is here said, will, I hope, suffice as a popular explanation. For some of my readers, however, the following definition may not, perhaps, be useless or unacceptable, That which, contemplated *objectively* (*i.e.* as existing *externally* to the mind), we call a LAW; the same contemplated *subjectively* (*i.e.* as existing in a subject or mind), is an idea. Hence Plato often names ideas laws; and Lord Bacon, the British Plato, describes the Laws of the material universe as the Ideas in nature. Quod in natura *naturata* LEX, in natura *naturante* IDEA dicitur.[26] By way of illustration take the following. Every reader of Rousseau, or of Hume's Essays, will understand me when I refer to the Original Social Contract, assumed by Rousseau, and by other and wiser men before him, as the basis of all legitimate government. Now, if this be taken as the assertion of an historical fact, or as the application of a conception, generalized from ordinary compacts between man and man, or nation and nation, to an

---

25. *concipimus*, id est, capimus hoc *cum* illo: we *conceive, i.e.* we take this thing *with* that thing.

26. Quod in natura *naturata* LEX, in natura *naturante* IDEA dicitur: that which in nature natured is a law is said, in nature naturing, to be an idea.

actual occurence in the first ages of the world; namely, the formation of
the first contract, in which men covenanted with each other to associate,
or in which a multitude entered into a compact with a few, the one to be
governed and the other to govern, under certain declared conditions; I
shall run little hazard at this time of day, in declaring the pretended fact a
pure fiction, and the conception of such a fact an idle fancy. It is at once
false and foolish.* For what if an original contract had actually been
entered into, and formally recorded? Still I cannot see what addition of
moral force would be gained by the fact. The same sense of moral
obligation which binds us to keep it, must have pre-existed in the same
force and in relation to the same duties, impelling our ancestors to make
it. For what could it do more than bind the contracting parties to act for
the general good, according to their best lights and opportunities? It is
evident, that no specific scheme or constitution can derive any other
claim to our reverence, than the presumption of its necessity or fitness for
the general good shall give it; and which claim of course ceases, or rather
is reversed, as soon this general presumption of its utility has given place
to as general a conviction of the contrary. From duties anterior to the
formation of the contract, because they arise out of the very constitution
of our humanity, which supposes the social state — in order to a rightful
removal of the institution, or law, thus agreed on, it is required that the
conviction of its inexpediency shall be as general, as the presumption of
its fitness was at the time of its establishment. This, the first of the two
great paramount interests of the social state demand, namely, that of
permanence; and to attribute more than this to any fundamental articles,
passed into law by any assemblage of individuals, is an injustice to their
successors, and a high offence against the other great interest of the social
state, namely, — its progressive improvement. The conception, therefore,
of an original contract, is, we repeat, incapable of historic proof as a fact,
and it is senselss as a theory.

But if instead of the *conception* or *theory* of an original social
contract, you say the *idea* of an ever-originating social contract, this is so
certain and so indispensable, that it constitutes the whole ground of the
difference between subject and serf, between commonwealth and a slave-
plantation. And this, again is evolved out of the yet higher idea of *person*,
in contra-distinction from *thing* — all social law and justice being
grounded on the principle, that a person can never, but by his own fault,
become a thing, or, without grievous wrong, be treated as such: and the

*I am not indeed certain, that some operatical farce, under the name of a Social
Contract or Compact, might not have been acted by the Illuminati and Constitution-
manufacturers, at the close of the eighteenth century; a period which how far it deserved
the name, so complacently affixed to it by the contemporaries of "this *enlightened age*",
may be doubted. That it was an age of *Enlighteners*, no man will deny.

distinction consisting in this, that a thing may be used altogether and merely as the *means* to an end; but the person must always be included in the *end*: his interest must form a part of the objects, a *means* to which, he, by consent, *i.e.* by his own act, makes himself. We plant a tree, and we fell it; we breed the sheep, and we shear or we kill it; in both cases wholly as means to *our* ends. For trees and animals are *things*. The woodcutter and the hind are likewise employed as *means*, but on agreement, and that too an agreement of reciprocal advantage, which includes them as well as their employer in the *end*. For they are *persons*. And the government, under which the contrary takes place, is not worthy to be called a STATE, if, as in the kingdom of Dahomy, it be unprogressive; or only by anticipation, where, as in Russia, it is in advance to a better and more *man-worthy* order of things. Now, notwithstanding the late wonderful spread of learning through the community, and though the schoolmaster and the lecturer are abroad, the hind and the woodman may, very conceivably, pass from cradle to coffin, without having once contemplated this idea, so as to be conscious of the same. And there would be an improbability in the supposition that they possessed the power of presenting it to the minds of others, or even to their own thoughts, verbally as a distinct proposition. But no man, who has ever listened to laborers of this rank, in any alehouse, over the Saturday night's jug of beer, discussing the injustice of the present rate of wages, and the iniquity of their being paid in part out of the parish poor-rates, will doubt for a moment that they are fully possessed by the idea.

...Now, in every country of civilized men, acknowledging the rights of property, and by means of determined boundaries and common laws, united into one people or nation, the two antagonist powers or opposite interests of the state, under which all other state interests are comprised, are those of PERMANENCE and of PROGRESSION.

It will not be necessary to enumerate the several causes that combine to connect the permanence of a state with the land and the landed property. To found a family, and to convert his wealth into land, are twin thoughts, births of the same moment, in the mind of the opulent merchant, when he thinks of reposing from his labours. From the class of the Novi Homines[27] he redeems himself by becoming the staple ring of the chain, by which the present will become connected with the past; and the test and evidence of permanency afforded. To the same principle appertain primogeniture and hereditary titles, and the influence which these exert in accumulating large masses of property, and in counteracting the antagonist and dispersive forces, which the follies, the vices, and misfortunes of individuals can scarcely fail to supply. To this, likewise, tends

27. Novi Homines: new men.

the proverbial obduracy of prejudices characteristic of the humbler tillers of the soil, and their aversion even to benefits that are offered in the form of innovations. But why need I attempt to explain a fact which no thinking man will deny, and where the admission of the fact is all that my argument requires?

On the other hand, with as little chance of contradiction, I may assert, that the progression of a state, in the arts and comforts of life, in the diffusion of the information and knowledge, useful or necessary for all; in short, all advances in civilization, and the rights and privileges of citizens, are especially connected with, and derived from the four classes of the mercantile, the manufacturing, the distributive, and the professional.

...That harmonious balance of the two great correspondent, at once supporting, and counterpoising, interests of the state, its permanence, and its progression: that balance of the landed and the personal interests was to be secured by a legislature of two Houses; the first consisting wholly of barons or landholders, permanent and hereditary senators; the second of the knights or minor barons, elected by, and as the representatives of, the remaining landed community, together with the burgesses, the representatives of the commercial, manufacturing, distributive, and professional classes, — the latter (the elected burgesses) constituting the major number. The king, meanwhile, in whom the executive power is vested, it will suffice at present to consider as the beam of the constitutional scales. A more comprehensive view of the kingly office must be deferred, till the remaining problem (the idea of a national church) has been solved.

I must here intreat the reader to bear in mind what I have before endeavoured to impress on him, that I am not giving an historical account of the legislative body; or can I be supposed to assert that such was the earliest mode or form in which the national council was constructed. My assertion is simply this, that its formation has advanced in this direction. The line of evolution, however sinuous, has still tended to this point, sometimes with, sometimes without, not seldom, perhaps, against, the intention of the individual actors, but always as if a power, greater, and better, than the men themselves had intended it for them. Nor let it be forgotten that every new growth, every power and privilege, bought or extorted, has uniformly been claimed by an antecedent right; not acknowledged as a boon conferred, but both demanded and received as what had always belonged to them, though withheld by violence and the injury of the times. This too, in cases, where, if documents and historical records, or even consistent traditions, had been required in evidence, the monarch would have had the better of the argument.

...After these introductory preparations, I can have no difficulty in setting forth the right idea of a national church as in the language of

Elizabeth the *third* great venerable estate of the realm. The first being the estate of the land-owners or possessors of fixed property, consisting of the two classes of the Barons and the Franklins; the second comprising the merchants, the manufacturers, free artizans, and the distributive class. To comprehend, therefore, this third estate, in whom the reserved nationalty was vested, we must first ascertain the end, or national purpose, for which it was reserved.

Now, as in the former state, the permanency of the nation was provided for; and in the second estate its progressiveness, and personal freedom; while in the king the cohesion by interdependence, and the unity of the country, were established; there remains for the third estate only that interest, which is the ground, the necessary antecedent condition, of both the former. All these depend on a continuing and progressive civilization; but civilization is itself but a mixed good, if not far more a corrupting influence, the hectic of disease, not the bloom of health, and a nation so distinguished more fitly to be called a varnished than a polished people; where this civilization is not grounded in *cultivation*, in the harmonious development of those qualities and faculties that characterize our *humanity*. In short, we must be men in order to be citizens.

The Nationalty, therefore, was reserved for the support and maintenance of a permanent class or order, with the following duties. A certain smaller number were to remain at the fountain heads of the humanities, in cultivating and enlarging the knowledge already possessed, and in watching over the interests of physical and moral science; being, likewise, the instructors of such as constituted, or were to constitute, the remaining more numerous classes of the order. This latter and far more numerous body were to be distributed throughout the country, so as not to leave even the smallest integral part or division without a resident guide, guardian, and instructor; the object and final intention of the whole order being thus to preserve the stores, to guard the treasures, of past civilization, and thus to bind the present with the past; to perfect and add to the same, and thus to connect the present with the future; but especially to diffuse through the whole community, and to every native entitled to its laws and rights, that quantity and quality of knowledge which was indispensable both for the understanding of those rights, and for the performance of the duties correspondent. Finally, to secure for the nation, if not a superiority over the neighbouring states, yet an equality at least, in that character of general civilization, which equally with, or rather more than, fleets, armies, and revenue, forms the ground of its defensive and offensive power. The object of the National Church, the third remaining estate of the realm, was to secure and improve that civilization, without which the nation could be neither permanent nor progressive.

That in all ages, individuals who have directed their meditations and their studies to nobler characters of our nature, to the cultivation of those powers and instincts which constitute the man, at least separate him from the animal, and distinguish the nobler from the animal part of his own being, will be led by the *supernatural* in themselves to the contemplation of a power which is likewise super-*human*; that science, and especially moral science, will lead to religion, and remain blended with it — this, I say, will, in all ages, be the course of things. That in the earlier ages, and in the dawn of civility, there will be a twilight in which science and religion give light, but a light refracted through the dense and the dark, a superstition — this is what we learn from history, and what philosophy would have taught us to expect. But we affirm, that in the spiritual purpose of the word, and as understood in reference to a future state and to the abiding essential interest of the individual as a person, and not as the citizen, neighbour, or subject, religion may be an indispensable ally, but is not the essential constitutive end of that national institute, which is unfortunately, at least improperly, styled a church — a name which, in its best sense is exclusively appropriate to the church of Christ. If this latter be ecclesia, the communion of such as are called out of the world, *i.e.* in reference to the especial ends and purposes of that communion; this other might more expressively have been entitled *enclesia*, or an order of men, chosen in and of the realm, and constituting an estate of that realm. And in fact, such was the original and proper sense of the more appropriately named CLERGY. It comprehended the learned of all names, and the CLERK was the synonyme of the man of learning. Nor can any fact more strikingly illustrate the conviction entertained by our ancestors, respecting the intimate connexion of this clergy with the peace and weal of the nation, than the privilege formerly recognized by our laws, in the well-known phrase, "benefit of clergy".[28]

From the narrow limits prescribed by my object in *compressing* the substance of my letters to you, I am driven to apologise for prolixity, even while I am pondering on the means of presenting, in three or four numbered paragraphs, the principal sides and aspects of a subject so large and multilateral as to require a volume for their full exposition. Regard the following, then, as the text. The commentary may be given hereafter:-

THE CLERISY of the nation (a far apter exponent of the thing meant, than the term which the usus norma loquendi forces on me), the clerisy, I say, or national church, in its primary acceptation and original intention comprehended the learned of all denominations; — the sages and professors of law and jurisprudence; of medicine and physiology; of

---

28. "benefit of clergy": exemption of clergymen and certain others from arrest or trial, abolished in 1827.

music; of military and civil architecture; of the physical sciences; with the mathematical as the common *organ* of the preceding; in short, all the so called liberal arts and sciences, the possession and application of which constitute the civilization of a country, as well as the Theological. The last was, indeed, placed at the head of all; and of good right did it claim the precedence. But why? Because under the name of Theology, or Divinity, were contained the interpretation of languages; the conservation and tradition of past events; the momentous epochs, and revolutions of the race and nation; the continuation of the records; logic, ethics, and the determination of ethical science, in application to the rights and duties of men in all their various relations, social and civil; and lastly, the ground-knowledge, the prima scientia as it was named, — PHILOS-OPHY, or the doctrine and discipline of *ideas*.

Theology formed only a part of the objects, the Theologians formed only a portion of the clerks or clergy of the national church. The theological order had precedency indeed, and deservedly; but not because its members were priests, whose office was to conciliate the invisible powers, and to superintend the interests that survive the grave; not as being exclusively, or even principally, sacerdotal or templar, which, when it did occur, is to be considered as an accident of the age, a misgrowth of ignorance and oppression, a falsification of the constitutive principle, not a constituent part of the same. No! The Theologians took the lead, because the SCIENCE of Theology was the root and the trunk of the knowledges that civilized man, because it gave unity and the circulating sap of life to all other sciences, by virtue of which alone they could be contemplated as forming, collectively, the living tree of knowledge. It had the precedency because under the name theology, were comprised all the main aids, instruments, and materials of NATIONAL EDUCATION, the *nisus formativus*[29] of the body politic, the shaping and informing spirit, which *educing, i.e.* eliciting, the latent *man* in all the natives of the soil, *trains them up* to citizens of the country, free subjects of the realm. And lastly, because to divinity belong those fundamental truths, which are the common ground-work of our civil and our religious duties, not less indispensable to a right view of our temporal concerns, than to a rational faith respecting our immortal well-being. (Not without celestial observations, can even terrestrial charts be accurately constructed.) And of special importance is it to the objects here contemplated, that only by the vital warmth diffused by these truths throughout the MANY, and by the guiding light from the philosophy, which is the basis of *divinity*, possessed by the FEW, can either the community or its rulers fully comprehend, or rightly appreciate, the permanent *distinction*, and the

29. *nisus formativus*: formative force.

occasional *contrast*, between cultivation and civilization; or be made to understand this most valuable of the lessons taught by history, and exemplified alike in her oldest and her most recent records — that a nation can never be a too cultivated, but may easily become an over-civilized race.

...our Eighth Henry would have acted in correspondence to the great principles of our constitution, if having restored the original balance on both sides, he had determined the nationalty to the following objects: 1st. To the maintenance of the Universities and the great liberal schools. 2ndly. To the maintenance of a pastor and schoolmaster in every parish. 3rdly. To the raising and keeping in repair of the churches, schools, &c., and, Lastly: to the maintenance of the proper, that is, the infirm, poor whether from age or sickness; one of the original purposes of the national Reserve being the alleviation of those evils, which in the best forms of worldly states must arise and must have been foreseen as arising from the institution of individual properties and primogeniture. If these duties were efficiently performed, and these purposes adequately fulfilled, the very increase of the population, (which would, however, by these very means have been prevented from becoming a vicious population),would have more than counterbalanced those savings in the expenditure of the nationalty occasioned by the detachment of the practitioners of law, medicine, etc., from the national clergy. That this transfer of the national reserve from what had become national evils to its original and inherent purpose of national benefits, instead of the sacrilegious alienation which actually took place — that this was impracticable, is historically true: but no less true is it philosophically that this impracticability, arising wholly from moral causes — that is, from loose manners and corrupt principles — does not rescue this wholesale sacrilege from deserving the character of the first and deadliest wound inflicted on the constitution of the kingdom: which term constitution in the body politic, as in bodies natural, expresses not only what has been actually evolved, but likewise whatever is potentially contained in the seminal principle of the particular body, and would in its due time have appeared but for emasculation or disease. Other wounds, by which indeed the constitution of the nation suffered, but which much more immediately concern the constitution of the church, we shall perhaps find another place to mention.

The mercantile and commercial class, in which I here comprise all the four classes that I have put in antithesis to the Landed Order, the guardian, and depository of the *Permanence* of the Realm, as more characteristically conspiring to the interests of its progression, the improvement and general freedom of the country — this class did as I have already remarked, in the earlier states of the constitution, exist but as in the bud. But during all this period of potential existence, or what we may call the minority of the burgess order, the National Church was the substitute for the most important national benefits resulting from the same. The National Church presented the only breathing hole of hope. The church alone relaxed the iron fate by which feudal dependency, primogeniture, and entail would otherwise have predestined every native of the realm to be lord or vassal. To the Church alone could the nation look for the benefits of existing knowledge, and for the means of future civilization. Lastly, let it never be forgotten, that under the fostering wings of the church, the class of free citizens and burgers were reared. To the feudal system we owe the *forms*, to the church the *substance*, of our liberty. We mention only two of many facts that would form the proof and comment of the above; first, the origin of towns and cities, in the privileges attached to the vicinity of churches and monasteries, and which preparing an asylum for the fugitive Vassal and oppressed Franklin, thus laid the first foundation of a class of freemen detached from the land. Secondly, the holy war which the national clergy, in this instance faithful to their national duties, waged against slavery and villenage, and with such success, that in the reign of Charles II., the law which declared every native of the realm free by birth, had merely to sanction an opus jam consummatum.[30] Our Maker has distinguished man from the brute that perishes, by making hope first an instinct of his nature; and secondly, an indispensable condition of his moral intellectual progression:

> For every gift of noble origin
> Is breathed upon by Hope's perpetual breath.
> WORDSWORTH.[31]

But a natural instinct constitutes a right, as far as its gratification is compatible with the equal rights of others in respect of the idea of the National Church.

Among the primary ends of a STATE, (in that highest sense of the word, in which it is equivalent to the nation, considered as one body politic, and therefore includes the National Church), there are two, of which the National Church (according to its idea), is the especial and constitutional organ and means. The one is, to secure to the subjects of the realm generally, the hope, the chance, of bettering their own or their children's condition. And though during the last three or four centuries, the National church has found a most powerful surrogate and ally for the

---

30. opus jam consummatum: task already achieved.
31. See Wordsworth's sonnet, "October 1803" ("These times..."), ll. 9-11.

...faith
That every gift of noble origin
Is breathed upon by Hope's perpetual breath;
  first published in his *Poems in Two Volumes* (1807).

effectuation of this great purpose in her former wards and foster-children, *i.e.* in trade, commerce, free industry, and the arts — yet still the nationalty, under all defalcations, continues to feed the higher ranks by drawing up whatever is worthiest from below, and thus maintains the principle of Hope in the humblest families, while it secures the possessions of the rich and noble. This is one of the two ends.

The other is, to develope, in every native of the country, those faculties, and to provide for every native that knowledge and those attainments, which are necessary to qualify him for a member of the state, the free subject of a civilized realm. We do not mean those degrees of moral and intellectual cultivation which distinguish man from man in the same civilized society, much less those that separate the Christian from the this-worldian; but those only that constitute the civilized man in contradistinction from the barbarian, the savage, and the animal.

...The power resulting from the acquisition of knowledge or skill, and from the superior development of the understanding is, doubtless, of a far nobler kind than mere physical strength and fierceness, the one being *peculiar* to the animal *Man*, the other common to him with the Bear, the Buffalo, and the Mastiff. And if superior Talents, and the mere possession of knowledges, such as can be learnt at Mechanics' Institutions were regularly accompanied with a Will in harmony with the Reason, and a consequent subordination of the appetites and passions to the ultimate ends of our Being: if intellectual gifts and attainments were infallible signs of wisdom and goodness in the same proportion, and the knowing, clever, and *talented* (a vile word!) were always *rational*; if the mere facts of science conferred or superseded the soft'ning humanizing influences of the moral world, that habitual presence of the beautiful or the seemly, and that exemption from all familiarity with the gross, the mean, and the disorderly, whether in look or language, or in the surrounding objects, in which the main efficacy of a liberal education consists; and if, lastly, these acquirements and powers of the understanding could be shared equally by the whole class, and did not, as by a necessity of nature they ever must do, fall to the lot of two or three in each several group, club, or neighbourhood; — then, indeed, by an enlargement of the Chinese system, political power might not unwisely be conferred as the honorarium or privilege on having passed through all the forms in the National Schools, without the security of political ties, without those fastenings and radical fibres of a collective and registrable property, by which the Citizen inheres in and belongs to the Commonwealth, as a constituent part either of the Proprietage, or of the Nationality; either of the State, or of the National Church. But as the contrary of all these suppositions may be more safely assumed, the practical conclusion will be — not that the requisite means of intellectual development and growth should be withheld from any native of the soil, which it was at all times wicked to wish, and which it would be now silly to attempt; but — that the gifts of the understanding, whether the boon of a genial nature, or the reward of more persistent application, should be allowed fair play in the acquiring of that proprietorship, to which a certain portion of political power belongs, as its proper function. For in this way there is at least a strong probability, that intellectual power will be armed with political power, only where it has previously been combined with and guarded by the moral qualities of prudence, industry, and self-control.

Political and Economic Reform

The age of the first industrial revolution witnessed increasingly urgent pressure for legal, electoral and social reform, less at first from the masses than from individuals with a variety of ideological commitments who put themselves at the head of notable campaigns. The Christian revival among the upper classes was led by the politician William Wilberforce (1759-1833), who underwent a conversion to evangelicism in 1785; according to his new priorities, he insisted on Sunday observance, moral purity, family prayer and abstention from gambling, swearing, drink, duelling and fornication. Wilberforce's social reformism was checked by the conservatism which became powerful after the outbreak of war in 1793, but, in company with members of the lay 'Clapham Sect', he campaigned successfully for the abolition of the Slave Trade (1807). In his *Practical View* he places great value on the established church, linking religious sincerity with political moderation and benevolence as key-factors in the improvement of a stable society. In the writings of Jeremy Bentham (1748-1832) and James Mill (1773-1836) the eighteenth-century philosophical interest in utilitarian ethics became channeled into a somewhat coldly argued programme for radical change. In the early *Introduction to the Principles of Morals and Legislation* Bentham tabulates precise guidelines for the regulation of the individual's conduct by himself and by the state, whereas in *The Book of Fallacies* he attacks the assumptions of his intuitionist and authoritarian opponents. In *The Constitutional Code* he gives detailed instructions for the working of a liberal representative democracy, attacking British reliance on unwritten tradition in this field as a disguised form of repression. James Mill in his articles on 'Government' and 'Education' stresses the moral benefits which arise from a voluntary, democratic system of government. The utilitarians' ambitious principle of the greatest happiness of the greatest number was applied in a number of projects aimed at rationalising government and stimulating self-reliance in the deprived of the community. The well-meaning rigour of these philosophic radicals' proposals for reform culminated in the Poor Law Reports, whose anonymous contributors included Nassau William Senior (1790-1864) and Edwin Chadwick (1800-1890) and which led ironically to the establishment of the unpopular Victorian workhouse system. Some of the most interesting prose of the period comes from writers who give humane, first-hand accounts of actual social conditions, such as the descriptions by Robert Southey (1774-1843) of the lives of manufacturing 'hands' in Manchester in his *Letters from England*, or the vindications by Robert Owen (1771-1858) of his own model industrial community at New Lanark, or the reports by William Cobbett (1763-1835) on the lot of agricultural labourers in his *Rural Rides*. Although Cobbett saw contemporary social evils with impressive clarity and campaigned effectively for Parliamentary Reform, his loyalty was to the rural values of the past. Owen, on the other hand, was in a position to confront the difficulties of the new industrial society, and his type of socialism with its faith in the viability of small-scale co-operative communities still has a distinct appeal. Political economy itself had at this period a reputation for a certain callousness and gloom, the 'dismal science', as it was called, partly because of the unsparing harshness of the economic laws which were confidently discerned and clearly formulated by Thomas Robert Malthus (1766-1834) in his *Principle of Population* and by David Ricardo (1772-1823) in his *Principles of Political Economy*. There was little dignity or hope in the category of labour as a 'commodity', and it was strongly believed by those economists that welfare-schemes designed to mitigate poverty only increased the problem by removing the natural motivation of fear from the labourer. The struggle of labour to organise itself and assert its rights was in its very early stages.

JEREMY BENTHAM

From *An Introduction to the Principles of Morals and Legislation* (The extracts, from Chs. 1, 2 and 4, are from the first edition, 1789).

The interest of the community is one of the most general expressions that can occur in the phraseology of morals: no wonder that the meaning of it is often lost. When it has a meaning, it is this. The community is a fictitious *body*, composed of the individual persons who are considered as constituting as it were its *members*. The interest of the community then is, what? the sum of the interests of the several members who compose it.

It is in vain to talk of the interest of the community, without understanding what is the interest of the individual. A thing is said to promote the interest, or to be *for* the interest of an individual, when it tends to add to the sum total of his pleasures: or, what comes to the same thing, to diminish the sum total of his pains.

An action then may be said to be conformable to the principle of utility, or, for shortness sake, to utility, (meaning with respect to the community at large) when the tendency it has to augment the happiness of the community is greater than any it has to diminish it.

A measure of government (which is but a particular kind of action, performed by a particular person or persons) may be said to be conformable to or dictated by the principle of utility, when in like manner the tendency which it has to augment the happiness of the community is greater than any which it has to diminish it.

When an action, or in particular a measure of government, is supposed by a man to be conformable to the principle of utility, it may be convenient, for the purpose of discourse, to imagine a kind of law or dictate, called a law or dictate of utility: and to speak of the action in question, as being conformable to such law or dictate.

A man may be said to be a partizan of the principle of utility, when the approbation or disapprobation he annexes to any action, or to any measure, is determined by and proportioned to the tendency which he conceives it to have to augment or to diminish the happiness of the community: or in other words, to its conformity or unconformity to the laws or dictates of utility.

...Among principles adverse to that of utility, that which at this day seems to have most influence in matters of government, is what may be called the principle of sympathy and antipathy. By the principle of sympathy and antipathy, I mean that principle which approves or disapproves of certain actions, not on account of their tending to augment the happiness, nor yet on account of their tending to diminish the happiness of the party whose interest is in question, but merely because a man finds himself disposed to approve or disapprove of them: holding up that approbation or disapprobation as a sufficient reason for itself, and disclaiming the necessity of looking out for any extrinsic ground. Thus far in the general department of morals: and in the particular department of politics, measuring out the quantum (as well as determining the ground) of punishment, by the degree of the disapprobation.

It is manifest, that this is rather a principle in name than in reality: it is not a positive principle of itself, so much as a term employed to signify the negation of all principle. What one expects to find in a principle is something that points out some external consideration, as a means of warranting and guiding the internal sentiments of approbation and disapprobation: this expectation is but ill fulfilled by a proposition, which does neither more nor less than hold up each of those sentiments as a ground and standard for itself.

In looking over the catalogue of human actions (says a partizan of this principle) in order to determine which of them are to be marked with the seal of disapprobation, you need but to take counsel of your own feelings:

whatever you find in youself a propensity to condemn, is wrong for that very reason. For the same reason it is also meet for punishment: in what proportion it is adverse to utility or whether it be adverse to utility at all, is a matter that makes no difference. In that same *proportion* also is it meet for punishment: if you hate much, punish much: if you hate little, punish little: punish as you hate. If you hate not at all, punish not at all: the fine feelings of the soul are not to be overborne and tyrannized by the harsh and rugged dictates of political utility.

The various systems that have been formed concerning the standard of right and wrong, may all be reduced to the principle of sympathy and antipathy. One account may serve for all of them. They consist all of them in so many contrivances for avoiding the obligation of appealing to any external standard, and for prevailing upon the reader to accept of the author's sentiment or opinion as a reason for itself. The phrases different, but the principle is the same.

...Pleasures then, and the avoidance of pains, are the *ends* which the legislator has in view: it behoves him therefore to understand their *value*. Pleasures and pains are the *instruments* he has to work with: it behoves him therefore to understand their force, which is again, in other words, their value.

To a person considered *by himself*, the value of a pleasure or pain considered *by itself*, will be greater or less, according to the four following circumstances:

1. Its *intensity*.
2. Its *duration*.
3. Its *certainty* or *uncertainty*.
4. Its *propinquity* or *remoteness*.

These are the circumstances which are to be considered in estimating a pleasure or a pain considered each of them by itself. But when the value of any pleasure or pain is considered for the purpose of estimating the tendency of any *act* by which it is produced there are two other circumstances to be taken into the account; these are,

5. Its *fecundity*, or the chance it has of being followed by sensations of the same kind: that is, pleasures, if it be a pleasure: pains, if it be a pain.

6. Its *purity*, or the chance it has of *not* being followed by sensations of the *opposite* kind: that is, pains, if it be a pleasure: pleasures, if it be a pain.

These two last, however, are in strictness scarcely to be deemed properties of the pleasure or the pain itself; they are not, therefore, in strictness to be taken into the account of the value of that pleasure or that pain. They are in strictness to be deemed properties only of the act, or other event, by which such pleasure or pain has been produced; and accordingly are only to be taken into the account of the tendency of such act or such event.

To a *number* of persons, with reference to each of whom the value of a pleasure or a pain is considered, it will be greater or less, according to seven circumstances: to wit, the six preceding ones; *viz.*

1. Its *intensity.*
2. Its *duration.*
3. Its *certainty* or *uncertainty.*
4. Its *propinquity* or *remoteness.*
5. Its *fecundity.*
6. Its *purity.*

And one other; to wit:

7. Its *extent*; that is the number of persons to whom it *extends*; or (in other words) who are affected by it.

To take an exact account then of the general tendency of any act, by which the interests of a community are affected, proceed as follows. Begin with any one person of those whose interests seem most immediately to be affected by it: and take an account,

1. Of the value of each distinguishable *pleasure* which appears to be produced by it in the *first* instance.

2. Of the value of each *pain* which appears to be produced by it in the *first* instance.

3. Of the value of each pleasure which appears to be produced by it after the first. This constitutes the *fecundity* of the first *pleasure* and the *impurity* of the first pain.

4. Of the value of each *pain* which appears to be produced by it after the first. This constitutes the *fecundity* of the first *pain*, and the *impurity* of the first pleasure.

5. Sum up all the values of all the *pleasures* on the one side, and those of all the pains on the other. The balance, if it be on the side of pleasure, will give the *good* tendency of the act upon the whole, with respect to the interests of that *individual* person; if on the side of pain, the *bad* tendency of it upon the whole.

6. Take an account of the *number* of persons whose interests appear to be concerned; and repeat the above process with respect to each. *Sum up* the numbers expressive of the degrees of *good* tendency, which the act has, with respect to each individual, in regard to whom the tendency of it is good upon the whole: do this again with respect to each individual in regard to whom the tendency of it is *bad* upon the whole. Take the *balance*; which, if on the side of *pleasure*, will give the general *good* tendency of the act, with respect to the total number or community of individuals concerned; if on the side of pain, the general *evil tendency*, with respect to the same community.

It is not to be expected that this process should be strictly pursued previously to every moral judgment, or to every legislative or judicial operation. It may, however, be always kept in view: and as near as the process actually pursued on these occasions approaches to it, so near will such process approach to the character of an exact one.

From *The Book of Fallacies*

(The extracts, from Parts 1, 2 and 4, are from the first edition, 1824).

In authority, defence, such as it is, has been found for every imperfection, for every abuse, for every most pernicious and most execrable abomination that the most corrupt system of government has ever husbanded in its bosom:-

And here may be seen the mischief necessarily attached to the course of him whose footsteps are regulated by the finger of this blind guide.

What is more, from hence may inferences be deduced — nor those illgrounded ones — respecting the probity or improbity, the sincerity, of him who, standing in a public situation, blushes not to look to this blind guide to the exclusion of, or in preference to reason — the only guide that does not begin by shutting his own eyes, for the purpose of closing the eyes of his followers.

As the world grows older, if at the same time it grows wiser (which it will do unless the time comes when experience, the mother of wisdom, becomes barren), the influence of authority will in each situation, and particularly in Parliament, become less and less.

Take any part of the field of moral science, private morality, constitutional law, private law, — go back a few centuries, and you will find argument consisting of reference to authority, not exclusively, but in as large a proportion as possible. As experience has increased, authority has gradually been set aside, and reasoning, drawn from facts and guided by reference to the end in view, true or false, has taken its place.

Of the enormous mass of Roman law heaped up in the school of Justinian,[1] — a mass, the perusal of which would employ several lives occupied by nothing else, — materials of this description constitute by far the greater part. A. throws out at random some loose thought: B. catching it up, tells you what A. thinks — at least, what A. said: C. tells you what has been said by A. and B.; and thus like an avalanche the mass rolls on.

1. Justinian I: Roman Emperor, from 527 to 565 at Constantinople; his digests and codes consolidated Roman Law into the four main books of the *Body of the Law* (*Corpus Iuris*).

Happily it is only in matters of law and religion that endeavours are made, by the favours shown and currently given to this fallacy, to limit and debilitate the exercise of the right of private inquiry in as great a degree as possible, although in these days the exercise of this essential right can no longer be suppressed in a complete and direct way by legal punishment.

In mechanics, in astronomy, in mathematics, in the new-born science of chemistry, — no one has at this time of day either effrontery or folly enough to avow, or so much as to insinuate, that the most desirable state of these branches of useful knowledge, the most rational and eligible course, is to substitute decision on the ground of authority, to decision on the ground of direct and specific evidence.

In every branch of physical art and science, the folly of this substitution or preference is a matter of demonstration, — is a matter of intuition, and as such is universally acknowledged. In the moral branch of science, religion not excluded, the folly of the like receipt for correctness of opinion would not be less universally recognized, if the wealth, the ease, and the dignity attached to and supported by the maintenance of the opposite opinion, did not so steadily resist such recognition.

...Could the wand of that magician be borrowed to whose potent touch the emissaries of his wicked antagonist threw off their several disguises, and made instant confession of their real characters and designs; — could a few of those ravens by whom the word *innovation* is uttered with a scream of horror, and the approach of the monster *Anarchy* denounced; — be touched with it, we should then learn their real character, and have the true import of these screams translated into intelligible language.

1. I am a lawyer (would one of them be heard to say), a fee-fed judge, who, considering that the money I lay up, the power I exercise, and the respect and reputation I enjoy, depend upon the undiminished continuance of the abuses of the law, the factitious delay, vexation, and expense with which the few who have money enough to pay for a chance of justice are loaded, and by which the many who have not the money, are cut off from the chance, — take this method of deterring men from attempting to alleviate those torments in which my comforts have their source.

2. I am a sinecurist (cries another) who, being in the receipt of 38,000 a year, public money, for doing nothing, and having no more wit than honesty, have never been able to open my mouth to pronounce an articulate sound for any other purpose, yet hearing a cry of "No sinecures!" am come to join in the shout of "No innovation! Down with the innovators!" in hopes of drowning, by these defensive sounds, the offensive ones which chill my blood and make me tremble.

3. I am a contractor (cries a third), who, having bought my seat that I

may sell my votes; and in return for them, being in the habit of obtaining with the most convenient regularity a succession of good jobs, foresee, in the prevalence of innovation, the ruin and destruction of this established branch of trade.

4. I am a country gentleman (cries a fourth), who, observing that from having a seat in a certain assembly a man enjoys more respect than he did before, on the turf, in the dog kennel, and in the stable, and having tenants and other dependents enough to seat me against their wills for a place in which I am detested, and hearing it said that if innovation were suffered to run on unopposed, elections would come in time to be as free in reality as they are in appearance and pretence; — have left for a day or two the cry of 'Tally-ho!" and "Hark forward!" to join in the cry of "No Anarchy!" "No Innovation!"

5. I am a priest (says a fifth), who, having proved the Pope to be Anti-Christ to the satisfaction of all orthodox divines whose piety prays for the cure of souls, or whose health has need of exoneration from the burden of residence; and having read my edition of the Gospel, that the apostles lived in palaces, which innovation and anarchy would cut down to parsonage-houses, though grown hoarse by screaming out "No reading!" "No writing!" "No Lancaster!"[2] and "No popery!" — for fear of coming change, am here to add what remains of my voice to the full chorus of "No Anarchy!" "No Innovation!"

...Among the several cloudy appellatives which have been commonly employed as cloaks for misgovernment, there is none more conspicuous in this atmosphere of illusion than the word *Order*.

The word *order* is in a peculiar degree adapted to the purpose of a cloak for *tyranny*; — the word *order* is more extensive than law, or even than government.

But, what is still more material, the word *order* is of the eulogistic cast; whereas the words *government* and *law*, howsoever the things signified may have been taken in the lump for subjects of praise, the complexion of the signs themselves is still tolerably neutral: just as in the case with the words *constitution* and *institutions*.

Thus, whether the measure or arrangement be a mere transitory measure or a permanent law, if it be a tyrannical one, be it ever so tyrannical, in the word *order* you have a term not only wide enough, but in every respect better adapted than any other which the language can supply, to serve as a cloak for it. Suppose any number of men, by a speedy death or a lingering one, destroyed for meeting one another for

---

2. Joseph Lancaster (1778-1838), Christian educationist, advocate of the monitorial system of teaching and of non-denominational or 'voluntary' elementary schools.

the purpose of obtaining a remedy for the absuses by which they are suffering, what nobody can deny is, that by their destruction, *order* is maintained; for the *worst* order is as truly *order* as the *best*. Accordingly, a clearance of this sort having been·effected, suppose in the House of Commons a Lord Castlereagh, or in the House of Lords a Lord Sidmouth,[3] to stand up and insist that by a measure so undeniably prudential order was maintained, with what truth could they be contradicted? And who is there that would have the boldness to assert that order ought not to be maintained?

To the word *order* add the word *good*, the strengh of the checks, if any there were, that were thus applied to tyranny would be but little if at all increased. By the word *good*, no other idea is brought to view than that of the sentiment of approbation, as attached by the person by whom it is employed to the object designated by the substantive to which this adjunct is applied. Order is any arrangement which exists with reference to the object in question;- good order is that order, be it what it may, which it is my wish to be thought to approve of.

Take the state of things under *Nero*, under *Caligula:* with as indisputable propriety might the word *order* be applied to it as to the state of things at present in Great Britain or the American United States.

What in the eyes of Bonaparte was good order? — That which it had been his pleasure to establish.

By the adjunct *social*, the subject *order* is perhaps rendered somewhat the less fit for the use of tyrants, but not much. Among the purposes to which the word *social* is employed, is indeed that of bringing to view a state of things favourable to the happiness of society: but a purpose to which it is also employed, is that of bringing to view a state of things no otherwise considered than as having place in society. By the war which, in the Roman history, bears the name of the social war, no great addition to the happiness of society was ever supposed to be made, yet it was not the less a social one.

As often as any measure is brought forward having for its object the making the slightest defalcation from the amount of the sacrifice made of the interest of the many to the interest of the few, *social* is the adjunct by which the *order* of things to which it is pronounced hostile is designated.

By a defalcation made from any part of the mass of factitious delay, vexation and expense, out of which and in proportion to which lawyers' profit is made to flow, — by any defalcation made from the mass of

3. Lord Castlereagh (1769-1822), Tory War Minister, Home Secretary and Foreign Secretary. Lord Sidmouth (1757-1844), Tory Home Secretary from 1812 till 1821, responsible for the Six Acts (Gag Acts) of 1819.

needless and worse than useless emolument to office, with or without service or pretence of service, — by any addition endeavoured to be made to the quantity or improvement in the quality of service rendered, or time bestowed in service rendered in return for such emolument, — by every endeavour that has for its object the persuading the people to place their fate at the disposal of any other agents than those in whose hands breach of trust is certain, due fulfilment of it morally and physically impossible, — *social order* is said to be endangered, and threatened to be destroyed.

Proportioned to the degree of clearness with which the only true and justifiable end of government is held up to view in any discourse that meets the public eye, is the danger and inconvenience to which those rulers are exposed, who, for their own particular interest, have been engaged in an habitual departure from that only legitimate and defensible course. Hence it is, that, when compared with the words *order, maintenance of order*, the use even of such words as *happiness, welfare, wellbeing*, is not altogether free from danger, wide-extending and comparatively indeterminate as the import of them is: to the single word *happiness* substitute the phrase *greatest happiness of the greatest number*, the description of the end becomes more determinate and even instructive, the danger and inconvenience to misgovernment, and its authors, and its instruments still more alarming and distressing; for then, for a rule whereby to measure the goodness or badness of a government, men are referred to so simple and universally apprehensible a standard as the numeration table. By the pointing men's attention to this end, and the clearness of the light thus cast upon it, the importance of such words as the word *order*, which by their obscurity substitute to the offensive light the useful and agreeable darkness, is more and more intimately felt.

From *Constitutional Code; for the Use of All Nations and All Governments professing Liberal Opinions*

(Volume I of the *Constitutional Code* was published in 1830; our extracts, from the Introduction, Sections I and II, and Chapter II, are from *The Works of Jeremy Bentham*, ed. John Bowring, 1843, vol. 9).

When I say the greatest happiness of the whole community, ought to be the end or object or pursuit, in every branch of the law — of the political rule of action, and of the constitutional branch in particular, what is it that I express? — this and no more, namely that it is my wish, my desire, to see it taken for such, by those who, in the community in question, are actually in possession of the powers of government; taken for such, on the occasion of every arrangement made by them in the exercise of such their powers, so that their endeavours shall be to render such their cause of action contributory to the obtainment of that same end.

...In saying, as above, the proper end of government is the greatest happiness of all, or, in case of competition, the greatest happiness of the greatest number, it seems to me that I have made a declaration of peace and good-will to all men.

On the other hand, were I to say, the proper end of government is the greatest happiness of some one, naming him, or of some few, naming them, it seems to me that I should be making a declaration of war against all men, with the exception of that one, or those few.

...A question that now immediately presents itself, is, whether to any individual, supposing him invested by the constitution in question with the supreme power, any inducement can be applied, by that same constitution, of sufficient force to overpower any sinister interest, to the operation of which, by his situation, he stands, exposed? Inducements, operating on interest, are all of them reducible to two denominations, — punishment and reward. Punishment in every shape his situation suffices to prevent his standing exposed to; so likewise reward. Being by the supposition invested with supreme power, the matter of reward cannot be applied to him in any shape, in which he has not already at his command, whatever it would be in the power of the constitution, by any particular arrangement, to confer on him. To him who has the whole, it is useless to give this or that part.

To a question to this effect, the only answer that can be given is sufficiently manifest. By reward, an individual so situated cannot be acted upon; for there exists no other individual in the community at whose hands he can receive more than he has in his own. By punishment as little; for there exists no individual at whose hands he is obliged to receive, or will receive any such thing.

The result is, that in a monarchy no such junction of interests can be effected, and that, therefore, by no means can monarchy be rendered conducive to the production of the greatest happiness of the greatest number; nor, therefore, according to the greatest happiness principle, be susceptible of the denomination of a good form of government.

What, then, is the best *form* of government? ...My opinion is, that so far as they go, the proposed arrangements which here follow would be in a higher degree conducive to it than any other could be, that could be proposed in a work which was not particularly adapted to the situation of any one country, to the exclusion of all others.

...In every community in which a constitutional code, generally acknowledged to be in force, is in existence, a really existing constitutional branch of law, and with it, as the offspring of it, a constitution, is so far in existence. In no community in which no constitutional code thus generally acknowledged to be in force is in existence, is any such branch of law as a constitutional branch, or any such thing as a constitution, really in existence.

In a community in which, as above, no such thing as a constitution is really to be found, things to each of which the name of a constitution is given, are to be found in endless multitudes. On each occasion, the thing designated by the phrase "the constitution", is a substitute for a constitution, — a substitute framed by the imagination of the person by whom this phrase is uttered, framed by him, and, of course, adapted to that which, in his mind, is the purpose of the moment, whatsoever that purpose be; in so far as the purpose is the promotion, the creation or preservation of an absolutely monarchical form of government, the constitution thus imagined and invented by him is of the absolutely monarchical cast; in so far as that purpose is the promoting the creation or preservation of a limitedly monarchical form of government, it is of the limitedly monarchical cast; in so far as the purpose is the creation or preservation of a democratical form of government, it is of the democratic cast.

The Anglo-American United States have a constitution. They have a constitutional code; the constitution is the system of arrangements delineated in that code.

It has for its object the greatest happiness of the greatest number, and in pursuit of that object, the powers of government are allotted to it by the greatest number.

The French and Spanish nations have constitutions. The English monarchy has no constitution, for it has no all-comprehensive constitutional code, nor in short, any constitutional code whatsoever generally acknowledged as such; nor by any one individual or the whole community acknowledged as such. Hence, so it is that of the assertion contained in the phrases, "excellent constitution", — "matchless constitution", an assertion by which every endeavour to produce the effect of the worst constitution possible is so naturally accompanied, no disproof can be opposed otherwise than by the assertion of a plain and universally notorious matter of fact, viz. — that the English people have no constitution at all belonging to them. England, not having any constitution at all, has no excellent, no matchless constitution; for nothing has no properties. If ever it has a constitution, that constitution will most probably be a democratical one; for nothing less than an insurrection on the part of the greatest number, will suffice to surmount and subdue so vast a power as that which is composed of the conjunct action of force, intimidation, corruption, and delusion.

THOMAS ROBERT MALTHUS

From *An Essay on the Principle of Population*

(The extracts are from Chs. 1, 4, 5 and 18 of the first edition, 1798).

...I think I may fairly make two postulata.

First, that food is necessary to the existence of man.

Secondly, That the passion between the sexes is necessary, and will remain nearly in its present state.

These two laws, ever since we have had any knowledge of mankind, appear to have been fixed laws of our nature; and, as we have not hitherto seen any alteration in them, we have no right to conclude that they will ever cease to be what they now are, without an immediate act of power in that Being who first arranged the system of the universe; and for the advantage of his creatures, still executes, according to fixed laws, all its various operations.

I do not know that any writer has supposed that on this earth man will ultimately be able to live without food. But Mr. Godwin has conjectured that the passion between the sexes may in time be extinguished.[4] As,

---

4. Mr. Godwin has conjectured that the passion between the sexes may in time be extinguished; in the first edition of *Political Justice* Godwin had considered the objection to his scheme from the principle of population to be sufficiently remote in time to be disregarded, and introduced his own most remote utopian vision of man's future dominance over his own body, the banishment of disease and sleep (one of our most conspicuous 'infirmities') and a vastly prolonged life: 'The men...who exist when the earth shall refuse itself to a more extended population, will cease to propagate, for they will no longer have any motive, either of error or duty, to induce them'. (Book VIII, Ch. VII). In later editions (1796 and 1798), although this 'deviation into the land of conjecture' is retained, Godwin relies on a natural 'principle' observed in the stabilisation of present populations, or the prospect of such future remedies 'as shall suggest themselves' to man's intellect. He also (Book I, Ch. V) affirms that 'no attempt ought to be made to eradicate' such universal characteristics as 'hunger and the propensity to the intercourse of the sexes'. They will be regulated by 'due exercise of the understanding.'

however, he calls this part of his work a deviation into the land of conjecture, I will not dwell longer upon it at present, than to say that the best arguments for the perfectibility of man are drawn from a contemplation of the great progress that he has already made from the savage state, and the difficulty of saying where he is to stop. But towards the extinction of the passion between the sexes, no progress whatever has hitherto been made. It appears to exist in as much force at present as it did two thousand, or four thousand years ago. There are individual exceptions now as there always have been. But, as these exceptions do not appear to increase in number, it would surely be a very unphilosophical mode of arguing, to infer merely from the existence of an exception, that the exception would, in time, become the rule, and the rule the exception.

Assuming then, my postulata as granted, I say, that the power of population is indefinitely greater than the power in the earth to produce subsistence for man.

Population, when unchecked, increases in a geometrical ratio. Subsistence increases only in an arithmetical ratio. A slight acquaintance with numbers will shew the immensity of the first power in comparison of the second.

By that law of our nature which makes food necessary to the life of man, the effects of these two unequal powers must be kept equal.

This implies a strong and constantly operating check on population from the difficulty of subsistence. This difficulty must fall some where; and must necessarily be severely felt by a large portion of mankind.

Through the animal and vegatable kingdoms, nature has scattered the seeds of life abroad with the most profuse and liberal hand. She has been comparatively sparing in the room and the nourishment necessary to rear them. The germs of existence contained in this spot of earth, with ample food, and ample room to expand in, would fill millions of worlds in the course of a few thousand years.

Necessity, that imperious all pervading law of nature, restrains them within the prescribed bounds. The race of plants, and the race of animals shrink under this great restrictive law. And the race of man cannot, by any efforts of reason, escape from it. Among plants and animals its effects are waste of seed, sickness, and premature death. Among mankind, misery and vice. The former, misery, is an absolutely necessary consequence of it. Vice is a highly probable consequence, and we therefore see it abundantly prevail; but it ought not, perhaps, to be called an absolutely necessary consequence. The ordeal of virtue is to resist all temptation to evil.

This natural inequality of the two powers of population, and of production in the earth and that great law of our nature which must constantly keep their effects equal, form the great difficulty that to me appears insurmountable in the way to the perfectibility of society. All other arguments are of slight and subordinate consideration in comparison of this. I see no way by which man can escape from the weight of this law which pervades all animated nature. No fancied equality, no agrarian regulations in their utmost extent, could remove the pressure of it even for a single century. And it appears, therefore, to be decisive against the possible existence of a society, all the members of which, should live in ease, happiness, and comparative leisure; and feel no anxiety about providing the means of subsistence for themselves and families.

Consequently, if the premises are just, the argument is conclusive against the perfectibility of the mass of mankind.

...In examining the principal states of modern Europe, we shall find that though they have increased very considerably in population since they were nations of shepherds, yet at the present, their progress is but slow; and instead of doubling their numbers every twenty-five years, they require three or four hundred years, or more for that purpose. Some, indeed, may be absolutely stationary, and others even retrograde. The cause of this slow progress in population cannot be traced to a decay of the passion between the sexes. We have sufficient reason to think that this natural propensity exists still in undiminished vigour. Why then do not its effects appear in a rapid increase of the human species? An intimate view of the state of society in any one country in Europe, which may serve equally for all, will enable us to answer this question, and to say, that a foresight of the difficulties attending the rearing of a family acts as a preventive check; and the actual distress of some of the lower classes, by which they are disabled from giving the proper food and attention to their children, acts as a positive check, to the natural increase of population.

...Hard as it may appear in individual instances, dependent poverty ought to be held disgraceful. Such a stimulus seems to be absolutely necessary to promote the happiness of the great mass of mankind, and every general attempt to weaken this stimulus, however benevolent its apparent intention, will always defeat its own purpose. If men are induced to marry from a prospect of parish provision, with little or no chance of maintaining their families in independence, they are not only unjustly tempted to bring unhappiness and dependence upon themselves and children; but they are tempted, without knowing it, to injure all in the same class with themselves. A labourer who marries without being able to support a family, may in some respects be considered as an enemy to all his fellow-labourers.

I feel no doubt whatever, that the parish laws[5] of England have contributed to raise the price of provisions, and to lower the real price of labour. They have therefore contributed to impoverish that class of people whose only possession is their labour. It is also difficult to suppose that they have not powerfully contributed to generate that carelessness, and want of frugality observable among the poor, so contrary to the disposition frequently to be remarked among petty tradesmen and small farmers. The labouring poor, to use a vulgar expression, seem always to live from hand to mouth. Their present wants employ their whole attention, and they seldom think of the future. Even when they have an opportunity of saving they seldom exercise it; but all that is beyond their present necessities goes, generally speaking, to the ale-house. The poor-laws of England may therefore be said to diminish both the power and the will to save among the common people, and thus to weaken one of the strongest incentives to sobriety and industry, and consequently to happiness.

It is a general complaint among master manufacturers that high wages ruin all their workmen; but it is difficult to conceive that these men would not save a part of their high wages for the future support of their families, instead of spending it in drunkenness and dissipation, if they did not rely on parish assistance for support in case of accidents. And that the poor employed in manufactures consider this assistance as a reason why they may spend all the wages they earn, and enjoy themselves while they can, appears to be evident from the number of families that, upon the failure of any great manufactory, immediately fall upon the parish, when perhaps the wages earned in this manufactory while it flourished, were sufficiently above the price of common country labour, to have allowed them to save enough for their support, till they could find some other channel for their industry.

A man who might not be deterred from going to the ale-house from the consideration that on his death, or sickness, he should leave his wife and family upon the parish, might yet hesitate in thus dissipating his earnings, if he were assured that, in either of these cases, his family must starve, or be left to the support of casual bounty.

...To prevent the recurrence of misery, is, alas! beyond the power of man. In the vain endeavour to attain what in the nature of things is impossible, we now sacrifice not only possible, but certain benefits. We tell the common people, that if they will submit to a code of tyrannical

5. Under the old Poor Law overseers in each parish levied a poor rate on all householders to relieve the aged, apprentice poor children and set the able poor on work, often in parish workhouses. After 1795 the poor rate was used also to supplement low wages in accordance with the price of bread and the number of dependents a man had.

regulations, they shall never be in want. They do submit to these regulations. They perform their part of the contract: but we do not, nay cannot, performs ours: and thus the poor sacrifice the valuable blessing of liberty, and receive nothing that can be called an equivalent in return.

Notwithstanding then, the institution of the poor-laws in England, I think it will be allowed, that considering the state of the lower classes altogether, both in the towns and in the country, the distresses which they suffer from the want of proper and sufficient food, from hard labour and unwholesome habitations, must operate as a constant check to incipient population.

To these two great checks to population, in all long occupied countries, which I have called the preventive and the positive checks, may be added, vicious customs with respect to women, great cities, unwholesome manufactures, luxury, pestilence, and war.

All these checks may be fairly resolved into misery and vice.

...It seems, however, every way probable, that even the acknowledged difficulties occasioned by the law of population, tend rather to promote, than impede the general purpose of Providence. They excite universal exertion, and contribute to that infinite variety of situations, and consequently of impressions, which seems, upon the whole, favourable to the growth of mind. It is probable, that too great, or too little excitement, extreme poverty, or too great riches, may be alike unfavourable in this respect. The middle regions of society seem to be best suited to intellectual improvement; but it is contrary to the analogy of all nature, to expect that the whole of society can be a middle region. The temperate zones of the earth seem to be the most favourable to the mental and corporeal energies of man; but all cannot be temperate zones. A world, warmed and enlightened but by one sun, must, from the laws of matter, have some parts chilled by perpetual frosts and others scorched by perpetual heats. Every piece of matter lying on a surface must have an upper and an under side: all the particles cannot be in the middle. The most valuable parts of an oak, to a timber merchant, are not either the roots, or the branches; but these are absolutely necessary to the existence of the middle part, or stem, which is the object in request. The timber merchant could not possibly expect to make an oak grow without roots or branches; but if he could find out a mode of cultivation which would cause more of the substance to go to stem, and less to root and branch, he would be right to exert himself in bringing such a system into general use.

In the same manner, though we cannot possibly expect to exclude riches and poverty from society; yet if we could find out a mode of government by which the numbers in the extreme regions would be lessened and the numbers in the middle regions increased, it would be undoubtedly our duty to adopt it. It is not, however, improbable that as in the oak, the roots and branches could not be diminished very greatly, without weakening the vigorous circulation of the sap in the stem; so in society the extreme parts could not be diminished beyond a certain degree, without lessening that animated exertion throughout the middle parts, which is the very cause that they are the most favourable to the growth of intellect. If no man could hope to rise, or fear to fall, in society; if industry did not bring with it its reward, and idleness its punishment, the middle parts would not certainly be what they now are. In reasoning upon this subject, it is evident that we ought to consider chiefly the mass of mankind, and not individual instances. There are undoubtedly many minds, and there ought to be many, according to the chances, out of so great a mass, that, having been vivified early by a peculiar course of excitements, would not need the constant action of narrow motives to continue them in activity. But if we were to review the various useful discoveries, the valuable writings, and other laudable exertions of mankind, I believe we should find that more were to be attributed to the narrow motives that operate upon the many, than to the apparently more enlarged motives that operate upon the few.

Leisure is, without doubt, highly valuable to man; but taking man as he is, the probability seems to be that, in the greater number of instances, it will produce evil rather than good. It has been not unfrequently remarked that talents are more common among younger brothers than among elder brothers; but it can scarcely be imagined that younger brothers are, upon an average, born with a greater original susceptibility of parts. The difference, if there really is any observable difference, can only arise from their different situations. Exertion and activity are in general absolutely necessary in the one case and are only optional in the other.

That the difficulties of life contribute to generate talents, every day's experience must convince us. The exertions that men find it necessary to make, in order to support themselves or families, frequently awaken faculties, that might otherwise have lain for ever dormant: and it has been commonly remarked that new and extraordinary situations generally create minds adequate to grapple with the difficulties in which they are involved.

WILLIAM WILBERFORCE

From *A Practical View of the Prevailing Religious System of Professed Christians, in the Higher and Middle Classes in this Country, contrasted with Real Christianity*

(The extract is from the first edition of 1797, Ch. 6).

...To provide...for the continuance of a state, by the admission of internal dissensions, or even by the chilling influence of poverty, seems to be in some sort sacrificing the end to the means. Happiness is the end for which men unite in civil society; but in societies thus constituted, little happiness, comparatively speaking, is to be found. The expedient, again, of preserving a state by the spirit of conquest, though even this has not wanted its admirers, is not to be tolerated for a moment, when considered on principles of universal justice. Such a state lives, and grows, and thrives by the misery of others, and becomes professedly the general enemy of its neighbours, and the scourge of the human race. All these devices are in truth but too much like the fabrications of man, when compared with the works of the Supreme Being, clumsy, yet weak in the execution of their purpose, and full of contradictory principles and jarring movements.

I might here enlarge with pleasure on the unrivalled excellence, in this very view, of the constitution under which we live in this happy country; and point out how, more perhaps than any which ever existed upon earth, it is so framed, as to provide at the same time for keeping up a due degree of public spirit, and yet for preserving unimpaired the quietness, and comfort, and charities of private life; how it even extracts from selfishness itself many of the advantages which, under less happily constructed froms of government, public spirit only can supply. But such a political discussion, however grateful to a British mind, would here be out of place. It is rather our business to remark, how much Christianity in every way sets herself in direct hostility to selfishness, the mortal distemper of political communities, and consequently, how their welfare must be inseparable from her prevalence. It might, indeed, be almost stated as the main object and chief concern of Christianity, to root out our natural selfishness, and to rectify the false standard which it imposes on us, with views, however, far higher than any which concern merely our temporal and social well-being; to bring us to a just estimate of ourselves, and of all around us, and to a due impression of the various claims and obligations resulting from the different relations in which we stand.

Benevolence, enlarged, vigorous, operative benevolence, is her master principle. Moderation in temporal pursuits and enjoyments, comparative indifference to the issue of wordly projects, diligence in the discharge of personal and civil duties, resignation to the will of God, and patience under all the dispensations of his Providence, are among her daily lessons. Humility is one of the essential qualities, which her precepts most directly and strongly enjoin, and which all her various doctrines tend to call forth and cultivate; and humility, as has been before suggested, lays the deepest and surest grounds for benevolence. In whatever class or order of society Christianity prevails, she sets herself to rectify the particular faults, or, if we would speak more distinctly, to counteract the particular mode of selfishness, to which that class is liable. Affluence she teaches to be liberal and beneficent; authority, to bear its faculties with meekness, and to consider the various cares and obligations belonging to its elevated station, as being conditions on which that station is conferred. Thus, softening the glare of wealth; and moderating the insolence of power, she renders the inequalities of the social state less galling to the lower orders, whom also she instructs, in their turn, to be diligent, humble, patient; reminding them that their more lowly path has been allotted to them by the hand of God; that it is their part faithfully to discharge its duties, and contendedly to bear its inconveniences; that the present state of things is very short; that the objects about which worldly men conflict so eagerly, are not worth the contest; that the peace of mind, which Religion offers to all ranks indiscriminately, affords more true satisfaction than all the expensive pleasures which are beyond the poor man's reach; that in this view, however, the poor have the advantage, and that if their superiors enjoy more abundant comforts, they are also exposed to many temptations from which the inferior classes are happily exempted; that "having food" and raiment, they should be therewith "content",[6] for that their situation in life, with all its evils, is better than they have deserved at the hand of God; finally, that all human distinctions will soon be done away, and the true followers of Christ will all, as children of the same father, be alike admitted to the possession of the same heavenly inheritance. Such are the blessed effects of Christianity on the temporal well-being of political communities.

But the Christianity which can produce effects like these must be real, not nominal, deep, not superficial. Such then is the Religion we should cultivate, if we would realize these pleasing speculations, and arrest the progress of political decay. But in the present circumstances of this country, it is a farther reason for endeavouring to cultivate this vital Christianity, still considering its effects merely in a political view, that,

6. I Timothy 6.8.

according to all human appearance, we must either have this or none; unless the prevalence of this be in some degree restored, we are likely not only to lose all the advantages which we might have derived from true Christianity, but to incur all the manifold evils which would result from the absence of all religion.

ROBERT SOUTHEY

From *Letters from England by Don Manuel Alvarez Espriella*

(The extract is from volume II of the first edition, 1807, which is in three volumes, from letter 38, omitting one footnote. Southey adopts the *persona* of a Spaniard, Don Manuel Alvarez Espriella, who is supposed to visit England from April, 1802 to October, 1803, staying at first with a London friend identified as 'J'. The letters are said to be addressed to 'my own family, and to my Father Confessor' in Spain, to have been intended for publication, and now to have been translated 'from the Spanish').

J. had provided us with letters to a gentleman in Manchester; we delivered them after breakfast, and were received with that courtesy which a foreigner when he takes with him the expected recommendations is sure to experience in England. He took us to one of the great cotton manufactories, showed us the number of children who were at work there, and dwelt with delight on the infinite good which resulted from employing them at so early an age. I listened without contradicting him, for who would lift up his voice against Diana in Ephesus! —[7] proposed my questions in such a way as not to imply, or at least not to advance, any difference of opinion, and returned with a feeling at heart which makes me thank God I am not an Englisman.

There is a shrub in some of the East Indian islands which the French call *veloutier*; it exhales an odour that is agreeable at a distance, becomes less so as you draw nearer, and, when you are quite close to it, is insupportably loathsome. Alciatus[8] himself could not have imagined an emblem more appropriate to the commercial prosperity of England.

Mr. — remarked that nothing could be so beneficial to a country as manufacturers. "You see these children, sir," said he. "In most parts of England poor children are a burthen to their parents and to the parish; here the parish, which would else have to support them, is rid of all

7. Diana: Roman equivalent of the Greek Artemis, who was worshipped as a maternal nature-goddess at Ephesus with a spring festival of games.
8. Alciatus: Andrea Alciati (1492-1550), Italian jurist, whose *Emblemata* (1522) were moral sayings written in Latin verse.

expense; they get their bread almost as soon as they can run about, and by the time they are seven or eight years old bring in money. There is no idleness among us: — they come at five in the morning; we allow them half an hour for breakfast, and an hour for dinner; they leave work at six, and another set relieves them for the night; the wheels never stand still." I was looking, while he spoke, at the unnatural dexterity with which the fingers of these little creatures were playing in the machinery, half giddy myself with the noise and the endless motion: and when he told me there was no rest in these walls, day nor night, I thought that if Dante had peopled one of his hells with children, here was a scene worthy to have supplied him with new images of torment.

"These children, then," said I, "have no time to receive instruction." "That, sir", he replied, "is the evil which we have found. Girls are employed here from the age you see them till they marry, and then they know nothing about domestic work, not even how to mend a stocking or boil a potatoe. But we are remedying this now, and send the children to school for an hour after they have done work." I asked if so much confinement did not injure their health. "No," he replied, "they are as healthy as any children in the world could be. To be sure, many of them as they grew up went off in consumptions, but consumption was the disease of the English." I ventured to inquire afterwards concerning the morals of the people who were trained up in this monstrous manner, and found, what was to be expected, that in consequence of herding together such numbers of both sexes, who are utterly uninstructed in the commonest principles of religion and morality, they were as debauched and profligate as human beings under the influence of such circumstances must inevitably be; the men drunken, the women dissolute; that however high the wages they earned, they were too improvident ever to lay-by for a time of need; and that, though the parish was not at the expense of maintaining them when children, it had to provide for them in diseases induced by their mode of life, and in premature debility and old age; the poor-rates were oppressively high, and the hospitals and workhouses always full and overflowing. I inquired how many persons were employed in the manufactory, and was told, children and all about two hundred. What was the firm of the house? — There were two partners. So! thought I, — a hundred to one!

"We are well off for hands in Manchester," said Mr. —; "manufactures are favourable to population, the poor are not afraid of having a family here, the parishes therefore have always plenty to apprentice, and we take them as fast as they can supply us. In new manufacturing towns they find it difficult to get a supply. Their only method is to send people round the country to get children from their parents. Women usually undertake this business; they promise the parents to provide for the children; one party is glad to be eased of a burthen, and it answers well to the other to find the young ones in food, lodging and clothes, and receive their wages." "But if these children should be ill-used?" said I. "Sir," he replied, "it never can be the interest of the women to use them ill, nor of the manufacturers to permit it."

It would have been in vain to argue had I been disposed to it. Mr. — was a man of humane and kindly nature, who would not himself use any thing cruelly, and judged of others by his own feelings. I thought of the cities in Arabian romance, where all the inhabitants were enchanted: here Commerce is the queen witch, and I had no talisman strong enough to disenchant those who were daily drinking of the golden cup of her charms.

We purchase English cloth, English muslins, English buttons, &c. and admire the excellent skill with which they are fabricated, and wonder that from such a distance they can be afforded to us at so low a price, and think what a happy country is England! A happy country indeed it is for the higher orders; no where have the rich so many enjoyments, no where have the ambitious so fair a field, no where have the ingenious such encouragement, no where have the intellectual such advantages; but to talk of English happiness is like talking of Spartan freedom, the Helots are overlooked. In no other country can such riches be acquired by commerce, but it is the one who grows rich by the labour of the hundred. The hundred, human beings like himself, as wonderfully fashioned by Nature, gifted with the like capacities, and equally made for immortality, are sacrificed body and soul. Horrible as it must needs appear, the assertion is true to the very letter. They are deprived in childhood of all instruction and all enjoyment; of the sports in which childhood instinctively indulges, of fresh air by day and of natural sleep by night. Their health physical and moral is alike destroyed; they die of diseases induced by unremitting task work, by confinement in the impure atmosphere of crowded rooms, by the particles of metallic or vegetable dust which they are continually inhaling; or they live to grow up without decency, without comfort, and without hope, without morals, without religion, and without shame, and bring forth slaves like themselves to tread in the same path of misery.

The dwellings of the labouring manufacturers are in narrow streets and lanes, blocked up from light and air, not as in our country to exclude an insupportable sun, but crowded together because every inch of land is of such value, that room for light and air cannot be afforded them. Here in Manchester a great proportion of the poor lodge in cellars, damp and dark, where every kind of filth is suffered to accumulate, because no exertions of domestic care can ever make such homes decent. These places are so many hotbeds of infection; and the poor in large towns are rarely or never without an infectious fever among them, a plague of their own, which leaves the habitations of the rich, like a Goshen[9] of cleanliness and comfort, unvisited.

Wealth flows into the country, but how does it circulate there? Not equally and healthfully through the whole system; it sprouts into wens and tumours, and collects in aneurisms which starve and palsy the extremities. The government indeed raises millions now as easily as it raised thousands in the days of Elizabeth: the metropolis is six times the size which it was a century ago; it has nearly doubled during the present reign; a thousand carriages drive about the streets of London, where, three generations ago there were not an hundred; a thousand hackney coaches are licensed in the same city, where at the same distance of time there was not one; they whose grandfathers dined at noon from wooden trenchers, and upon the produce of their own farms, sit down by the light of waxen tapers to be served upon silver, and to partake of delicacies from the four quarters of the globe. But the number of the poor, and the sufferings of the poor, have continued to increase; the price of every thing which they consume has always been advancing, and the price of labour, the only commodity which they have to dispose of, remains the same. Workhouses are erected in one place, and infirmaries in another; the poor-rates increase in proportion to the taxes; and in times of dearth the rich even purchase food, and retail it to them at a reduced price, or supply them with it gratuitously: still every year adds to their number. Necessity is the mother of crimes; new prisons are built, new punishments enacted; but the poor become year after year more numerous, more miserable, and more depraved; and this is the inevitable tendency of the manufacturing system.

This system is the boast of England, — long may she continue to boast it before Spain shall rival her! Yet this is the system which we envy, and which we are so desirous to imitate. Happily our religion presents one obstacle; that incessant labour which is required in these task-houses can never be exacted in a Catholic country, where the Church has wisely provided so many days of leisure for the purposes of religion and enjoyment. Against the frequency of these holydays much has been said; but Heaven forbid that the clamour of philosophizing commercialists should prevail, and that the Spaniard should ever be brutalized by unremitting task-work, like the negroes in America and the labouring manufacturers in England! Let us leave to England the boast of supplying all Europe with her wares; let us leave to these lords of the sea the distinction of which they are so tenacious, that of being the white slaves of the rest of the world, and doing for it all its dirty work. The poor must

9. Goshen: a place of light and plenty, as in Genesis 45.10.

be kept miserably poor, or such a state of things could not continue; there must be laws to regulate their wages, not by the value of their work, but by the pleasure of their masters; laws to prevent their removal from one place to another within the kingdom, and to prohibit their emigration out of it. They would not be crowded in hot task-houses by day, and herded together in damp cellars at night; they would not toil in unwholesome employments from sun-rise till sun-set, whole days, and whole days and quarters, for with twelve hours labour the avidity of trade is not satisfied; they would not sweat night and day, keeping up this *laus perennis*[10] of the Devil, before furnaces which are never suffered to cool, and breathing-in vapours which inevitably produce disease and death; — the poor would never do these things unless they were miserably poor, unless they were in that state of abject poverty which precludes instruction, and by destroying all hope for the future, reduces man, like the brutes, to seek for nothing beyond the gratification of present wants.

How England can remedy this evil, for there are not wanting in England those who perceive and confess it to be an evil, it is not easy to discover, nor is it my business to inquire. To us it is of more consequence to know how other countries may avoid it, and, as it is the prevailing system to encourage manufactures every where, to inquire how we may reap as much good and as little evil as possible. The best methods appear to be by extending to the utmost the use of machinery, and leaving the price of labour to find its own level: the higher it is the better. The introduction of machinery in an old manufacturing country always produces distress by throwing workmen out of employ, and is seldom effected without riots and executions. Where new fabrics are to be erected it is obvious that this difficulty does not exist, and equally obvious that, when hard labour can be performed by iron and wood, it is desirable to spare flesh and blood. High wages are a general benefit, because money thus distributed is employed to the greatest general advantage. The labourer, lifted up one step in society, acquires the pride and the wants, the habits and the feelings, of the class now next above him. Forethought, which the miserably poor necessarily and instinctively shun, is, to him who earns a comfortable competence, new pleasure; he educates his children, in the hope that they may rise higher than himself, and that he is fitting them for better fortunes. Prosperity is said to be more dangerous than adversity to human virtue; both are wholesome when sparingly distributed, both in the excess perilous always, and often deadly: but if prosperity be thus dangerous, it is a danger which falls to the lot of few; and it is sufficiently

---

10. I am informed by a catholic, that those convents in which the choir service is never discontinued are said to have laus perennis there (Southey's note), *i.e.* perpetual praise.

proved by the vices of those unhappy wretches who exist in slavery, under whatever form or in whatever disguise, that hope is essential to prudence, and to virtue, as to happiness.

ROBERT OWEN

From *A New View of Society*

(The extracts are from the second essay, in the first edition, 1813).

...At that time the lower classes in Scotland, like those of other countries, had strong prejudices against strangers having any authority over them, and particularly against the English; few of whom had then settled in Scotland, and not one in the neighbourhood of the scenes under description. It is also well known that even the Scotch peasantry and working classes possess the habit of tracing cause and effect with great acuteness; and in the present case, those employed naturally concluded that the new purchasers intended merely to make the utmost profit by the establishment, on the abuses of which many of them were then deriving support. The persons employed at these works were therefore strongly prejudiced against the new director of the establishment: prejudiced, because he was a stranger and from England: because he succeeded Mr. Dale[11], under whose proprietorship they were allowed their own way; because his religious creed was not theirs: and because they concluded that the works would be governed by new laws and regulations, calculated to squeeze, as they often termed it, the greatest sum of gain out of their labour.

In consequence, from the day he arrived among them, every means which ingenuity could devise was set to work to counteract the plan which he attempted to introduce; and for two years it was a regular attack and defence of prejudices and mal-practices between the manager and population of the place, without the former being able to make much progress, or convince the latter of the sincerity of his good intentions for their welfare. He, however, did not lose his patience, his temper, or his confidence in the certain success of the principles on which he founded his conduct. And these principles did ultimately prevail: the population could not continue to resist a firm well-directed kindness, administering justice to all. They therefore slowly and cautiously began to give him

11. David Dale (1739-1806), Owen's father-in-law, mill-owner at New Lanark, who built a village for his employees.

some portion of their confidence; and, as this increased, he was enabled more and more to develop his plans for their amelioration. It may with truth be said, that at this period they possessed almost all the vices and very few of the virtues of a social community. Theft and the receipt of stolen goods was their trade, idleness and drunkenness their habit, falsehood and deception their garb, dissensions, civil and religious, their daily practice: and they were united only in a jealous systematic opposition to their employers.

Here, then, was a fair field on which to try the efficacy in practice of principles supposed capable of altering any characters. The manager formed his plans accordingly: he spent some time in finding out the full extent of the evil against which he had to contend, and in tracing the true causes which had produced these effects, and were continuing them. He found that all was distrust, disorder, and disunion; and he wished to introduce confidence, regularity, and harmony: he therefore began to bring forward his various expedients to withdraw the unfavourable circumstances by which they had been hitherto surrounded, and replace them by others calculated to produce a more happy result. He soon discovered that theft was extended through almost all the ramifications of the community, and the receipt of stolen goods through all the country around. To remedy this evil, not one legal punishment was inflicted, not one individual imprisoned, even for an hour: but checks and other regulations of prevention were introduced; a short plain explanation of the immediate benefits they would derive from a different conduct was inculcated by those instructed for the purpose, who had the best powers of reasoning among themselves. They were at the same time instructed how to direct their industry in legal and useful occupations; by which, without danger or disgrace, they could really earn more than they had previously obtained by dishonest practices. — Thus the difficulty of committing the crime was increased, the detection afterwards rendered more easy, the habit of honest industry formed, and the pleasure of good conduct experienced.

...The same principles were applied to correct the irregular intercourse of the sexes; — such conduct was discountenanced and held in disgrace; fines were levied upon both parties for the use of the support fund of the community.* But because they had once unfortunately offended against the established laws and customs of society, they were not forced to become vicious, abandoned, and miserable. The door was left open for them to return to the comforts of kind friends and respected ac-

---

* This fund arose from each individual contributing one-sixtieth part of their wages, which, under their management, was applied to support the sick, the injured by accident, and the aged.

quaintances; and, beyond any previous expectation, the evil became greatly diminished.

The system of receiving apprentices from public charities was abolished; permanent settlers with large families were encouraged, and comfortable houses were built for their accommodation.

The practice of employing children in the mills, of six, seven, and eight years of age, was prevented, and their parents advised to allow them to acquire health and education until they were ten years old. **

The children were taught reading, writing, and arithmetic, during five years, that is, from five to ten, in the village school, without expense to their parents. All the modern improvements in education have been adopted, or are in process of adoption.*** Some facilities in teaching arithmetic have been also introduced, which were peculiar to this school, and which have been found very advantageous. They may therefore be taught and well-trained before they engage in any regular employment. Another important consideration is, that all their instruction is rendered a pleasure and delight to them; they are much more anxious for the hour of school-time to arrive than to end: they therefore make a rapid progress; and it may be safely asserted, that if they shall not be trained to form such characters as may be the most wished and desired, not one particle of the fault will proceed from the children; the cause will rest in the want of a true knowledge of human nature in those who have the management of them and their parents.

During the period that these changes were going forward, attention was given to the domestic arrangements of the community. Their houses were rendered comfortable, their streets were improved, the best provisions were purchased, and sold to them at low rates, yet covering the original expense; and under such regulations as taught them how to proportion their expenditure to their income. Fuel and clothes were

---

** It may be remarked, that even this age is too early to keep them at constant employment in manufactories, from six in the morning to seven in the evening. Far better would it be for the children, their parents, and for society, that the first should not commence employment until they attain the age of twelve, when their education might be finished, and their bodies would be more competent to undergo the fatigue and exertions required of them. When parents can be trained to afford this additional time to their children without inconvenience, they will, of course, adopt the practice now recommended.

*** To avoid the inconveniences which must ever arise from the introduction of a particular creed into a school, the children are taught to read in such books as inculcate those precepts of the Christian religion which are common to all denominations; and on Sunday the school is opened for the express purpose of teaching the catechisms, psalms, etc. of the established church to those children whose parents are of that persuasion, while the remainder attend their respective places of worship.

obtained for them in the same manner; and no advantage was ever attempted to be taken of them, or means used to deceive them.

In consequence, their animosity and opposition to a stranger subsided, their full confidence was given, and they became satisfied that no evil was intended them: on the contrary they were convinced that a real desire existed to increase their happiness upon those grounds on which alone it could be permanently increased. All difficulties in the way of future improvement vanished. They were taught to be rational, and they acted rationally, and thus both parties experienced the incalculable advantages of the system which had been adopted. Those employed became industrious, temperate, healthy, faithful to their employers, and kind to each other; while the proprietors were deriving services from their attachment, almost without inspection, far beyond those which could be obtained by any other means, without those mutual principles of confidence and kindness existing between the parties. Such was the effect of these principles on the adults, on those whose previous habits had been as ill-formed as habits could be; and certainly the application of the principles to practice was made under the most unfavourable circumstances.****

I have thus, at the urgent request of many respected friends and individuals proceeded to give a more detailed account of this experiment than I should otherwise have deemed necessary; because these details of the application of the principles to any local situation, are of far less importance than to give a clear and accurate knowledge of the principles themselves; that they may be so well understood as to be easily applicable to practice in any community, and under any circumstances. Without this being done, particular facts may indeed amuse or astonish, but they would not contain that high degree of substantial value which the principles will be found to possess. But if it shall forward this object, the experiment cannot fail to prove the certain means of renovating the moral and religious principles of the world, by showing whence arise the various opinions, manners, vices, and virtues of mankind, and how the best or the worse of them may be with mathematical precision taught to the rising generations.

Let it not, therefore, be longer said that evil or injurious actions cannot be prevented; or that the most rational habits in the rising generation cannot be universally formed. In those characters which now exhibit crime, the fault is obviously not in the individual, but the defect proceeds

---

**** It may be supposed that this community was separated from other society; but the supposition would be erroneous, for it had daily and hourly communication with a population exceeding itself. The royal borough of Lanark is only one mile distant from the works; many individuals came daily from the former to be employed at the latter; and a general intercourse is constantly maintained between the old and new towns.

from the system in which those individuals have been trained. Withdraw those circumstances which tend to create crime in the human character, and crime will not be created. Replace them with such as are calculated to form habits of order, regularity, temperance, industry, and upon the most certain data these qualities may be formed. Adopt measures of fair equity and justice, and you will readily acquire the full and complete confidence of the lower orders: nay, more; proceed systematically on principles of undeviating persevering kindness, yet retaining and using, though with the least possible severity, the means of restraining full-formed crime from immediately injuring society; and by degrees, even the crimes now existing in the adults will also gradually disappear: for the worst formed disposition, short of incurable insanity, will not long resist a firm, determined, well-directed, persevering kindness. Such a proceeding, whenever practised, will be found the most powerful and effective corrector of crime, of all injurious and improper habits.

From *Report to the County of Lanark, of a Plan for relieving Public Distress and Removing Discontent, etc.*

(The extracts are from Part III, in the first edition, 1821).

As it will afterwards appear that the food for the whole population can be provided better and cheaper, under one general arrangement of cooking, and that the children can better be trained and educated together, under the eye of their parents than under any other circumstances, a large square, or rather parallelogram will be found to combine the greatest advantage, in its form, for the domestic arrangements of the association. This form, indeed, affords so many advantages for the comfort of human life, that if great ignorance, respecting the means necessary to secure good conduct and happiness among the working classes, had not prevailed in all ranks, it must long ago have become universal. It admits of a most simple, easy, convenient, and economical arrangement for all the purposes required. The four sides of this figure may be adapted to contain all the private apartments, or sleeping and sitting rooms for the adult part of the population; general sleeping apartments for the children while under tuition; store-rooms, or warehouses in which to deposit various products, an inn, or house, for the accommodation of strangers, an infirmary, &c, &c. In a line across the centre of the parallelogram, leaving free space for air and light, and easy communication, might be erected the church, or places of worship;

kitchen and apartments for eating; all in the most convenient situation for the whole population, and under the best possible public super-intendence, without trouble, expense, or inconvenience to any part.

The advantages of this general domestic arrangement can only be known and appreciated by those who have had great experience in the beneficial results of extensive combinations, in improving the condition of the working classes: and whose minds, advancing beyond the petty range of individual party interests, have been calmly directed to consider what may now be attained by a well-devised association of human powers, for the benefit of all ranks. It is such individuals only, who can detect the present total want of foresight in the conduct of society, and its gross misapplication of the most valuable and abundant means of securing prosperity. They can distinctly perceive, that the blind are leading the blind from difficulties to dangers, which they feel to increase at every step.

The parallelogram being found to be the best form in which to dispose the dwelling and chief domestic arrangements for the proposed as-sociations of cultivators, it will be useful now to explain the principles on which those arrangements have been formed. The first in order, and the most necessary, are those respecting food.

It has been, and still is, a received opinion among theorists in political economy, that man can provide better for himself, and more advan-tageously for the public, when left to his own individual exertions, opposed to and in competition with his fellows, than when aided by any social arrangement which shall unite his interests individually and generally with society. This principle of individual interest, opposed, as it is perpetually, to the public good, is considered, by the most celebrated political economists, to be the corner-stone of the social system, and without which, society could not subsist. Yet when they shall know themselves, and discover the wonderful effects, which combination and union can produce, they will acknowledge that the present arrangement of society is the most anti-social, impolitic, and irrational, that can be devised; that under its influence all the superior and valuable qualities of human nature are repressed from infancy, and that the most unnatural means are used to bring out the most injurious propensities; in short, that the utmost pains are taken to make that which by nature is the most delightful compound for producing excellence and happiness, absurd, imbecile, and wretched.

...The peculiar mode of governing these establishments will depend on the parties who form them. Those founded by land-owners and capit-alists, public companies, parishes, or counties will be under the direction of the individuals whom these powers may appoint to superintend them, and will, of course, be subject to the rules and regulations laid down by their founders. Those formed by the middle and working classes, upon a complete reciprocity of interests, should be governed by themselves, upon principles that will *prevent* divisions, opposition of interests, jealousies, or any of the common and vulgar passions which a contention for power is certain to generate. Their affairs should be conducted by a committee, composed of all the members of the association between certain ages — for instance, of those between 35 and 45, or between 40 and 50. Perhaps the former will unite more of the activity of youth with the experience of age than the latter; but it is of little moment which period of life may be fixed upon. In a short time the ease with which these associations will proceed in all their operations will be such as to render the business of governing a mere recreation; and as the parties who govern will in a few years again become the governed, they must always be conscious that at a future period they will experience the good or evil effects of the measures of their administration. By this equitable and natural arrangement, all the numberless evils of elections and electioneering will be avoided. As all are to be trained and educated together, and without distinction, they will be delightful companions and associates, intimately acquainted with each other's inmost thoughts. There will be no foundation for disguise or deceit of any kind; all will be as open as the hearts and feelings of young children before they are trained (as they necessarily are under the present system) in complicated arts of deception. At the same time their whole conduct will be regulated by a sound and rational discretion, and intelligence, such as human beings trained and placed as they have hitherto been will deem it visionary to expect, and impossible to attain, in every-day practice.

The superior advantages which these associators will speedily possess, and the still greater superiority of knowledge which they will rapidly acquire, will preclude on their parts the smallest desire for what are now called honours and peculiar privileges. They will have minds so well informed — their power of accurately tracing cause and effect will be so much increased, that they must clearly perceive, that to be raised to one of the privileged orders, would be to themselves a serious evil, and to their posterity would certainly occasion an incalculable loss of intellect and enjoyment, equally injurious to themselves and to society. They will, therefore, have every motive not to interfere with the honours and privileges of the existing higher orders, but remain well satisfied with their own station in life. The only distinction which can be found of the least utility in these associations, is that of age or experience. It is the only just and natural distinction; and any other would be inconsistent with the enlarged and superior acquirements of the individuals who would compose these associations. The deference to age or experience will be natural, and readily given; and any advantageous regulations may be formed in consequence, for apportioning the proper employments to the period of life best calculated for them, and diminishing the labour of the individual, as age advances beyond the term when the period of governing is concluded.

WILLIAM COBBETT

From *Rural Rides*

(Our extracts are from *Rides* dated 6 November, 1821, 27 September, 1822, 20 October, 1825 and 30 August, 1826, in the first volume-edition, 1830. The first publication of the *Rides* was in contemporary numbers of the *Political Register*).

I left Uphusband this morning at 9, and came across to this place Marlborough in a post-chaise. Came up the valley of Uphusband, which ends at about 6 miles from the village, and puts one out upon the Wiltshire downs, which stretch away towards the west and south-west, towards Devizes and towards Salisbury. After about half a mile of down we came down into a level country; the flints cease, and the chalk comes nearer the top of the ground. The labourers along here seem very poor indeed. Farm houses with twenty ricks round each, besides those standing in the fields; pieces of wheat, 50, 60, or 100 acres in a piece; but a group of women labourers, who were attending the measurers to measure their reaping work, presented such an assemblage of rags as I never before saw even amongst the hoppers at Farnham, many of whom are common beggars. I never before saw *country* people, and reapers too, observe, so miserable in appearance as these. There were some very pretty girls, but ragged as colts and as pale as ashes. The day was cold too, and frost hardly off the ground; and their blue arms and lips would have made any heart ache but that of a seatseller or a loan-jobber. A little after passing by these poor things, whom I left, cursing, as I went, those who had brought them to this state, I came to a group of shabby houses upon a hill. While a boy was watering his horses, I asked the ostler the *name* of the place; and, as the old women say, 'you might have knocked me down with a feather', when he said, *'Great Bedwin'*. The whole of the houses are not intrinsically worth a thousand pounds. There stood a thing out in the middle of the place, about 25 feet long and 15 wide, being a room stuck up on unhewed stone pillars about 10 feet high. It was the Town Hall, where the ceremony of choosing the *two members*[12] is performed.

...In quitting Tilford we came on to the land belonging to Waverley Abbey, and then, instead of going on to the town of Farnham, veered away to the left towards *Wrecklesham,* in order to cross the Farnham and Alton turnpike-road, and to come on by the side of *Crondall* to *Odiham.* We went a little out of the way to go to a place called the *Bourne,* which lies in the heath at about a mile from Farnham. It is a winding narrow valley, down which, during the wet season of the year, there runs a stream beginning at the *Holt Forest,* and emptying intself into the *Wey* just below Moor-Park, which was the seat of *Sir William Temple*[13], when *Swift* was residing with him. We went to this Bourne in order that I might show my son the spot where I received the rudiments of my education. There is a little hop-garden in which I used to work when from eight to ten years' old; from which I have scores of times run to follow the hounds, leaving the hoe to do the best that it could to destroy the weeds; but the most interesting thing was, a *sand-hill,* which goes from a part of the heath down to the rivulet. As a due mixture of pleasure with toil, I, with two brothers, used occasionally to *desport* ourselves, as the lawyers call it, at this sand-hill. Our diversion was this: we used to go to the top of the hill, which was steeper than the roof of a house; one used to draw his arms out of the sleeves of his smock-frock, and lay himself down with his arms by his sides; and then the others, one at head and the other at feet, sent him rolling down the hill like a barrrel or a log of wood. By the time he got to the bottom, his hair, eyes, ears, nose and mouth, were all full of this loose sand; then the others took their turn, and at every roll, there was a monstrous spell of laughter. I had often told my sons of this while they were very little, and I now took one of them to see the spot. But, that was not all. This was the spot where I was receiving my *education;* and this was the sort of education; and I am perfectly satisfied that if I had not received such an education, or something very much like it; that, if I had been brought up a milksop, with a nursery-maid everlastingly at my heels; I should have at this day been as great a fool, as inefficient a mortal, as any of those frivolous idiots that are turned out from Winchester and Westminister School, or from any of those dens of dunces called Colleges and Universities. It is impossible to say how much I owe to that sand-hill; and I went to return it may thanks for the ability which it probably gave me to be one of the greatest terrors, to one of the greatest and most powerful bodies of knaves and fools, that ever were permitted to afflict this or any other country.

From the Bourne we proceeded on to *Wrecklesham,* at the end of

---

12. *two members*: *i.e.* of Parliament, representing a 'Rotten Borough'.
13. Sir William Temple (1628-1699), diplomat, essayist and memoirist.

which, we crossed what is called the river *Wey*. Here we found a parcel of labourers at parish-work. Amongst them was an old playmate of mine. The account they gave of their situation was very dismal. The harvest was over early. The hop-picking is now over; and now they are employed *by the Parish;* that is to say, not absolutely digging holes one day and filling them up the next; but at the expense of half-ruined farmers and tradesmen and landlords, to break stones into very small pieces to make nice smooth roads lest the jolting, in going along them, should create bile in the stomachs of the overfed tax-eaters. I call upon mankind to witness this scene; and to say, whether ever the like of this was heard before. It is a state of things, where all is out of order; where self-preservation, that great law of nature, seems to be set at defiance; for here are farmers *unable* to pay men for working for them, and yet compelled to pay them for working in doing that which is really of no use to any human being. There lie the hop-poles unstripped. You see a hundred things in the neighbouring fields that want doing. The fences are not nearly what they ought to be. The very meadows, to our right and our left in crossing this little valley, would occupy these men advantageously until the setting in of the frost; and here are they, not, as I said before, actually digging holes one day and filling them up the next; but, to all intents and purposes, as uselessly employed. Is this Mr. Canning's *'Sun of Prosperity?'* Is this the way to increase or preserve a nation's wealth? Is this a sign of wise legislation and of good government? Does this thing *'work well'*, Mr. Canning?[14] Does it prove, that we want no change? True, you were born under a Kingly Government; and so was I as well as you; but I was not born under *Six-Acts;* nor was I born under a state of things like this. I was not born under it, and I do not wish to live under it; and, with God's help, I will change it if I can.

...Having done my business at Hartswood to-day about eleven o'clock, I went to a *sale* at a farm, which the farmer is quitting. Here I had a view of what has long been going on all over the country. The farm, which belongs to *Christ's Hospital,* has been held by a man of the name of CHARINGTON,in whose family the lease has been, I hear, a great number of years. The house is hidden by trees. It stands in the Weald of Surrey, close by the *River Mole*, which is here a mere rivulet, thought just below this house this rivulet supplies the very prettiest flour-mill I ever saw in my life.

Every thing about this farm-house was formerly the scene of *plain manners* and *plentiful living.* Oak clothes-chests, oak bedsteds, oak chests of drawers, and oak tables to eat on, long, strong, and

14. George Canning (1770-1827), Foreign Secretary in 1822 and Prime Minister in 1827, whose somewhat complacent phrases in his political speeches are often quoted contemptuously by Cobbett.

well supplied with joint stools. Some of the things were many hundreds of years old. But all appeared to be in a state of decay and nearly of *disuse*. There appeared to have been hardly any *family* in that house, where formerly there were, in all probability, from ten to fifteen men, boys, and maids: and, which was the worst of all, there was a *parlour*! Aye, and a *carpet* and *bell-pull* too! One end of the front of this once plain and substantial house had been moulded into a "*parlour;*" and there was the mahogany table, and the fine chairs, and the fine glass, and all as bare-faced upstart as any stock-jobber in the kingdom can boast of. And, there were the decanters, the glasses, the "dinner-set" of crockery ware, and all just in the true stock-jobber style. And I dare say it has been '*Squire* Charington and the *Miss* Charingtons; and not plain Master Charington, and his son Hodge, and his daughter Betty Charington, all of whom this accursed system has, in all likelihood, transmuted into a species of mock gentlefolks, while it has ground the labourers down into real slaves. Why do not farmers now *feed* and *lodge* their work-people, as they did formerly? Because they cannot keep them *upon so little* as they give them in wages. This is the real cause of the change. There needs no more to prove that the lot of the working classes has become worse than it formerly was. This fact alone is quite sufficient to settle this point. All the world knows, that a number of people, boarded in the same house, and at the same table, can, with as good food, be boarded much cheaper than those persons divided into twos; threes, or fours, can be boarded. This is a well-known truth: therefore, if the farmer now shuts his pantry against his labourers, and pays them wholly in money, is it not clear, that he does it because he thereby gives them a living *cheaper* to him; that is to say a *worse* living than formerly? Mind he has *a house* for them; a kitchen for them to sit in, bed rooms for them to sleep in, tables and stools, and benches, of everlasting duration. All these he has: all these *cost him nothing;* and yet so much does he gain by pinching them in wages that he lets all these things remain as of no use, rather than feed the labourers in the house. Judge, then, of the *change* that has taken place in the condition of these labourers! And, be astonished, if you can, at the *pauperism* and the *crimes* that now disgrace this once happy and moral England.

The land produces, on an average, what it always produced; but, there is a new distribution of the produce. This 'Squire Charington's father used, I dare say, to sit at the head of the oak-table along with his men, say grace to them, and cut up the meat and the pudding. He might take a cup of *strong beer* to himself, when they had none; but, that was pretty nearly all the difference in their manner of living. So that *all* lived well. But, the 'Squire had many *wine-decanters* and *wine-glasses* and "*a dinner set*", and a "*breakfast set*", and "*desert knives*"; and these evidently imply carryings on and a consumption that must of necessity have greatly robbed the long oak table if it had remained fully tenanted. That long table could not share in the work of the decanters and the dinner set. Therefore, it became almost untenanted; the labourers retreated to hovels, called cottages; and, instead of board and lodging, they got money; so little of it as to enable the employer to drink wine; but, then, that he might not reduce them to *quite starvation,* they were enabled to come to him, in the *king's name,* and demand food *as paupers.* And, now, mind, that which a man received in the *king's name,* he knows well he has *by force;* and it is not in nature that he should *thank* any body for it, and least of all the party *from whom it is forced.* Then, if this sort of force be insufficient to obtain him *enough* to eat and to keep warm, is it surprising, if he think it *no great offence against God* (who created no man to starve) to use *another sort of force* more within his own controul? Is it, in short, surprising, if he resort to *theft* and *robbery*?

...I could not quit this farm-house without reflecting on the thousands of scores of bacon and thousands of bushels of bread that had been eaten from the long oak-table which, I said to myself, is now perhaps, going, at last, to the bottom of a bridge that some stock-jobber will stick up over an artificial river in his cockney garden. *'By – it shant',* said I, almost in a real passion: and so I requested a friend to buy it for me; and if he do so, I will take it to Kensington, or to Fleet-street, and keep it for the good it has done in the world.

...At one farm, between PEWSEY and UPAVON, I counted more than 300 hogs in one stubble. This is certainly the most delightful farming in the world. No *ditches*, no *water-furrows*, no *drains*, hardly any *hedges*, no *dirt* and *mire*, even in the wettest seasons of the year; and though the *downs* are *naked* and *cold,* the valleys are snugness itself. They are, as to the downs, what *ah-ahs!*[15] are, in parks or lawns. When you are going over the downs, you look *over* the valleys, as in the case of the *ah-ah*; and, if you be not acquainted with the country, your surprise, when you come to the edge of the hill, is very great. The *shelter*, in these valleys, and particularly where the downs are *steep* and *lofty* on the sides, is very complete. Then, the trees are every where *lofty.* They are generally *elms,* with some *ashes*, which delight in the soil that they find here. There are, almost always, two or three large clumps of trees in every parish, and a rookery or two (not *rag*-rookery[16]) to every parish. By the water's edge there are *willows;* and to almost every farm, there is a fine *orchard*, the trees being, in general, very fine, and, this year, they are, in general, well loaded with fruit. So that, all taken together, it seems

15. *ah-ahs:* ha-has, or sunken fences.
16. *rag*-rookery: cluster of mean tenements inhabited by ragged paupers.

impossible to find a more beautiful and pleasant country than this, or to imagine any life more easy and happy than men might here lead, if they were untormented by an accursed system that takes the food from those that raise it, and gives it to those that do nothing that is useful to man.

DAVID RICARDO

From *On the Principles of Political Economy and Taxation*
(Our extracts are from Ch. V., 'On Wages', in the first edition, 1817).

Labour, like all other things which are purchased and sold, and which may be increased or diminished in quantity, has its natural and its market price. The natural price of labour is that price which is necessary to enable the labourers, one with another, to subsist and to perpetuate their race, without either increase or diminution.

The power of the labourer to support himself, and the family which may be necessary to keep up the number of labourers, does not depend on the quantity of money which he may receive for wages, but on the quantity of food, necessaries, and conveniences become essential to him from habit, which that money will purchase. The natural price of labour, therefore, depends on the price of the food, necessaries, and conveniences required for the support of the labourer and his family. With a rise in the price of food and necessaries, the natural price of labour will rise; with the fall in their price, the natural price of labour will fall.

With the progress of society the natural price of labour has always a tendency to rise, because one of the principal commodities by which its natural price is regulated, has a tendency to become dearer, from the greater difficulty of producing it. As, however, the improvements in agriculture, the discovery of new markets, whence provisions may be imported, may for a time counteract the tendency to a rise in the price of necessaries, and may even occasion their natural price to fall, so will the same causes produce the correspondent effects on the natural price of labour.

The natural price of all commodities, excepting raw produce and labour, has a tendency to fall, in the progress of wealth and population; for though, on one hand, they are enhanced in real value, from the rise in the natural price of the raw material of which they are made, this is more than counterbalanced by the improvements in machinery, by the better division and distribution of labour, and by the increasing skill, both in science and art, of the producers.

The market price of labour is the price which is really paid for it, from the natural operation of the proportion of the supply to the demand;

labour is dear when it is scarce, and cheap when it is plentiful. However much the market price of labour may deviate from its natural price, it has, like commodities, a tendency to conform to it.

It is when the market price of labour exceeds its natural price, that the condition of the labourer is flourishing and happy, that he has it in his power to command a greater proportion of the necessaries and enjoyments of life, and therefore to rear a healthy and numerous family. When, however, by the encouragement which high wages give to the increase of population, the number of labourers is increased, wages again fall to their natural price, and indeed from a re-action sometimes fall below it.

When the market price of labour is below its natural price, the condition of the labourers is most wretched: then poverty deprives them of those comforts which custom renders absolute necessaries. It is only after their privations have reduced their number, or the demand for labour has increased, that the market price of labour will rise to its natural price, and that the labour will have the moderate comforts which the natural price will afford.

Notwithstanding the tendency of wages to conform to their natural rate, their market rate may, in an improving society, for an indefinite period, be constantly above it; for no sooner may the impulse, which an increased capital gives to a new demand for labour be obeyed, than another increase of capital may produce the same effect; and thus, if the increase of capital be gradual and constant, the demand for labour may give a continued stimulus to an increase of people.

...It is not by raising in any manner different from the present, the fund from which the poor are supported, that the evil can be mitigated. It would not only be no improvement, but it would be an aggravation of the distress which we wish to see removed, if the fund were increased in amount, or were levied according to some late proposals, as a general fund from the country at large. The present mode of its collection and application has served to mitigate its pernicious effects. Each parish raises a separate fund for the support of its own poor. Hence it becomes an object of more interest and more practicability to keep the rates low, than if one general fund were raised for the relief of the poor of the whole kingdom. A parish is much more interested in an economical collection of the rate, and a sparing distribution of relief, when the whole saving will be for its own benefit, than if hundreds of other parishes were to partake of it.

It is to this cause, that we must ascribe the fact of the poor laws not having yet absorbed all the net revenue of the country; it is to the rigour with which they are applied, that we are indebted for their not having become overwhelmingly oppressive. If by law every human being wanting support could be sure to obtain it, and obtain it in such a degree as to make life tolerably comfortable, theory would lead us to expect that all other taxes together would be light compared with the single one of poor rates. The principle of gravitation is not more certain than the tendency of such laws to change wealth and power into misery and weakness; to call away the exertions of labour from every object, except that of providing mere subsistence; to confound all intellectual distinction; to busy the mind continually in supplying the body's wants; until at last all classes should be infected with the plague of universal poverty. Happily these laws have been in operation during a period of progressive prosperity, when the funds for the maintenance of labour have regularly increased, and when an increase of population would be naturally called for. But if our progress should become more slow; if we should attain the stationary state, from which I trust we are yet far distant, then will the pernicious nature of these laws become more manifest and alarming; and then, too, will their removal be obstructed by many additional difficulties.

JAMES MILL

From 'Government'

(The extract is from *Supplement to the Fourth, Fifth and Sixth Editions of the Encyclopaedia Britannica*, 1824).

...We may allow, for example, in general terms, that the lot of every human being is determined by his pains and pleasures; and that his happiness corresponds with the degree in which his pleasures are great, and his pains are small.

Human pains and pleasures are derived from two sources. They are produced, either by our fellow-men, or by causes independent of other men.

We may assume it as another principle, that the concern of Government is with the former of these two sources; that its business is to increase to the utmost the pleasures, and diminish to the utmost the pains, which men derive from one another.

Of the laws of nature, on which the condition of man depends, that which is attended with the greatest number of consequences, is the necessity of labour for obtaining the means of subsistence, as well as the means of the greatest part of our pleasures. This is, no doubt, the primary cause of government; for, if nature had produced spontaneously all the objects which we desire, and in sufficient abundance for the desires of all, there would have been no source of dispute or of injury among men; nor would any man have possessed the means of ever acquiring authority over another.

The results are exceedingly different, when nature produces the objects of desire not in sufficient abundance for all. The source of dispute is then exhaustless; and every man has the means of acquiring authority over others, in proportion to the quantity of those objects which he is able to possess. In this case, the end to be obtained, through Government as the means, would be to make that distribution of the scanty materials of happiness which would insure the greatest sum of it in the members of the community taken altogether; and to prevent every individual, or combination of individuals, from interfering with that distribution, or making any man to have less than his share.

An element of great importance is taken into the calculation, when it is considered that most of the objects of desire, and even the means of subsistence, are the product of labour. The means of insuring labour must, in that case, be provided for as the foundation of all.

The means for the insuring of labour are of two sorts; the one made out of the matter of evil, the other made out of the matter of good. The first sort is commonly denominated force; and, under its application, the labourers are slaves. This mode of procuring labour we need not consider; for, if the end of Government be to produce the greatest happiness of the greatest number, that end cannot be attained by making the greatest number slaves.

The other mode of obtaining labour is by allurement, or the advantage which it brings. If we would obtain all the objects of desire in the greatest possible quantity, we must obtain labour in the greatest possible quantity; and, if we would obtain labour in the greatest possible quantity, we must raise the advantage attached to labour to the greatest possible height. It is impossible to attach to labour a greater degree of advantage than the whole of the product of labour. Why so? Because, if you give more to one man than the produce of his labour, you can do so only by taking it away from the produce of some other man's labour. The greatest possible happiness of society is, therefore, attained by insuring to every man the greatest possible quantity of the produce of his labour.

How is this to be accomplished? for it is obvious that every man, who has not all the objects of his desire, has inducement to take them from any other man who is weaker than himself. And how is this to be prevented? One mode is sufficiently obvious; and it does not appear that there is any other. It is the union of a certain number of men, agreeing to protect one another; and the object is best accomplished when a great number of men combine together, and delegate to a small number the power necessary for protecting them all. This is Government. And it thus appears, that it is for the sake of property that government exists.

From 'Education'

(The extracts are from *Supplement to the Fourth, Fifth and Sixth Editions of the Encyclopaedia Britannica*, 1824).

...The order of the impressions which are made upon the child by the spontaneous order of events, is, to a certain degree, favourable to benevolence. The pleasures of those who are about him are most commonly the cause of pleasure to himself, their pains of pain. When highly pleased, they are commonly more disposed to exert themselves to gratify him. A period of pain or grief in those about him, is a period of gloom, — a period in which little is done for pleasure, — a period in which the pleasures of the child are apt to be overlooked. Trains of pleasurable ideas are thus apt to arise in his mind, at the thought of the pleasurable condition of those around him; trains of painful ideas at the thought of the reverse; and he is thus led to have an habitual desire for the one, — aversion to the other. But if pleasures, whencesoever derived, of those about him, are apt to be the cause of good to himself, those pleasures which they derive from himself are in a greater degree the cause of good to himself. If those about him are disposed to exert themselves to please him when they are pleased themselves, they are disposed to exert themselves in a much greater degree to please *him*, in particular, when it is he who is the cause of the pleasure they enjoy. A train of ideas, in the highest degree pleasurable, may thus habitually pass through his mind at the thought of happiness to others produced by himself; a train of ideas, in the highest degree painful, at the thought of misery to others, produced by himself. In this manner the foundation of a life of beneficience is laid.

The business of a skilful education is, so to arrange the circumstances by which the child is surrounded, that the impressions made upon him shall be in the order most conducive to this happy result. The impressions, too, which are made originally upon the child, are but one of the causes of the trains which are rendered habitual to him, and which therefore obtain a leading influence in his mind. When he is often made to conceive the trains of other men, by the words, or other signs by which their feelings are betokened, those borrowed trains become also habitual, and exert a similar influence on the mind. This, then, is another of the instruments of education. When the trains signified to the child of the ideas in the minds of those about him are trains of pleasure at the thought of happiness of other human beings, trains of the opposite kind at the conception of their misery; and when such trains are still more pleasurable or painful as the happiness or misery is produced by themselves, the association becomes in time sufficiently powerful to govern the life.

The grand object of human desire is a command over the wills of other men. This may be attained, either by qualities and acts which excite their love and admiration, or by those which excite their terror. When the education is so wisely conducted as to make the train run habitually from the conception of the good end to the conception of the good means; and as often, too, as the good means are conceived, viz, the useful and beneficial qualities, to make it run on to the conception of the great reward, the command over the wills of men; an association is formed which impels the man through life to pursue the great object of desire, fitting himself to be, and by actually becoming the instrument of the greatest possible benefit to his fellow men.

But, unhappily, a command over the wills of men may be obtained by other means than by doing them good; and these, when a man can command them, are the shortest, the easiest, and the most effectual. These other means are all summed up in a command over the pains of other men. When a command over the wills of other men is pursued by the instrumentality of pain, it leads to all the several degress of vexation, injustice, cruelty, oppression, and tyranny. It is, in truth, the grand source of all wickedness, of all the evil which man brings upon man. When the education is so deplorably bad as to allow an association to be formed in the mind of the child between the grand object of desire, the command over the wills of other men, and the fears and pains of other men, as the means; the foundation is laid of the bad character, — the bad son, the bad brother, the bad husband, the bad father, the bad neighbour, the bad magistrate, the bad citizen, — to sum up all in one word, the bad man. Yet, true it is, a great part of education is still so conducted as to form that association. The child, while it yet hangs at the breast, is often allowed to find out by experience, that crying, and the annoyance which it gives, is that by which chiefly it can command the services of its nurse, and obtain the pleasures which it desires. There is not one child in fifty who has not learned to make its cries and wailings an instrument of power, and very often an instrument of absolute tyranny. When the evil grows to excess, the vulgar say the child is spoiled. Not only is the child allowed to exert an influence over the wills of others by means of their pains; it finds, that frequently, sometimes most frequently, its own will is needlessly and unduly commanded by the same means, pain, and the fear of pain. All these sensations concur in establishing a firm association between the idea of the grand object of desire, command over the acts of other men, and those of pain and terror, as the means of acquiring it. That those who have been subject to tyranny are almost always desirous of being tyrants in their turn; that is to say, that a strong association has been formed in their minds, between the ideas of pleasure and dignity, on the one hand, and those of the exercise of tyranny, on the other, is a matter of old and invariable observation. An anecdote has just been mentioned to us, so much in point, that we will repeat it, as resting on its own probability, though it is hearsay evidence (very good, however, of its kind) on which we have received it. At Eton, in consequence, it is probable, of the criticisms which the press has usefully made upon the system of *fagging* (as it is called), at the public schools, a proposition was lately made, among the boys themselves, for abolishing it. The idea originated with the elder boys, who were in possession of the power; — a power of very unlimited and formidable description; and was by them warmly supported; but it was opposed with still greater vehemence by the junior boys, the boys who were then the victims of it, so much did the expected pleasure of tyrannizing in their turn outweigh the pain of their present slavery. — In this case, too, as in most others, the sources of those trains which govern our lives are two, — the impressions made upon ourselves, and the trains which we copy from others. Besides the impressions just recounted, if the trains which pass in the minds of those by whom the child is surrounded, and which he is made to conceive by means of their words, and other signs, lead constantly from the idea of command over the wills of other men, as the grand object of desire, to the idea of pain and terror as the means, the repetition of the copied trains increases the effect of the native impressions, and establishes and confirms the maleficent character.

...It is a common observation, that such as is the direction given to the desires and passions of men, such is the character of the men. The direction is given to the desires and passions of men by one thing, and one alone; the means by which the grand objects of desire may be attained. Now this is certain, that the means by which the grand objects of desire may be attained, depend almost wholly upon the political machine. When the political machine is such, that the grand objects of desire are seen to be the natural prizes of great and virtuous conduct — of high services to mankind, and of the generous and amiable sentiments from which great endeavours in the service of mankind naturally proceed — it is natural to see diffused among mankind a generous ardour in the acquisition of all those admirable qualities which prepare a man for admirable actions; great intelligence, perfect self-command, and over-ruling benevolence. When the political machine is such that the grand objects of desire are seen to be the reward, not of virtue, not of talent, but of subservience to the will, and command over the affections of the ruling few; that interest with the *man above* is the only sure means to the next step in wealth, or power, or consideration, and so on; the means of pleasing the man above become, in that case, the great object of pursuit. And as the favours of the man above are necessarily limited — as some, therefore, of the candidates for his favour can only obtain the objects of their desire by disappointing others — the arts of supplanting rise into importance; and the whole tribe of faculties which is expressed by the words intrigue, flattery, back-biting, treachery, &c., are the fruitful offspring of that political education, which a government, in which the interests of the subject many are but a secondary object, cannot fail to produce.

VARIOUS AUTHORS INCLUDING NASSAU WILLIAM SENIOR AND EDWIN CHADWICK

From *Report of the Royal Commission on the Poor Laws*

(The extracts are from 'Operation of the Law as administered' and 'Principle of Legislation', in the first edition, 1834).

...The services of the labourer are by far the most important of all the instruments used in agriculture. In the management of live and dead stock much must always be left to his judgement. Only a portion, and that not a very large portion, of the results of ordinary farm labour is susceptible of being immediately valued so as to be paid by the piece. The whole farm is the farmer's workshop and storehouse; he is frequently obliged to leave it, and has no partner on whom he can devolve its care during his absence, and its extent generally makes it impossible for him to stand over and personally inspect all the labourers employed on it. His property is scattered over every part, with scarcely any protection against depredation or injury. If his labourers, therefore, want the skill and intelligence necessary to enable them to execute those details for which no general and unvarying rules can be laid down; if they have not the diligence necessary to keep them steadily at work when their master's eye is off; if they have not sufficient honesty to resist the temptation to plunder when the act is easy and the detection difficult, it follows that neither the excellence or abundance of the farmer's agricultural capital, nor his own skill or diligence, or economy, can save him from loss or perhaps from ruin.

Now it is obvious that the tendency of the allowance system is to diminish, we might almost say to destroy, all these qualities in the labourer. What motive has the man who is to receive 10s. every Saturday, not because 10s. is the value of his week's labour, but because his family consists of five persons, who knows that his income will be increased by nothing but by an increase of his family, that it has no reference to his skill, his honesty, or his diligence — what motive has he to acquire or to preserve any of these merits? Unhappily, the evidence shows not only that these virtues are rapidly wearing out, but that their place is assumed by the opposite vices; and that the very labourers among whom the farmer has to live, on whose merits as workmen and on whose affection as friends he ought to depend, are becoming not merely idle and ignorant and dishonest, but positively hostile; not merely unfit for his service and indifferent to his welfare, but actually desirous to injure him.

...The most favourable state of things is when the farmer is himself the proprietor. The owner of land, unless it be covered with cottages occupied by the poor, never has any permanent interest in introducing Poor Law abuses into the parish in which that land is situated. He may, indeed, be interested in introducing them into the neighbouring parishes, if he can manage, by pulling down cottages, or other expedients to keep down the number of persons having settlements in his own parish. Several instances have been mentioned to us, of parishes nearly depopulated, in which almost all the labour is performed by persons settled in the neighbouring villages or towns; drawing from them, as allowance, the greater part of their subsistence; receiving from their employer not more than half wages, even in summer, and much less than half in winter; and discharged whenever their services are not wanted. But with the exception of similar cases, a good administration of the Poor Laws is the landlord's interest; and where he is a man of sense, is acquainted with what is going on, and being an occupier is allowed a vote, he may be expected to oppose the introduction of allowance, knowing that for giving up an immediate accession to his income he will be repaid by preserving the industry and morality of his fellow-parishioners and by saving his estate from being gradually absorbed by pauperism. Even when that system has been introduced, he may, in some stages of the disease, refuse to allow his labourers to be infected by it; pay them full wages, and insist on their taking nothing from the parish. Such conduct, however, can seldom be hoped for; both because it must be exceedingly difficult to preserve a set of labourers uncontaminated by the example of all around them; and because the person who pursues it must submit to pay his proportion of the rates, without being, like the other farmers, indemnified.

The effects of the system on the manufacturing capitalist are very different. The object of machinery is to diminish the want not only of physical, but of moral and intellectual qualities on the part of the workman. In many cases it enables the master to confine him to a narrow routine of similar operations in which the least error or delay is capable of immediate detection. Judgement or intelligence are not required for processes which can be performed only in one mode, and which constant repetition has made mechanical. Honesty is not necessary where all the property is under one roof, or in one inclosure, so that its abstraction would be very hazardous; and where it is, by its incomplete state, difficult of sale. Diligence is insured by the presence of a comparatively small number of over-lookers, and by the almost universal adoption of piece-work.

Under such circumstances, it is not found that parish assistance necessarily destroys the efficacy of the manufacturing labourer. Where that assistance makes only a part of his income, and the remainder is derived from piece-work, his employer insists, and sometimes successfully, that he shall not earn that remainder but by the greatest exertion. We have seen that in agriculture this is impossible, and that consequently the allowance system becomes ultimately mischievous to the farmer who adopts or submits to it; but the manufacturer, who can induce or force others to pay part of the wages of his labourers, not only appears to be, but actually may be, a pure gainer by it; he really can obtain cheap labour. On whom, then, does the loss fall? Partly, of course, on the owners of rateable property, partly on the labourers who are unmarried, or with families of less than the average number, and who are in fact robbed of a portion of the natural price of their labour, but principally on those manufacturers who do not enjoy the same advantages. A manufactory worked by paupers is a rival with which one paying ordinary wages, of course, cannot compete, and in this way a Macclesfield manufacturer may find himself undersold and ruined in consequence of the mal-administration of the Poor Laws in Essex.

...We are not aware that our communications display one instance of out-door pauperism having been permanently repressed by the mere exercise of individual knowledge acting on a limited area. What our evidence does show is that where the administration of relief is brought nearer to the door of the pauper, little advantage arises from increased knowledge on the part of the distributors, and great evil from their increased liability to every sort of pernicious influence. It brings tradesmen within the influence of their customers, small farmers within that of their relations and connections, and not unfrequently of those who have been their fellow workmen, and exposes the wealthier classes to solicitations from their own dependants for extra allowances, which might be meritoriously and usefully given as private charity, but are abuses when forced from the public. Under such circumstances, to continue out-door relief is to continue a relief which will generally be given ignorantly or corruptly, frequently procured by fraud, and, in a large and rapidly increasing proportion of cases, extorted by intimidation — an intimidation which is not more powerful as a source of profusion than as an obstacle to improvement. We shall recur to this subject when we submit the grounds for withdrawing all local discretionary power, and appointing a new agency to superintend the administration of relief.

Many apparent difficulties in the proposed plan, will be considered, and we hope removed, in a subsequent part of this Report. One objection, however, we will answer immediately; and that is that it implies that the whole, or a large proportion of the present paupers must become inmates of the workhouse. One of the most encouraging of the results of our inquiry is the degree in which the existing pauperism arises from fraud, indolence, or improvidence. If it had been principally the result of unavoidable distress, we must have inferred the existence of an organic disease, which, without rendering the remedy less necessary, would have fearfully augmented its difficulty. But when we consider how strong are the motives to claim public assistance, and how ready are the means of obtaining it, independently of real necessity, we are surprised, not at the number of paupers, but at the number of those who have escaped the contagion. A person who attributes pauperism to the inability to procure employment, will doubt the efficiency of the means by which we propose to remove it, tried as they have been, and successful as they have always proved.... In answer to all objections founded on the supposition that the present number of able-bodied paupers will remain permanently chargeable, we refer to the evidence which shows the general causes of pauperism, and to the effects produced by administration on a correct principle, as guaranteeing the effects to be anticipated from the general application of measures which have been tried by so many experiments. But we cannot expect that such evidence will satisfy the minds of those who sincerely disbelieve the possibility of a class of labourers subsisting without rates in aid of wages; and we have found numbers who have sincerely disbelieved that possibility, notwithstanding they have had daily presented to their observation the fact that labourers of the same class, and otherwise no better circumstanced, do live well without such allowances; still less can we expect that such evidence will abate the clamours of those who have a direct interest in the abuses which they defend under the mask of benevolence.

Such persons will, no doubt, avail themselves of the michievous ambiguity of the word *poor*, and treat all diminution of the expenditure for the relief of the poor as so much taken from the labouring classes, as if those classes were naturally pensioners on the charity of their superiors, and relief, not wages, were the proper fund for their support; as if the independent labourers themselves were not, directly or indirectly, losers by all expenditure on paupers; as if those who would be raised from pauperism to independence would not be the greatest gainers by the change; as if, to use the expression of one of the witnesses whom we have quoted, the meat of industry were worse than the bread of idleness.

We have dealt at so much length on the necessity of abolishing out-door relief to the able-bodied, because we are convinced that it is the master evil of the present system. The heads of settlement[17] may be

---

17. heads of settlement: rules by which incoming persons were permitted to settle or restrained from settling in a parish.

reduced and simplified; the expense of litigation may be diminished; the procedure before the magistrates may be improved; uniformity in parochial accounts may be introduced; less vexatious and irregular modes of rating may be established; systematic peculation and jobbing on the parts of the parish officers may be prevented: the fraudulent impositions of undue burthens by one class upon another class — the tampering with the labour-market by the employers of labour — the abuse of the public trust for private or factious purposes, may be corrected; all the other collateral and incidental evils may be remedied;- but if the vital evil of the system, relief to the able-bodied, on terms more eligible than regular industry, be allowed to continue, we are convinced that pauperism with its train of evils, must steadily advance; as we find it advancing in parishes where all or most of its collateral and incidental evils are, by incessant vigilance and exertion, avoided or mitigated.

COSTERUS. Essays in English and American Language and Literature.

Volume 1. Amsterdam 1972. 240 p. Hfl. 40.–
GARLAND CANNON: Sir William Jones's Translation-Interpretation of Sanskrit Literature. SARAH DYCK: The Presence of that Shape: Shelley's *Prometheus Unbound*. MARJORIE ELDER: Hawthorne's *The Marble Faun:* A Gothic Structure. JAMES L. GOLDEN: Adam Smith as a Rhetorical Theorist and Literary Critic. JACK GOODSTEIN: Poetry, Religion and Fact: Matthew Arnold. JAY L. HALIO: Anxiety in *Othello.* JOHN ILLO: Miracle in Milton's Early Verse. F. SAMUEL JANZOW: De Quincey's "Danish Origin of the Lake Country Dialect" Republished. MARTIN L. KORNBLUTH: The Degeneration of Classical Friendship in Elizabethan Drama. VIRGINIA MOSELY: The "Dangerous" Paradox in Joyce's "Eveline". JOHN NIST: Linguistics and the Esthetics of English. SCOTT B. RICE: Smollett's *Travels* and the Genre of Grand Tour Literature. LISBETH J. SACHS and BERNARD H. STERN: The Little Preoedipal Boy in Papa Hemingway and How He Created His Artistry.

Volume 2. Amsterdam 1972. 236 p. Hfl. 40.–
RALPH BEHRENS: Mérimée, Hemingway, and the Bulls. JEANNINE BOHL-MEYER: Mythology in Sackville's "Induction" and "Complaint". HAROLD A. BRACK: Needed – a new language for communicating religion. LEONARD FEINBERG: Satire and Humor: In the Orient and in the West. B. GRANGER: The Whim-Whamsical Bachelors in Salmagundi. W. M. FORCE: The What Story? or Who's Who at the Zoo? W. N. KNIGHT: To Enter lists with God. Transformation of Spencerian Chivalric Tradition in Paradise Regained. MARY D. KRAMER: The Roman Catholic Cleric on the Jacobean Stage. BURTON R. POLLIN: The Temperance Movement and Its Friends Look at Poe. SAMUEL J. ROGAL: Two Translations of the Iliad, Book I: Pope and Tickell. J. L. STYAN: The Delicate Balance: Audience Ambivalence in the Comedy of Shakespeare and Chekhov. CLAUDE W. SUMERLIN: Christopher Smart's A Song to David: its influence on Robert Browning. B.W. TEDFORD: A Recipe for Satire and Civilization. H. H. WATTS: Othello and the Issue of Multiplicity. GUY R. WOODALL: Nationalism in the Philadelphia National Gazette and Literary Register: 1820–1836.

Volume 3. Amsterdam 1972. 236 p. Hfl. 40.–
RAYMOND BENOIT: In Dear Detail by Ideal Light: "Ode on a Grecian Urn". E. F. CALLAHAN: Lyric Origins of the Unity of 1 Henry IV. FRASER DREW: John Masefield and Juan Manuel de Rosas. LAURENCE GONZALEZ: Persona Bob: seer and fool. A. HIRT: A Question of Excess: Neo-Classical Adaptations of Greek Tragedy. EDWIN HONIG: Examples of

Poetic Diction in Ben Jonson. ELSIE LEACH: T. S. Eliot and the School of Donne. SEYMOUR REITER: The Structure of 'Waiting for Godot'. DANIEL E. VAN TASSEL: The Search for Manhood in D. H. Lawrence's 'Sons and Lovers'. MARVIN ROSENBERG: Poetry of the Theatre. GUY R. WOODALL: James Russell Lowell's "Works of Jeremy Taylor, D.D.'

Volume 4. Amsterdam 1972. 233 p. Hfl. 40.–
BOGDDY ARIAS: Sailor's Reveries. R. H. BOWERS: Marlowe's 'Dr. Faustus', Tirso's 'El Condenado por Desconfiado', and the Secret Cause. HOWARD O. BROGAN: Satirist Burns and Lord Byron. WELLER EMBLER: Simone Weil and T. S. Eliot. E. ANTHONY JAMES: Defoe's Autobiographical Apologia: Rhetorical Slanting in 'An Appeal to Honour and Justice'. MARY D. KRAMER: The American Wild West Show and "Buffalo Bill" Cody. IRVING MASSEY: Shelley's "Dirge for the Year": The Relation of the Holograph to the First Edition. L. J. MORRISSEY: English Street Theatre: 1655–1708. M. PATRICK: Browning's Dramatic Techniques and 'The Ring and the Book': A Study in Mechanic and Organic Unity. VINCENT F. PETRONELLA: Shakespeare's 'Henry V' and the Second Tetralogy: Meditation as Drama. NASEEB SHAHEEN: Deriving Adjectives from Nouns. TED R. SPIVEY: The Apocalyptic Symbolism of W. B. Yeats and T. S. Eliot. EDWARD STONE: The Other Sermon in 'Moby–Dick'. M. G. WILLIAMS: 'In Memoriam': A Broad Church Poem.

Volume 5. Amsterdam 1972. 236 p. Hfl. 40.–
PETER G. BEIDLER: Chaucer's Merchant and the Tale of January. ROBERT A. BRYAN: Poets, Poetry, and Mercury in Spenser's Prosopopia: Mother Hubberd's Tale. EDWARD M. HOLMES: Requiem For A Scarlet Nun. E. ANTHONY JAMES: Defoe's Narrative Artistry: Naming and Describing in Robinson Crusoe. MICHAEL J. KELLY: Coleridge's "Picture, or The Lover's Resolution": its Relationship to "Dejection" and its Sources in the Notebooks. EDWARD MARGOLIES: The Playwright and his Critics. MURRAY F. MARKLAND: The Task Set by Valor. RAYMOND S. NELSON: Back to Methuselah: Shaw's Modern Bible. THOMAS W. ROSS: Maimed Rites in Much Ado About Nothing. WILLIAM B. TOOLE: The Metaphor of Alchemy in Julius Caesar. PAUL WEST: Carlyle's Bravura Prophetics. GLENA D. WOOD: The Tragi-Comic Dimensions of Lear's Fool. H. ALAN WYCHERLEY: "Americana": The Mencken – Lorimer Feud.

Volume 6. Amsterdam 1972. 235 p. Hfl. 40.–
GEORG W. BOSWELL: Superstition and Belief in Faulkner. ALBERT COOK: Blake's Milton. MARSHA KINDER: The Improved Author's Farce: An Analysis of the 1734 Revisions. ABE LAUFE: What Makes Drama Run? (Introduction to Anatomy of a Hit). RICHARD L. LOUGHLIN: Laugh and Grow Wise with Oliver Goldsmith. EDWARD MARGOLIES: The American Detective Thriller & The Idea of Society. RAYMOND S. NELSON: Shaw's Heaven, Hell, and Redemption. HAROLD OREL: Is Patrick White's Voss the Real Leichhardt of Australia? LOUIS B. SALOMON: A Walk With Emerson On The Dark Side. H. GRANT SAMPSON: Structure in the Poetry of Thoreau. JAMES H. SIMS, Some Biblical Light on Shakespeare's Hamlet.

olume 9. **GERALD LEVIN: Richardson the Novelist: Th** **atterns.** Amsterdam 1978. 172 p. Hfl. 30.—

nts: Preface. Chapter One. The Problem of Criticism. Chapter *ting Trends" in *Pamela.* Chapter Three. Lovelace's Dream. The "Family Romance" of *Sir Charles Grandison.* Chapter *n's Art. Chapter Six. Richardson and Lawrence: the Rhetoric . Appendix. Freud's Theory of Masochism. Bibliography.

lume 10. **WILLIAM F. HUTMACHER: Wynkyn de Worde and** *erbury Tales.* **A Transcription and Collation of the 1498 Edi-** **on² from the General Prologue Through the Knights Tale.** *'8. 224 p. Hfl. 40,—

nts: Introduction. Wynkyn's Life and Works. Wynkyn De *ution to Printing. Significance of Wynkyn's *The Canterbury* *ice of Wynkyn's Order of the Tales. Scheme of the Order of *Tales.* Wynkyn's Variants from CX². Printer's Errors. Spelling. *ynkyn's Edition. Additions in Wynkyn's Edition. Transposi- *n's Edition. Miscellaneous Variants in the Reading. Biblio- *ation of the Scheme of the Transcription and Recording of *ie Transcription and Collation.

lume 11. **WILLIAM R. KLINK: S. N. Behrman: The Major** *m 1978. 272 p. Hfl. 45,—

ts: Introduction. *The Second Man. Brief Moment. Biography.* *iven. End of Summer. No Time for Comedy. The Talley r Whom Charlie.* Language. Conclusion. Bibliography.

ume 12. **VALERIE BONITA GRAY:** *Invisible Man's* **Literary** *Cereno* and *Moby Dick.* Amsterdam 1978. 145p. Hfl. 30,— *ts:* Democracy: The Politics of "Affirming the Principle" and Individual. The Spectrum of Ambiguity: From Mask Wearing g. Whiteness or Blackness: Which Casts the Shadow? Melvil- 's Methodology: Bird Imagery and Whale and Circus Lore. Bibliography.

ume 13. **VINCENT DIMARCO and LESLIE PERELMAN: The** **Letter of Alexander to Aristotle.** Amsterdam 1978. 194p.

ume 14. **JOHN W. CRAWFORD: Discourse: Essays on English** **iterature.** Amsterdam 1978. 200p. 40,—

*cer's Use of Sun Imagery. The Fire from Spenser's Faerie Queene," I.xi. The Changing Renaissance World *oney's Fiction. Shakespeare's Falstaff: A Thrust at Plato- *us Question in *Julius Caesar.* Teaching *Julius Caesar:* A Study *ision. Shakespeare: A Lesson in Communications. Intuitive *ymbeline.* White Witchcraft in Tudor-Stuart Drama. Another

ROBERT F. WILLSON, Jr.: Lear's Auction. JAMES N. WISE: Emerson's "Experience" and "Sons and Lovers". JAMES D. YOUNG: Aims in Reader's Theatre.

Volume 7. Amsterdam 1973. 235 p. Hfl. 40.—
HANEY H. BELL Jr.: Sam Fathers and Ike McCaslin and the World in Which Ike Matures. SAMUEL IRVING BELLMAN: The Apocalypse in Literature. HALDEEN BRADDY: England and English before Alfred. DAVID R. CLARK: Robert Frost: "The Thatch" and "Directive". RALPH MAUD: Robert Crowley, Puritan Satirist. KATHARINE M. MORSBERGER: Haw- thorne's "Borderland": The Locale of the Romance. ROBERT E. MORS- BERGER: The Conspiracy of the Third International. "What is the metre of the dictionary? " — Dylan Thomas. RAYMOND PRESTON: Dr. Johnson and Aristotle. JOHN J. SEYDOW: The Sound of Passing Music: John Neal's Battle for American Literary Independence. JAMES H. SIMS: Enter Satan as Esau, Alone; Exit Satan as Belshazzar: *Paradise Lost,* BOOK (IV). MICHAEL WEST, Dryden and the Disintegration of Renaissance Heroic Ideals. RENATE C. WOLFF: Pamela as Myth and Dream.

Volume 8. Amsterdam 1973. 231 p. Hfl. 40.—
SAMUEL I. BELLMAN: Sleep, Pride, and Fantasy: Birth Traumas and Socio-Biologic Adaptation in the American-Jewish Novel. PETER BUITEN- HUIS: A Corresponding Fabric: The Urban World of Saul Bellow. DAVID R. CLARK: An Excursus upon the Criticism of Robert Frost's "Directive". FRANCIS GILLEN: Tennyson and the Human Norm: A Study of Hubris and Human Commitment in Three Poems by Tennyson. ROBERT R. HARSON: H. G. Wells: The Mordet Island Episode. JULIE B. KLEIN: The Art of Apology: "An Epistle to Dr. Arbuthnot" and "Verses on the Death of Dr. Swift". ROBERT E. MORSBERGER: The Movie Game in Who's Afraid of Virginia Woolf and The Boys in the Band. EDWIN MOSES: A Reading of "The Ancient Mariner". JOHN H. RANDALL: Romeo and Juliet in the New World. A Study in James, Wharton, and Fitzgerald "Fay ce que vouldras". JOHN E. SAVESON: Conrad as Moralist in Victory. ROBERT M. STROZIER: Politics, Stoicism, and the Development of Elizabethan Tragedy. LEWIS TURCO: Manoah Bodman: Poet of the Second Awakening.

Volume 9. Amsterdam 1973. 251 p. Hfl. 40.—
THOMAS E. BARDEN: Dryden's Aims in *Amphytryon.* SAMUEL IRVING BELLMAN: Marjorie Kinnan Rawling's Existentialist Nightmare *The Year-* *ling.* SAMUEL IRVING BELLMAN: Writing Literature for Young People. Marjorie Kinnan Rawlings' "Secret River" of the Imagination. F. S. JANZOW: "Philadelphus," A New Essay by De Quincey. JACQUELINE KRUMP: Robert Browning's Palace of Art. ROBERT E. MORSBERGER: The Winning of Barbara Undershaft: Conversion by the Cannon Factory, or "Wot prawce selvytion nah? " DOUGLAS L. PETERSON: Tempest-Tossed Barks and Their Helmsmen in Several of Shakespeare's Plays. STANLEY POSS: Serial Form and Malamud's Schlemihls. SHERYL P. RUTLEDGE: Chaucer's Zodiac of Tales. CONSTANCE RUYS: John Pickering—Merchant Adventurer and Playwright. JAMES H. SIMS: Death in Poe's Poetry: Varia-

tions on a Theme. ROBERT A. SMITH: A Pioneer Black Writer and the Problems of Discrimination and Miscegenation. ALBERT J. SOLOMON: The Sound of Music in "Eveline": A Long Note on a Barrel-Organ. J. L. STYAN: Goldsmith's Comic Skills. ARLINE R. THORN: Shelley's *The Cenci* as Tragedy. E. THORN: James Joyce: Early Imitations of Structural Unity. LEWIS TURCO: The Poetry of Lewis Turco. An Interview by Gregory Fitzgerald and William Heyen.

New Series. Volume 1. Edited by James L. W. West III. Amsterdam 1974. 194 p. Hfl. 40.—
D. W. ROBERTSON, Jr.: Chaucer's Franklin and His Tale. CLARENCE H. MILLER and CARYL K. BERREY: The Structure of Integrity: The Cardinal Virtues in Donne's "Satyre III". F. SAMUEL JANZOW: The English Opium-Eater as Editor. VICTOR A. KRAMER: Premonition of Disaster: An Unpublished Section for Agee's *A Death in the Family*. GEORGE L. GECKLE: Poetic Justice and *Measure for Measure*. RODGER L. TARR: Thomas Carlyle's Growing Radicalism: The Social Context of *The French Revolution*. G. THOMAS TANSELLE: Philip Gaskell's *A New Introduction to Bibliography*. Review Essay. KATHERINE B. TROWER: Elizabeth D. Kirk's *The Dream Thought of Piers Plowman*. Review Essay. JAMES L. WEST III: Matthew J. Bruccoli's *F. Scott Fitzgerald a Descriptive Bibliography*. Review Essay. JAMES E. KIBLER: R. W. Stallman's *Stephen Crane: A Critical Bibliography*. Review. ROBERT P. MILLER: Jonathan Saville's *The Medieval Erotic Alba*. Review.

New Series. Volume 2. **THACKERY. Edited by Peter L. Shillingsburg.** Amsterdam 1974. 359 p. Hfl. 70.—
JOAN STEVENS: *Vanity Fair* and the London Skyline. JANE MÍLLGATE: History *versus* Fiction: Thackeray's Response to Macaulay. ANTHEA TRODD: Michael Angelo Titmarsh and the Knebworth Apollo. PATRICIA R. SWEENEY: Thackeray's Best Illustrator. JOAN STEVENS: Thackeray's Pictorial Capitals. ANTHONY BURTON: Thackeray's Collaborations with Cruikshank, Doyle, and Walker. JOHN SUTHERLAND: A *Vanity Fair* Mystery: The Delay in Publication. JOHN SUTHERLAND: Thackeray's Notebook for *Henry Esmond*. EDGAR F. HARDEN: The Growth of *The Virginians* as a Serial Novel: Parts 1–9. GERALD C. SORENSEN: Thackeray Texts and Bibliographical Scholarship. PETER L. SHILLINSBURG: Thackeray Texts: A Guide to Inexpensive Editions. RUTH apROBERTS: Thackeray Boom: A Review. JOSEPH E. BAKER: Reading Masterpieces in Isolation: Review. ROBERT A. COLBY and JOHN SUTHERLAND: Thackeray's Manuscripts: A Preliminary Census of Library Locations.

New Series. Volume 3. Edited by James L. W. West III. Amsterdam 1975. 184 p. Hfl. 40.—
SAMUEL J. ROGAL: Hurd's Editorial Criticism of Addison's Grammar and Usage. ROBERT P. MILLER: Constancy Humanized: Trivet's Constance and the Man of Law's Custance. WELDON THORNTON: Structure and Theme in Faulkner's *Go Down, Moses*. JAYNE K. KRIBBS: John Davis: A Man For His Time. STEPHEN E. MEATS: The Responsibilities of an Editor of Correspon-

dence. Review Essay. RODGER L[...] Carlyle. Review. CHAUNCEY WO[...] Review.

New Series. Volume 4. Edited b[...] 179 p. Hfl. 40.—
JAMES L. W. WEST III: A Biblic[...] TIMOTHY HOBBS: The Doctrine[...] STEFFENSEN HAGEN: Tennyso[...] Court". CLIFFORD CHALME[...] University and Popular Drama in [...] MAN: Textual Editing and the [...] HILL: The Bard in Chains: *The Ha[...] Essay. BRUCE HARKNESS: C[...] Review Essay. MIRIAM J. SHILLI[...] or, The Machine Makes Another [...] DAMMERS: Explicit Statement a[...] Medieval Madness and Medieval Lit[...] ner's Faulkner. Review.

New Series. Volume 5–6. GYAS[...] **Humorous and Sporting Writing. E**[...] 1978.
NOEL POLK: The Blind Bull, [...] Damned Human Race. HERBERT [...] as Playwright. LELAND .H. COX,[...] *Young Sportsmen*. ALAN GRIB[...] *Georgia Scenes*. T. B. THORPE's F[...] Unknown Tale by GEORGE WA[...] JOHNSON JONES HOOPER's "The[...] West III. SOUTH CAROLINA WI[...] Stephen E. Meats. A NEW MOCI[...] ANOTHER NEW MOCK SERMON [...] Correspondence ed. Edgar E. Thomp[...]

New Series. Volume 7. **SANFORD** [...] **rad.** Amsterdam 1978. 87 p. Hfl. 20.[...]
Table of Contents: Foreword. Intro[...] East. The Language of Narration. T[...] Politics. *Victory* As Afterword.

New Series. Volume 8. **GARLAN**[...] **mational Grammar of the English** [...] Hfl. 60.—
Table of Contents: Preface. 1) A Chil[...] Man's Use of Language. 3) Syntacti[...] Component: Lexicon. 5) Syntactic [...] Semantic Component. 7) Phonologic[...] of His Language. Appendix: the [...] Index.

ROBERT F. WILLSON, Jr.: Lear's Auction. JAMES N. WISE: Emerson's "Experience" and "Sons and Lovers". JAMES D. YOUNG: Aims in Reader's Theatre.

Volume 7. Amsterdam 1973. 235 p. Hfl. 40.—
HANEY H. BELL Jr.: Sam Fathers and Ike McCaslin and the World in Which Ike Matures. SAMUEL IRVING BELLMAN: The Apocalypse in Literature. HALDEEN BRADDY: England and English before Alfred. DAVID R. CLARK: Robert Frost: "The Thatch" and "Directive". RALPH MAUD: Robert Crowley, Puritan Satirist. KATHARINE M. MORSBERGER: Hawthorne's "Borderland": The Locale of the Romance. ROBERT E. MORSBERGER: The Conspiracy of the Third International. "What is the metre of the dictionary? " — Dylan Thomas. RAYMOND PRESTON: Dr. Johnson and Aristotle. JOHN J. SEYDOW: The Sound of Passing Music: John Neal's Battle for American Literary Independence. JAMES H. SIMS: Enter Satan as Esau, Alone; Exit Satan as Belshazzar: *Paradise Lost*, BOOK (IV). MICHAEL WEST, Dryden and the Disintegration of Renaissance Heroic Ideals. RENATE C. WOLFF: Pamela as Myth and Dream.

Volume 8. Amsterdam 1973. 231 p. Hfl. 40.—
SAMUEL I. BELLMAN: Sleep, Pride, and Fantasy: Birth Traumas and Socio-Biologic Adaptation in the American-Jewish Novel. PETER BUITEN-HUIS: A Corresponding Fabric: The Urban World of Saul Bellow. DAVID R. CLARK: An Excursus upon the Criticism of Robert Frost's "Directive". FRANCIS GILLEN: Tennyson and the Human Norm: A Study of Hubris and Human Commitment in Three Poems by Tennyson. ROBERT R. HARSON: H. G. Wells: The Mordet Island Episode. JULIE B. KLEIN: The Art of Apology: "An Epistle to Dr. Arbuthnot" and "Verses on the Death of Dr. Swift". ROBERT E. MORSBERGER: The Movie Game in Who's Afraid of Virginia Woolf and The Boys in the Band. EDWIN MOSES: A Reading of "The Ancient Mariner". JOHN H. RANDALL: Romeo and Juliet in the New World. A Study in James, Wharton, and Fitzgerald "Fay ce que vouldras". JOHN E. SAVESON: Conrad as Moralist in Victory. ROBERT M. STROZIER: Politics, Stoicism, and the Development of Elizabethan Tragedy. LEWIS TURCO: Manoah Bodman: Poet of the Second Awakening.

Volume 9. Amsterdam 1973. 251 p. Hfl. 40.—
THOMAS E. BARDEN: Dryden's Aims in *Amphytryon*. SAMUEL IRVING BELLMAN: Marjorie Kinnan Rawling's Existentialist Nightmare *The Yearling*. SAMUEL IRVING BELLMAN: Writing Literature for Young People. Marjorie Kinnan Rawlings' "Secret River" of the Imagination. F. S. JANZOW: "Philadelphus," A New Essay by De Quincey. JACQUELINE KRUMP: Robert Browning's Palace of Art. ROBERT E. MORSBERGER: The Winning of Barbara Undershaft: Conversion by the Cannon Factory, or "Wot prawce selvytion nah? " DOUGLAS L. PETERSON: Tempest-Tossed Barks and Their Helmsmen in Several of Shakespeare's Plays. STANLEY POSS: Serial Form and Malamud's Schlemihls. SHERYL P. RUTLEDGE: Chaucer's Zodiac of Tales. CONSTANCE RUYS: John Pickering—Merchant Adventurer and Playwright. JAMES H. SIMS: Death in Poe's Poetry: Varia-

tions on a Theme. ROBERT A. SMITH: A Pioneer Black Writer and the Problems of Discrimination and Miscegenation. ALBERT J. SOLOMON: The Sound of Music in "Eveline": A Long Note on a Barrel-Organ. J. L. STYAN: Goldsmith's Comic Skills. ARLINE R. THORN: Shelley's *The Cenci* as Tragedy. E. THORN: James Joyce: Early Imitations of Structural Unity. LEWIS TURCO: The Poetry of Lewis Turco. An Interview by Gregory Fitzgerald and William Heyen.

New Series. Volume 1. Edited by James L. W. West III. Amsterdam 1974. 194 p. Hfl. 40.–
D. W. ROBERTSON, Jr.: Chaucer's Franklin and His Tale. CLARENCE H. MILLER and CARYL K. BERREY: The Structure of Integrity: The Cardinal Virtues in Donne's "Satyre III". F. SAMUEL JANZOW: The English Opium-Eater as Editor. VICTOR A. KRAMER: Premonition of Disaster: An Unpublished Section for Agee's *A Death in the Family*. GEORGE L. GECKLE: Poetic Justice and *Measure for Measure*. RODGER L. TARR: Thomas Carlyle's Growing Radicalism: The Social Context of *The French Revolution*. G. THOMAS TANSELLE: Philip Gaskell's *A New Introduction to Bibliography*. Review Essay. KATHERINE B. TROWER: Elizabeth D. Kirk's *The Dream Thought of Piers Plowman*. Review Essay. JAMES L. WEST III: Matthew J. Bruccoli's *F. Scott Fitzgerald a Descriptive Bibliography*. Review Essay. JAMES E. KIBLER: R. W. Stallman's *Stephen Crane: A Critical Bibliography*. Review. ROBERT P. MILLER: Jonathan Saville's *The Medieval Erotic Alba*. Review.

New Series. Volume 2. **THACKERY**. Edited by Peter L. Shillingsburg. Amsterdam 1974. 359 p. Hfl. 70.–
JOAN STEVENS: *Vanity Fair* and the London Skyline. JANE MÍLLGATE: History *versus* Fiction: Thackeray's Response to Macaulay. ANTHEA TRODD: Michael Angelo Titmarsh and the Knebworth Apollo. PATRICIA R. SWEENEY: Thackeray's Best Illustrator. JOAN STEVENS: Thackeray's Pictorial Capitals. ANTHONY BURTON: Thackeray's Collaborations with Cruikshank, Doyle, and Walker. JOHN SUTHERLAND: A *Vanity Fair* Mystery: The Delay in Publication. JOHN SUTHERLAND: Thackeray's Notebook for *Henry Esmond*. EDGAR F. HARDEN: The Growth of *The Virginians* as a Serial Novel: Parts 1–9. GERALD C. SORENSEN: Thackeray Texts and Bibliographical Scholarship. PETER L. SHILLINSBURG: Thackeray Texts: A Guide to Inexpensive Editions. RUTH apROBERTS: Thackeray Boom: A Review. JOSEPH E. BAKER: Reading Masterpieces in Isolation: Review. ROBERT A. COLBY and JOHN SUTHERLAND: Thackeray's Manuscripts: A Preliminary Census of Library Locations.

New Series. Volume 3. Edited by James L. W. West III. Amsterdam 1975. 184 p. Hfl. 40.–
SAMUEL J. ROGAL: Hurd's Editorial Criticism of Addison's Grammar and Usage. ROBERT P. MILLER: Constancy Humanized: Trivet's Constance and the Man of Law's Custance. WELDON THORNTON: Structure and Theme in Faulkner's *Go Down, Moses*. JAYNE K. KRIBBS: John Davis: A Man For His Time. STEPHEN E. MEATS: The Responsibilities of an Editor of Correspon-

dence. Review Essay. RODGER L. TARR: Carlyle and Dickens *or* Dickens and Carlyle. Review. CHAUNCEY WOOD: Courtly Lovers: An Unsentimental View. Review.

New Series. Volume 4. Edited by James L. W. West III. Amsterdam 1975. 179 p. Hfl. 40.—
JAMES L. W. WEST III: A Bibliographer's Interview with William Styron. J. TIMOTHY HOBBS: The Doctrine of Fair Use in the Law of Copyright. JUNE STEFFENSEN HAGEN: Tennyson's Revisions of the Last Stanza of "Audley Court". CLIFFORD CHALMERS HUFFMAN: *The Christmas Prince*: University and Popular Drama in the Age of Shakespeare. ROBERT L. OAKMAN: Textual Editing and the Computer. Review Essay. T.H. HOWARD-HILL: The Bard in Chains: *The Harvard Concordance to Shakespeare*. Review Essay. BRUCE HARKNESS: Conrad Computerized and Concordanced. Review Essay. MIRIAM J. SHILLINGSBURG: A Rose is a Four-Letter Word; or, The Machine Makes Another Concordance. Review Essay. RICHARD H. DAMMERS: Explicit Statement as Art. Review Essay. A. S. G. EDWARDS: Medieval Madness and Medieval Literature. Review Essay. NOEL POLK: Blotner's Faulkner. Review.

New Series. Volume 5–6. **GYASCUTUS. Studies in Antebellum Southern Humorous and Sporting Writing. Edited by James L. W. West III. Amsterdam 1978.**
NOEL POLK: The Blind Bull, Human Nature: Sut Lovingood and the Damned Human Race. HERBERT P. SHIPPEY: William Tappan Thompson as Playwright. LELAND H. COX, Jr.: Porter's Edition of *Instructions to Young Sportsmen*. ALAN GRIBBEN: Mark Twain Reads Longstreet's *Georgia Scenes*. T. B. THORPE's Far West Letters, ed. Leland H. Cox, Jr. An Unknown Tale by GEORGE WASHINGTON HARRIS ed. William Starr. JOHNSON JONES HOOPER's "The 'Frinnolygist' at Fault" ed. James L. W. West III. SOUTH CAROLINA WRITERS in the *Spirit of the Times* ed. Stephen E. Meats. A NEW MOCK SERMON ed. James L. W. West III. ANOTHER NEW MOCK SERMON ed. A. S. Wendel. The PORTER-HOOPER Correspondence ed. Edgar E. Thompson.

New Series. Volume 7. **SANFORD PINSKER: The Languages of Joseph Conrad.** Amsterdam 1978. 87 p. Hfl. 20.—
Table of Contents: Foreword. Introductory Language. The Language of the East. The Language of Narration. The Language of the Sea. The Language of Politics. *Victory* As Afterword.

New Series. Volume 8. **GARLAND CANNON: An Integrated Transformational Grammar of the English Language.** Amsterdam 1978. 315 p. Hfl. 60.—
Table of Contents: Preface. 1) A Child's Acquisition of His First Language. 2) Man's Use of Language. 3) Syntactic Component: Base Rules. 4) Syntactic Component: Lexicon. 5) Syntactic Component: Transformational Rules. 6) Semantic Component. 7) Phonological Component. 8) Man's Understanding of His Language. Appendix: the Sentence-Making Model. Bibliography. Index.

New Series: Volume 9. **GERALD LEVIN: Richardson the Novelist: The Psychological Patterns.** Amsterdam 1978. 172 p. Hfl. 30.—

Table of Contents: Preface. Chapter One. The Problem of Criticism. Chapter Two. "Conflicting Trends" in *Pamela.* Chapter Three. Lovelace's Dream. Chapter Four. The "Family Romance" of *Sir Charles Grandison.* Chapter Five. Richardson's Art. Chapter Six. Richardson and Lawrence: the Rhetoric of Concealment. Appendix. Freud's Theory of Masochism. Bibliography.

New Series: Volume 10. **WILLIAM F. HUTMACHER: Wynkyn de Worde and Chaucer's Canterbury Tales. A Transcription and Collation of the 1498 Edition with Caxton^2 from the General Prologue Through the Knights Tale.** Amsterdam 1978. 224 p. Hfl. 40,—

Table of Contents: Introduction. Wynkyn's Life and Works. Wynkyn De Word's Contribution to Printing. Significance of Wynkyn's *The Canterbury Tales*. Significance of Wynkyn's Order of the Tales. Scheme of the Order of *The Canterbury Tales*. Wynkyn's Variants from CX^2. Printer's Errors. Spelling. Omissions in Wynkyn's Edition. Additions in Wynkyn's Edition. Transpositions in Wynkyn's Edition. Miscellaneous Variants in the Reading. Bibliography. Explanation of the Scheme of the Transcription and Recording of the Variants. The Transcription and Collation.

New Series: Volume 11. **WILLIAM R. KLINK: S. N. Behrman: The Major Plays.** Amsterdam 1978. 272 p. Hfl. 45,—

Table of Contents: Introduction. *The Second Man. Brief Moment. Biography. Rain From Heaven. End of Summer. No Time for Comedy. The Talley Method. But For Whom Charlie.* Language. Conclusion. Bibliography.

New Series: Volume 12. **VALERIE BONITA GRAY:** *Invisible Man's* **Literary heritage:** *Benito Cereno* **and** *Moby Dick.* Amsterdam 1978. 145p. Hfl. 30,—

Table of Contents: Democracy: The Politics of "Affirming the Principle" and Celebrating the Individual. The Spectrum of Ambiguity: From Mask Wearing to Shape-shifting. Whiteness or Blackness: Which Casts the Shadow? Melville's and Ellison's Methodology: Bird Imagery and Whale and Circus Lore. Social Protest. Bibliography.

New Series: Volume 13. **VINCENT DIMARCO and LESLIE PERELMAN: The Middle English Letter of Alexander to Aristotle.** Amsterdam 1978. 194p. Hfl. 40,—

New Series: Volume 14. **JOHN W. CRAWFORD: Discourse: Essays on English and American Literature.** Amsterdam 1978. 200p. 40,—

Contents: Chaucer's Use of Sun Imagery. The Fire from Spenser's Dragon: "The Faerie Queene," I.xi. The Changing Renaissance World in Thomas Deloney's Fiction. Shakespeare's Falstaff: A Thrust at Platonism. The Religious Question in *Julius Caesar.* Teaching *Julius Caesar:* A Study in Poetic Persuasion. Shakespeare: A Lesson in Communications. Intuitive Knowledge in *Cymbeline.* White Witchcraft in Tudor-Stuart Drama. Another

Biblical Allusion in *Paradise Lost*. *Absalom and Achitophel;* and Milton's *Paradise Lost*. Asem-Goldsmith's Solution to Timon's Dilemma. Dr. Johnson: A Modern Example of Christian Constancy. A Unifying Element in Tennyson's *Maud*. Arnold's Relevancy to the Twentieth Century. Sophocles' Role in "Dover Beach". Lest We Forget, Lest We Forget: Kipling's Warning to Humanity. The Garden Imagery in *Great Expectations*. "Victorian" Women in *Barchester Towers*. Another Look at "Youth". Forster's "The Road from Colonus". Biblical Influences in *Cry, the Beloved Country*. Huxley's *Island:* A Contemporary *Utopia*. The Generation Gap in Literature. Bred and Bawn in a Briar Patch — Deception in the Making. Success and Failure in the Poetry of Edwin Arlington Robinson. Naturalistic Tendencies in *Spoon River Anthology*. Primitiveness in "The Bravest Boat". Theme of Suffering in "Sonny's Blues". Nabokov's "First Love". The Temper of Romanticism in *Travels with Charley*. Unrecognized Artists in American Literature: Chicano Renaissance.

New Series: Volume 15. **ROBERT F. WILLSON, JR.: Landmarks of Shakespeare Criticism.** Amsterdam 1979. 113p. 25,–
Contents: Introduction. Thomas Rymer: On *Othello* (1692). Nicholas Rowe: Preface (1709-14). Alexander Pope: Preface (1725). Lewis Theobald: Preface (1740). Samuel Johnson: Preface (1765). Richard Farmer: Essay on the Learning of Shakespeare (1767). Gotthold Lessing: On Ghosts (1769). Walter Whiter: On Hell and Night in *Macbeth* (1794). William Richardson: On the Faults of Shakespeare (1797). August Wilhelm von Schlegel: Lecture XXIII. Shakespeare (1809-11). Johann Wolfgang von Goethe: Shakespeare ad Infinitum (1812?). Samuel Taylor Coleridge: On Shakespeare as a Poet (1811-12). William Hazlitt: On Shakespeare and Milton (1818). Thomas de Quincey: On the Knocking at the Gate in *Macbeth* (1823). Thomas Carlyle: The Hero as a Poet (1841). Ivan Turgenev: Hamlet and Don Quixote: the Two Eternal Human Types (1860). Edward Dowden: Shakespeare's Portraiture of Women (1888). Walter Pater: Shakespeare's English Kings (1889). Bernard ten Brink: Shakespeare as a Comic Poet (1895). Richard Moulton: Supernatural Agency in the Moral World of Shakespeare (1903). Leo Tolstoy: Shakespeare and the Drama (1906). J.J. Jusserand: What to Expect of Shakespeare (1911-12). Sigmund Freud: On Lady Macbeth (1916). George Bernard Shaw: On Cutting Shakespear (1919). Edmund Blunden: Shakespeare's Significances (1929). Selected Bibliography.

New Series: Volume 16. **A.H. Qureshi: Edinburgh Review and Poetic Truth.** Amsterdam 1979. 61p. 15,–

New Series: Volume 17. **RAYMOND J.S. GRANT: Cambridge Corpus Christi College 41: The Loricas and the Missal.** Amsterdam 1979. 127p. 30,–
Contents: Chapter I: The Loricas of Corpus 41. Chapter II: Corpus 41 — An 11th-Century English Missal. Appendix: Latin Liturgical material contained in

the Margins of Cambridge, Corpus Christi College 41. Endnotes: Chapter I and Chapter II.

New Series: Volume 18. **CARLEE LIPPMAN**: Lyrical Positivism. Amsterdam 1979. 195p. 40,–
Contents: Chapter I: Some Tenets. Chapter II: The Rape of *The Rape of the Lock*. Chapter III: García Márquez' Language Laboratory. Chapter IV: The Syntax of Persuasion. Afterword. Bibliography.

New Series: Volume 19. **EVELYN A. HOVANEC: Henry James and Germany.** Amsterdam 1979. 149p. 30,–
Contents: Preface. Introduction. Chapter I: A Travel Sketch. Chapter II: The Analytic Tourist. Chapter III: Life Into Fiction. Chapter IV: Value, Inconsistency, and Resolution. Bibliography. Index.

New Series: Volume 20. **SANDY COHEN: Norman Mailer's Novels.** Amsterdam 1979. 133p. 25,–
Contents: Chapter One: Norman Mailer in Context. Chapter Two: The Naked and the Dead. Chapter Three: Barbary Shore. Chapter Four: The Deer Perk. Chapter Five: An American Dream. Chapter Six: History As Novel As History: Armies of the Night. Chapter Seven: Why Are We In Vietnam? A Novel. Chapter Eight: Marilyn. A Biographical Note.

New Series: Volume 21. **HANS BERTENS: The Fiction of Paul Bowles.** Amsterdam 1979. 260p. 50,–
Contents: Chapter One: Introduction. Chapter Two: The Sheltering Sky. Chapter Three: Let It Come Down. Chapter Four: The Spider's House. Chapter Five: Up Above the World. Chapter Six: The Stories. Chapter Seven: Conclusion. Selected Bibliography. Index.

New Series: Volume 22. **RICHARD MANLEY BLAU: The Body Impolitic.** Amsterdam 1979. 214p. 45,–
Contents: Preface. Chapter I. Typee: In Search of Plump Sphericity. Chapter II. White Jacket: To Scourge a Man that is a Roman. Chapter III. Moby-Dick: Beware of the Spinal Complaint. Chapter IV. Pierre: Let them look out for me now! Epilogue. Bibliography.

New Series: Volume 23. From Caxton to Beckett, Essays presented to W.H. Toppen on the occasion of his seventieth birthday, Edited by Jacques B.H. Alblas and Richard Todd. With a foreword by A.J. Fry. Amsterdam 1979. 133p. 30,–
Contents: List of Plates. Foreword. Acknowledgements. Hans H. Meier: Middle English Styles in Translation: A Note on *Everyman* and Caxton's *Reynard*. Richard Todd: The Passion Poems of George Herbert. Jacques B.H. Alblas: The Earliest Editions of *The Pilgrim's Progress* as Source Texts for the First Dutch Translation of Bunyan's Allegory. Peter J. de Voogd et al.: A Reading of William Hogarth's *Marriage à la Mode*. M. Buning: *Lessness* Magnified. A.J. Fry: On the Agonies of Elitism.

New Series: Volume 24. **CAROL JOHNSON**: The Disappearance of Literature. Amsterdam 1980. 123p. 25,–

Contents: Chapter One: The Disappearance of Literature. Chapter Two: Randall Jarrell and the Art of Self Defense. Chapter Three: Paul Valery: The Art of Concealment. Chapter Four: Hart Crane's Unimproved Infancy. Chapter Five: John Berryman: The Will to Exceed. Chapter Six: The Poetics of Disregard: Homage to Basil Bunting. Chapter Seven: The Translator as Poet. Chapter Eight: An Adjunct to the Poet's Dossier. Chapter Nine: The Consummation of Consciousness: The Poetry of Delmore Schwartz. Chapter Ten: Mrs. Wharton's Profession: The Reef. Reconnoitered. Chapter Eleven: Eça De Queiroz: The Arbitrations of Irony. Chapter Twelve: Nabokov's Ada: Word's End. Chapter Thirteen: Hysteria Naturalized.

New Series. Volume 25. **LINGUISTIC STUDIES offered to Berthe Siertsema,** edited by D.J. van Alkemade, A. Feitsma, W.J. Meys, P. van Reenen en J.J. Spa Amsterdam 1980. 382p. 56,–

Contents: D.J. van Alkemade: Referentiality and definiteness of NP's. D.M. Bakker: On *a*-generic sentences in Dutch. F. Balk-Smit Duyzentkunst: Metaphor and linguistic theory. R.A. Blust: Iban antonymy: a case from diachrony? S.C. Dik: On term coordination in functional grammar. A. Hurkmans: De Saussure and Wittgenstein. J.G. Kooij: Preposed PP's in Dutch and the definition of grammatical relations. P. Pitha: Case Frames of Nouns. S.R. Slings: 'KAI adversativum' – some thoughts on the semantics of coordination. E.M. Uhlenbeck: Observations in semantics is not easy. P.A. Verburg: Discipline versus philosophy. R. Botha: Allen's theory of synthetic compounding: a critical appraisal. H.H. Meier: Agnimals in English: group words in word groups. W.J. Meys: Morphemic make-up and lexical dynamics. Q.I.M. Mok: Le préfixe *RE*-re-regardé: productivité et potentialité. P. van Reenen/ J. Voorhoeve: Gender in Limbum. H. Schultink: On stacking up affixes, mainly in Dutch words. W. Zwanenburg: Regards du 17e siècle français sur la productivité morphologique. A. Cohen: The word as a processing unit in speech perception. A. Dees/ P. van Reenen: L'interprétation des graphies -o- et -ou- à la lumière des formes trouvées dans les chartes françaises du 13e siècle. H.D. Meijering: *D(e)*-deletion in the past tense of the class II weak verbs in Old Frisian. H. Mol: Gesture phonetics. J. Stewart: The feature Advanced Tongue Root and the Lepsius diacritics. J. Vachek: Writing and the glossematicists. B.P.F. Al: Sur la richesse lexicale du corpus d'Orléans. Contribution à l'analyse sociolinguistique d'un vocabulaire oral. J.T. Bendor-Samuel: Is a sociolinguistic profile necessary? A. Feitsma: The Frisian native speaker between Frisian and Dutch. G.J. Hartman: The goal-directedness of the process of sentence perception. E.A. Nida: The contribution of linguistics to the theory and practice of translating. J.J. Spa: Le langage et la sémiologie. Quelques réflexions nouvelles. B.T. Tervoort: What is the native language of a deaf child?

New Series. Volume 26. **FROM COOPER TO PHILIP ROTH**, Essays on American Literature, Presented to J.G. Riewald, on the occasion of his seventieth brithday. Edited by J. Bakker and D.R.M. Wilkinson, with a foreword by J. Gerritsen. Amsterdam 1980. 118p. 25,–

Contents: Foreword; T.A. Birrell: A Preface to Cooper's *The Last of the Mohicans*; A.J. Fry: *Writing New Englandy*: A Study of Diction and Technique in the Poetry of Emily Dickinson; D.R.M. Wilkinson: A Complete Image: James's *The Bostonians*; S. Betsky-Zweig: From Pleached Garden to Jungle and Waste Land: Henry James's Beast; J. Bakker: Faulkner's World as the Extension of Reality: *As I Lay Dying* Reconsidered; H.I. Schvey: Madonna at the Poker Night: Pictorial Elements in Tennessee Williams' *A Streetcar Named Desire;* G.A.M. Janssens: Styron's Case and "Sophie's Choice"; J.W. Bertens: "The Measured Self vs. The Insatiable Self:" Notes on Philip Roth; Curriculum Vitae; Publications; Tabula Gratulatorum.

Editions Rodopi N.V., Keizersgracht 302-304, Amsterdam, The Netherlands